# The Governance of Not-for-Profit Organizations

A National Bureau
of Economic Research
Conference Report

# The Governance of
# Not-for-Profit Organizations

Edited by      **Edward L. Glaeser**

**The University of Chicago Press**

Chicago and London

EDWARD L. GLAESER is professor of economics at Harvard
University and a research associate of the National Bureau of
Economic Research.

The University of Chicago Press, Chicago 60637
The University of Chicago Press, Ltd., London
© 2003 by the National Bureau of Economic Research
All rights reserved. Published 2003
Printed in the United States of America
12  11  10  09  08  07  06  05  04  03    1  2  3  4  5
ISBN: 0-226-29785-3 (cloth)


Library of Congress Cataloging-in-Publication Data

The governance of not-for-profit organizations / edited by Edward L.
    Glaeser.
        p.   cm. — (A National Bureau of Economic Research conference
    report)
        ISBN 0-226-29785-3 (cloth : alk. paper)
        1. Nonprofit organizations—Management—Congresses.
    I. Glaeser, Edward L. (Edward Ludwig), 1967–   II. Series

    HD62.6.G68 2003
    658′.048—dc21

                                                              2002045166

# Contents

# Acknowledgments

This book is part of a multiyear project on nonprofits at the National Bureau of Economic Research (NBER). I was a relative latecomer to this project; essentially, I came in as a pinch editor for R. Glenn Hubbard. Glenn, Martin Feldstein, and an anonymous donor are the true parents of this book. Glenn was the original ringleader of the project, and he would have edited this volume if he had not gone to serve as chairman of the Council of Economic Advisors. His intellectual fingerprints are everywhere in this volume and he deserves much credit for making this book happen.

Martin Feldstein not only was one of the originators of this project, but was an intellectual guide throughout the book's development. His wisdom and vast understanding of this subject area have been enormously helpful. Finally, an anonymous donor contributed both financially and intellectually. This donor ultimately deserves credit for the existence of this book.

A number of discussants at the conference where this material was originally presented improved the volume. David Cutler, Jerry Green, Thomas Hubbard, Fiona Scott Morton, Sendhil Mullainathan, Antoinette Schoar, and Bruce Weinberg all gave excellent comments. I am especially grateful to Jerry Green and to an anonymous reviewer, both of whom read through the entire manuscript and made helpful suggestions.

I am also grateful to the NBER staff, particularly Helena Fitz-Patrick and Brett Maranjian, for their invaluable help at making this happen. I would have been lost without them. Finally, I would like to thank Nancy Schwartz for her gentle support and sage guidance.

This book is not formally dedicated to anyone, but I like to think of this book as a thank-you note to our nonprofit employers. All of the authors in this volume are part of the nonprofit sector and we all have been treated well by that sector. In a sense, this volume is a chance to give something back to the universities and other nonprofit organizations (especially the NBER) that trained us and that continue to provide a supportive and stimulating atmosphere in which we can investigate our world.

# Introduction

Edward L. Glaeser

What makes not-for-profit organizations different from their for-profit alternatives? Nonprofit organizations have tax privileges: Donations to them are tax deductible, and nonprofit organizations are themselves free from many tax burdens. These tax advantages are at the heart of nonprofit status, and the nonprofit sector owes its strength, in part, to tax deductibility. A second difference between nonprofits and for-profits is the nondistribution constraint. Nonprofit organizations cannot disburse profits to owners or employees. This constraint affects the nature of nonprofits in important ways, and may enable nonprofits to commit not to cheat customers or workers (see Hansmann 1996; Weisbrod 1988; Glaeser and Shleifer 2001).

As striking as these differences between nonprofits and for-profits may be, a third difference is as important in explaining the behavior of nonprofit organizations: Nonprofit organizations do not have owners. The people who fund nonprofits, through donations, do not explicitly gain control rights over the firm. Nonprofit organizations do have boards, which do have control rights, and these boards are often partially composed of donors and their representatives.

But nonprofit boards are self-perpetuating and not accountable to share-

Edward L. Glaeser is professor of economics at Harvard University and a research associate of the National Bureau of Economic Research.

The National Science Foundation provided helpful funding. David Cutler, Martin Feldstein, and Andrei Shleifer provided enormously helpful conversations. This research comes out of the National Bureau of Economic Research's nonprofits project and will be the introduction of a volume of governance in the nonprofit sector. All of the participants in the nonprofits project provided helpful insights into these issues.

holders. They are rarely subject to elections or never to takeovers.[1] Board members cannot sell or transfer their control rights, so they do not own an asset the value of which is tied to the organization's success. There is certainly no legal rule requiring boards to act as custodians of the interests of past investors or donors. The law constrains itself to generally vaguely worded requirements about the nonprofit's mission. Moreover, given the murky missions of many nonprofits, their managers are inherently harder to incentivize. A for-profit manager's income can be tied to the stock price of his firm, but no similar benchmarks exist for most nonprofits. Indeed, many forms of incentive pay are illegal for nonprofit organizations.

The result of these factors is that the managers of nonprofit organizations—the chief executive officer (CEO) and the board—have an almost unmatched degree of autonomy. Donors often recognize that they have little influence on the institutions that they endow and they make their donations accepting that the only effects of their gifts will be to increase the budget of the recipient nonprofit. Furthermore, while nonprofit managers do not inherently maximize the objectives of either investors/donors or society as a whole, it is less clear what these managers do maximize or what ultimately drives the decisions of nonprofit organizations. This book represents an attempt to shed some new light on the objectives that govern nonprofit organizations.

Indeed, given the weak nature of corporate control in nonprofits, the most surprising thing to me about these organizations is that they function as well as they do. Widespread looting of endowments is almost unheard of. Nonprofit universities and hospitals generally do a credible job of educating students and curing the sick. While I will argue that workers do tend to subvert the mission of nonprofits, I also think that this subversion is ultimately modest and in some cases creates its own social benefits. Indeed, I suspect that, as the model suggests, competition in the market for customers and donors ultimately disciplines nonprofit organizations in a way that keeps them reasonably honest. If this suspicion is correct then it suggests that understanding the ability of competition to solve agency problems deserves much more research.

This introductory essay begins with a simple model of the choices made by nonprofit organizations. I consider a model with four types of actors: a manager (meant to represent the CEO and the board), workers, donors, and customers. Each of these actors has different preferences about the nature of the organization's product. The model focuses on whose preferences come to dominate the firm's decision making. Does the firm ultimately hew toward the preferences of donors, customers, workers, or management?

---

1. There are certainly minor exceptions to this claim. Many churches and synagogues have boards elected by parishioners. Alumni groups are frequently entitled to elect some members of university boards.

I assume that in the nonprofit organization, the manager decides on the nature of production and maximizes preferences over both the amount of output and its attributes. The level of donations, workers' salaries, and the sale price are all functions of the output attributes. Furthermore, workers are assumed to directly influence, lobby, or punish the manager if he or she deviates from their preferences. In some cases (think of the student riots in the 1960s), customers are also able to cause pain to management as well.

The most central result of this model is that worker preferences tend to be more important in nonprofits than in for-profit firms. In a profit-maximizing firm, worker preferences only matter to the extent that workers are willing to accept lower salaries. Even if workers are able to lobby managers, shareholders should be able to create incentives to undo the influence of elite workers. Of course, in reality, for-profit firms are often subverted by workers, especially top management. But the weak incentives in nonprofit organizations means that workers will have more influence within nonprofits. Indeed, as Glaeser and Shleifer (2001) argue, the ability of workers to protect themselves from ex post appropriation in nonprofits may be a major reason for the success of nonprofit organizations.[2]

Within and across nonprofit organizations, there will be a wide degree of variation in the extent to which workers are able to influence outcomes. Across workers, the ability to impact decision making depends on the amount of direct contact with the manager, the extent to which the CEO comes from a specific class of workers (e.g., professors, doctors), and the extent to which individual workers are able to punish or reward the CEO, especially through the press. As such, the model predicts that elite workers who interact with the CEO will have influence. Lower-level workers will not.

Across nonprofit organizations, the degree of worker control will rise with the wealth of the firm. Firms that are wealthy can afford to cater to their own interests rather than focusing on courting new donors or on making money through customers. Indeed, the model suggests that non-profits will have a life cycle where they are originally controlled by initial donors who select the board and continue to provide financing for the firm. However, over time, as the initial donors die off and as the firm becomes richer, the preferences of workers will tend to dominate the preferences of donors. If there is a shock to the income level of the firm, caused by an exogenous fall in price or increase in costs of production, then nonprofit organizations will become more commercial (i.e., cater more to the interests of consumers), and the preferences of management and workers will become less important.

---

2. Indeed, one aspect of the model in that paper is that nonprofit managers care less about profits than about embarrassment. This preference comes ultimately from the weak governance of nonprofits.

The model implies that the Pauly and Redisch (1973) view of hospitals as doctors' cooperatives is likely to be applied to many areas of nonprofits.[3] Instead, the generally weak governance of nonprofit organizations means that if the organizations get wealthier over time, they will almost invariably become oriented toward the interests of their elite workers. Indeed, in many of the most important nonprofit sectors, including religion, art museums, and academia, the growth of the industry was closely linked to at least a partial capture of the wealthier organizations by their workers. Certainly, as we have known since Berle and Means, for-profit corporations also face this problem. But the mechanisms that have made for-profit firms at least somewhat accountable to shareholders are ultimately much weaker in nonprofit organizations, and as such elite workers in nonprofit become much more dominant.[4]

Of course, there are many factors that limit the extent to which nonprofits deviate from their social goals. Boards do include representatives of at least relatively recent donors, and management is certainly motivated to attracting new donors. The nonprofits that actually sell to the public generally must pay some attention to consumer demand, especially if their prices are close to market rates.[5] Legal restrictions are also important. Nonprofits that pay their workers too much or that diverge too far from their mission statement may be subject to legal challenges. Finally, worker preferences are often themselves altruistic and often internalize the stated goals of the organization. Nonprofits are not organizations that selfishly maximize the income of their workers, but they are organizations where the preferences of elite workers come to have a very large and perhaps undue amount of influence.

Board control is strongest in areas that are clearly observable, such as the size of salaries and decisions about construction. This will tend to limit the extent to which workers are able to lobby for higher salaries and will induce workers to focus on less measurable amenities. Indeed, if boards are able to force salaries to be competitive (i.e., to make sure that there are not huge queues for jobs in the nonprofit), then the degree of worker influence over firm production can explain the well-known fact that salaries in nonprofits are generally lower. If the salaries of nonprofit workers are limited by competition, then salaries in nonprofits will be pushed down to reflect workers' greater ability to influence the organization. Even if full compensation doesn't occur, and nonprofit workers end up with rents, competition

3. McCormick and Meiners (1988) discuss the property rights that professors have over universities and essentially point to universities as being close to faculty-run institutions.

4. One view is that since the mid-1970s, a number of institutions including takeovers and incentive pay have served to reorient for-profit managers toward shareholder value. No comparable changes have occurred for nonprofits.

5. In many cases, nonprofit firms appear to price at far below market rates. This both serves a charitable function and also gives them the freedom to control the product without worrying about having to cater excessively to consumer preferences.

for jobs generally will mean that greater control over production is accompanied by lower wages.

Another implication of the model is that the composition of donors to nonprofit organizations will differ with the endowment level of the organization. Donors who are interested in impacting firm behavior will go to small nonprofits that they can control. The donors who give to large nonprofits cannot expect to affect the organization very much, except in cases where they can write a legally or reputationally enforceable contract. As such, donors to large nonprofits will either have preferences that are well matched with the preferences of elite workers or they will be driven by a desire to signal generosity and wealth. Donors to smaller nonprofits generally will be driven by a desire to impact the organization's behavior. Donors to wealthy nonprofits will also tend to have tastes that are more in line with the tastes of the workers in those nonprofits.

A third set of implications concerns the determinants of commercialism in nonprofits. One of the major topics in nonprofit research has been the convergence of nonprofit and for-profit behavior, especially in the medical sector. The model suggests that this type of convergence occurs in two different ways. First, negative shocks to the earnings of nonprofits will cause them to behave in a way that is more calculated to appeal to consumer tastes. Certainly, some of the commercialism of hospitals has occurred because of declining rents in that industry. Second, nonprofits will always be attuned to money-making opportunities, and a rise in the returns to commercialism will also make nonprofits more commercial. In Duggan (2000), nonprofit organizations seem perfectly able to take advantage of a clear money-making opportunity. This helps us to understand Barro's chapter in this volume showing that advertising rose most among the rich, university hospitals, not among the cash-strapped hospitals. He explains this by arguing that the returns to this form of commercial activity have risen most for nonprofits with the highest quality level.

Finally, the general freedom of nonprofit managers will tend to mean that there is much more variance over time and across companies in the structure and methods of nonprofits (relative to for-profits). If there is a profit-maximizing way to produce, then our models predict that profit maximizing should generally follow that strategy. However, nonprofits are much more likely to follow whatever quirky ideas dominate the opinions of their CEO. This variance will be limited if workers as a group are homogeneous across nonprofits and if CEO behavior tends to cater to the elite workers. As such, the model predicts that managerial style, which Bertrand and Schoar (2002) find to be important in for-profit firms, should be even more important in nonprofit organizations.

After presenting the model, I discuss donor-worker-customer conflicts in four key nonprofit industries: academia (particularly the better-endowed universities), hospitals, art museums, and the Catholic Church. I argue that all four industries support the basic point of the model: Weak incentives mean that workers come to greatly influence the practices of nonprofits. However, competition still acts to check massive rent extraction and to keep nonprofits oriented toward customers. Universities generally were originally dominated by their donors and the clergy. From 1900 to 1960 academics and higher-level administrators came to dominate these institutions. In 1890, donors and customers were the dominant figures in the life of the university. Professors were freely dismissed if their views differed from those of trustees, even on religious matters that were unrelated to their teaching. One hundred years later, academics and elite administrators exercise an incomparably larger degree of control over the nature of the university. Universities still cater to customers, and competition has certainly limited the growth of faculty salaries, but the rise of the research university is intimately related to professors gaining influence over the management of the academy.

Hospitals were also initially dominated by donors who supported them as charitable institutions for the poor. Initially, doctors often had little control over their management. Again, as they grew richer, they became much more oriented toward the interests and objectives of elite doctors. Hospitals for the indigent became elite research hospitals focused on the interests of their most impressive doctors. Only in the past thirty years have recent changes in the industry caused a re-orientation of these hospitals (see Weisbrod 1998). As the model predicts, this reorientation appears to be the result of a substantial decline in the amount of available rents.

Art museums likewise have seen a transformation from donor-controlled institutions to institutions where curators wield more power, but the transition has been more modest. Donors are still quite dominant in many institutions. This relatively large amount of continuing donor control occurs because art museums generally have limited free cash (their endowments are primarily in nontransferable works of art) and they depend on donors for new purchases. Of course, this is itself endogenous—donors know better than to give museums unrestricted cash. Art museums have generally been less effective in funding themselves with customers, but perhaps the financial success of blockbuster exhibitions will end up freeing museum management from donors and giving them more autonomy.

My final example of the transformation from donor to worker control is the Catholic Church. One thousand years ago, lay leaders—the founders of the church—exercised a phenomenal amount of control over the institution: They chose bishops, they determined church policy, and even the pope was ultimately beholden to the secular authorities who supported him. Over the last three hundred years, the wealth of the church grew significantly and with it the degree of priestly power. In recent years as well, the rise of various churches in the United States and elsewhere has been accompanied by church workers freeing themselves from lay control.

Finally, I end the paper by reviewing the seven subsequent chapters in this volume. These papers relate to various aspects of nonprofit behavior. Two of these are general: Fisman and Hubbard examine endowments, and Malani, Philipson, and David review the empirical literature on what nonprofits maximize. Three are focused on the medical sector: Hansmann, Kessler, and McClellan show that nonprofits are slower to respond to negative demand shocks than their for-profit competitors, Erus and Weisbrod look at bonuses in nonprofits, and Barro examines hospital advertising. Goetzman and Oster examine the behavior of art museums, and Nelson and Zeckhauser examine donor-church relations in Renaissance Florence.

## The Model

I consider a nonprofit an organization that produces a good (e.g., health care, education, etc.) that is characterized by number of units sold, denoted $N$, and a production attribute, denoted $X$. This $X$ attribute is meant to capture things like the research orientation of medical care in hospitals, the spending decisions of universities, the degree of openness of art museums, or the style in which ministers preach. Different values of $X$ will impact the utility of managers, workers, donors, and customers. $X$ is a continuous scalar variable that lies between $-1$ and $1$. In a more realistic model, $X$ would be a rich vector of characteristics.

This production attribute, $X$, will have different interpretations in different settings. For example, in a university, the value of $X$ might correspond to the extent to which the university focuses on research or teaching. In hospitals, the value of $X$ might capture the amount of attention paid to reputation-making rare diseases versus the amount of attention paid to more common ailments. In churches, $X$ might capture the degree to which sermons focus on what the clerics believe relative to what the congregation wants to hear.

The good is sold for a price $P(|X - X_C|)$ where $P(.)$ is a strictly decreasing function and $|X - X_C|$ is the absolute value operator. In the case of some nonprofits $P$ may be fixed at zero. In the case of for-profits, $P$ is unlikely to be zero. The value of $X_C$ represents the ideal nature of the good to consumers. Thus, in a university context, customer willingness to pay for classes might depend on the extent to which those classes are entertaining or cater toward productivity in the workplace.

The organization produces using a manager, exactly one unit of labor, and a flexible amount of capital. The cost of capital is $K(N)$, where $K(.)$ is an increasing, weakly convex function (in most cases, I will assume that $K[N]$ is linear). The wage rate of labor is denoted $W$, so that total costs of production are $W + K(N)$. The utility of workers' utility equals their wage, $W$, plus $BX$. I assume that $X$ is ordered so that workers always prefer higher values of $X$. The parameter $B$ captures the degree to which workers care about this aspect of production.

The reservation utility of workers equals $\underline{W}$. One key issue is the degree to which wages are set by market forces and the degree to which wages will respond to the level of $X$. Given that I am assuming a fair amount of divergence from profit-maximizing behavior, in principle, it might be possible for workers to capture the organization and pay themselves extremely high wages. In line with the experience of most nonprofit organizations, I assume that this does not occur and that wages must be at least somewhat responsive to the degree of competition for the jobs. In essence, I am assuming that if the queues for nonprofit jobs get too long, someone in management notices and cuts salaries, at least a little. This is the first place in the model where I implicitly assume that competition (in this case labor market competition) serves to limit rent appropriation in nonprofits.

However, I do allow that workers in nonprofits will be able to receive rents. The form this will take is that, in some nonprofits, workers' perquisites will rise and wages will not fall one-for-one. In the language of the model, wages may not respond fully to changes in the level of $X$. To capture the range of possibilities, we assume that wages, $W$, equal $\underline{W} - \sigma BX$, where $\sigma$ can range from zero to 1. Low values of $\sigma$ imply that workers are actually able to appropriate rents from the job if they influence the character of the organization's production. High values of $\sigma$ imply that workers' utility levels are determined entirely by their outside opportunities. Lower values of $\sigma$ imply that workers are able to keep more of the rents that their lobbying activities generate.

Recognizing that for-profit firms often face their own incentive problems and fail to maximize profits, I still begin with the benchmark case of a purely profit-maximizing firm. Such a firm will choose $X$ and $N$ to maximize $P(|X - X_C|)N - K(N) - (\underline{W} - \sigma BX)$, which implies that the firm will choose output so that $P(|X - X_C|) = K'(N)$, and $X$ so that $P'(|X - X_C|)N + \sigma B = 0$. This implies that profit-maximizing firms will choose a level of $X$ that is greater than $X_C$ (to reduce their wage bill), and, generally, the value of $X$ will rise with $\sigma$ and $B$. Profit-maximizing firms will internalize the preferences of their workers more as workers care more about the attribute and as their wages respond more to workplace amenities.

In the case of nonprofit organizations, no simple profit-maximizing rule can be assumed. Instead, I assume that the choices of $X$ and $N$ are made by a manager with his or her own preferences over the value of $X$. In the nonprofit context, this manager is meant to represent a combination of the CEO and the board. I assume that the direct utility for the manager from production equals $f(N) - g|X - X_M|$. Thus, the manager receives utility both from the scale of production and from the extent to which the good aligns well with his own preferences. The scale maximization assumption is somewhat arbitrary, but given the lack of evidence about the objectives of nonprofit boards, it seems as good an assumption as any. The value of $X_M$ reflects the manager's preferences about the product, and I will assume that this lies between zero and 1.

The nonprofit must earn exactly zero profits. Positive profits would violate the non-distribution constraint. Negative profits would lead to bankruptcy. The organization's revenues come from sales, the endowment (equal to $E$), and new donations. The supply of endowment is exogenous, but the flow of new donations is determined by donors who also respond to the value of $X$. In the case of a new nonprofit, the donors might themselves be able to choose the board and select the value of $X$. However, for more mature organizations, donors rarely exercise strong control and as such are probably best seen as "price" or $X$ takers who accept the characteristics of the organization as given and then allocate funds more to nonprofits who fit their preferences. To highlight the potential conflict between donors and workers, I assume that donors' preferences are opposed to those of workers and that the donor would ideally like $X$ to equal zero. The level of donations will be a function $D - d|X|$.

The value of $d$ reflects the degree to which donations respond to the organization's product. Higher levels of $d$ should be interpreted as reflecting a more competitive market for donations. If this market is more competitive and if the organizations stray from providing the goods that donors want, donations will tumble. If the organization has a monopoly on its donors, then the level of donations will be invariant with respect to $X$ (i.e., $d$ will be small).

A nonprofit organization faces a break-even constraint that implies that total profits, or $P(|X - X_C|)N + D - d|X| + E - (\underline{W} - \sigma BX) - K(N)$, must equal zero. Competition in three markets impacts profitability: the eventual product market, the market for donations, and the labor market. All three of these markets will act to discipline nonprofits and keep them from catering to the whims of top management. Some nonprofits, for example, large foundations that do not look for new donations and that give money away, only compete in one market. As a result, their profits will only be influenced by competition for labor, not by competition in either of the other two markets.

Workers' preferences are internalized by management in two ways. First, just like for-profit firms, nonprofit organizations will respond to the impact that catering to employees will have on wages. Second, I assume that workers can impose a cost of $C$ times $(1 - X)$ on management. The level of cost is increasing in the distance between the actual attribute of the good and the workers' desired nature of the good. Examples of this cost would include publicly embarrassing the CEO by talking negatively about him to newspapers or just impeding his progress through obstructionist tactics. This is meant to reflect the power that workers generally have over the quality of life of their bosses. In principle, workers in for-profit firms can also influence their CEOs, but in the case of for-profit firms, shareholders may be able to cause the CEO to care more about profits than about elite worker influence.

Because managers are workers who are selected by boards, I will assume that the preferences of managers lie between the preferences of workers and donors, i.e., $X_M$ lies between zero and 1. I consider a nonprofit organization where the manager solely maximizes his own utility subject to the constraint that total net revenues are nonnegative. The manager then maximizes $f(N) - g|X - X_M| - C(1 - X)$ over $N$ and $X$ subject to this constraint. The first-order condition for the level of $N$ yields $P(|X - X_C|) + f'(N)/\lambda = K'(N)$, where $\lambda$ is the multiplier on the balanced budget constraint.

If we let $X_N$ refer to the value of $X$ chosen by the nonprofit organization, then the following proposition holds:

PROPOSITION 1. *The level of production will be greater in the nonprofit organization than in the for-profit firm if and only if* $P(0) < P(|X_N - X_C|) + f'(N)/\lambda$.

As long as $P(0) < P(|X - X_C|) + f'(N)/\lambda$, then this first-order condition gives us the familiar result (shown in Malani, Philipson, and David, chapter six in this volume) that nonprofits will produce more than for-profits because they have a direct taste for production (the $f'(N)$ term in this equation). This proposition also suggests that nonprofits will be slower to shut down hospitals in the face of declining profitability, as found by Hansmann, Kessler, and McClellan (chap. 1 in this volume).

However, if $P(0) > P(|X - X_C|) + f'(N)/\lambda$, then for-profit firms produce at a larger scale than nonprofit organizations. The intuition of this result is that for-profits end up making goods that appeal more to consumers. As such, the price that for-profit firms receive will be higher, and the marginal benefit to them of producing is also higher than the marginal benefit of producing to the nonprofit organization. One example of this phenomenon might be nonprofits that produce very elite products, such as public radio and television, which have less market appeal than their for-profit alternatives.

To focus on the determinants of $X$, I now assume that $K(N) = KN$ and that $K > P(0)$. This assumption, combined with the zero profit assumption, means that nonprofits produce in areas where for-profits would lose money and shut down. If $X > 0$, then the level of $N$ for the nonprofit firm will equal $(E + D - d|X| - W)/(K - P[|X - X_C|])$. Values of $X$ that please consumers will increase scale by raising the overall revenues. Values of $X$ that appeal to donors will increase scale by raising the level of donations. Thus, the managers will have to decide on a value of $X$, taking into account that they can either cater to their own wishes (or the wishes of workers) and produce at a smaller scale, or they can cater to the wishes of donors and customers and produce at a larger scale.

The manager chooses $N$ and $X$ to maximize $f(N) - g|X - X_M| - C(1 - X)$ subject to the constraint that $N$ equals $(E + D - \underline{W} - d|X| + \sigma BX)/(K - P[|X - X_C|])$, which yields the first-order condition

$$(1) \quad P'(|X - X_C|)N + \sigma B = d \cdot I(X > 0) - [C - g \cdot I(X > X_M)]\frac{(K - P)}{f'(N)},$$

where $I(X > k)$ is an indicator function that takes on a value of 1 if $X > k$ and $-1$ otherwise. I assume that $d$ is greater than $\sigma B$ to avoid a corner solution where workers' preferences completely dominate the organization's choices.

Comparing this first-order condition with the first-order condition for the profit-maximizing firm (i.e., $P'[|X - X_C|]N + \sigma B = 0$) shows that nonprofits will not produce the same products as for-profit firms. Their output will be directed toward the interests of donors and workers in a way that is different from for-profits. If $d$ is small, and $X_M > X_C$, then nonprofits will cater to worker and manager taste more than for-profits will. As such, all nonprofits, not just Pauly and Redisch's (1973) hospitals, will resemble workers' cooperatives.

The forces that mitigate this effect will be the preferences of customers and donors. Again the degree of competition in the product or donation markets is crucial. If the level of donations is quite susceptible to the attributes of the product, then the organization will end up catering to donors. If the product market is highly competitive, which would be represented by a higher value of $P'(.)$, then the organization will end up catering to customers. Worker capture is a real possibility in nonprofits, but this capture will be tempered by competition.

PROPOSITION 2. *If $P'(|X - X_C|) = P$ then $X > 0$ and if $d > \sigma B$, then the value of $X$ is rising with $\sigma$, $B$, $C$, $D$, $E$, and falling with $d$ and $\underline{W}$. The value of $X$ is falling with $K$ and rising with $P$ if and only if $f'(N) > -Nf''(N)$.*

The assumption is that $P'(|X - X_C|) = P$ eliminates the role of competition for consumers at this stage. I will return to this form of competition later in the model. Here, this assumption implies that $X$ will be positive, since a negative value of $X$ would only hurt the manager through direct utility loss, higher wages, punishment from workers, and lost donations.

These comparative statics are the heart of the model. The manager faces a tradeoff between accommodating the donors and accommodating the workforce. The manager's interest in accommodating the workforce is naturally driven by the extent to which the workers can cause pain to the manager and by the extent to which their wages can be reduced by catering to their desires. Thus, if the manager is particularly dependent on the workers or if the workers have the ability to embarrass the manager, then the manager will be likely to accommodate their desires, not the desires of the donors.

In profit-maximizing firms, worker preferences only change firm behavior if they impact wages. In nonprofits without incentives, worker preferences will matter because of the ability of workers to influence or punish management. As such, nonprofits and profit-maximizing firms are predicted to cater to different workers. Profit-maximizing firms are predicted to change working conditions if those changes can reduce the wage bill. Nonprofits are predicted to change working conditions to cater to those workers who are able to directly influence or punish the CEO and board.

A more complicated model would allow different groups to have different abilities or willingnesses to engage in different forms of lobbying. In that case, we would expect those workers with a particular ability to influence management to receive the biggest amenities. The workers that are physically closest to the CEO or that have the best ability to use the press to embarrass the CEO are likely to acquire the most rents.

If the division of labor increases in the largest nonprofits, then CEOs will mainly interact with other administrators. In smaller nonprofits, CEOs will have more direct contact with the actual workers in the organization. As such, the CEOs in the largest nonprofits may tend to be more oriented toward the desires of administrators while the CEOs in smaller (but still wealthy) nonprofits may be more oriented toward other elite workers. This might explain why many observers argue that the University of Chicago is more faculty oriented, while larger universities, such as Harvard or Stanford, might be more oriented toward the desires of top administrators.

Given that CEOs will cater to their friends, forward-looking nonprofit boards should choose CEOs from different interest groups over time if they are interested in maintaining balance in the orientation of the firm. Perhaps it might make sense to alternate between an administrator and an academic in choosing university presidents. Given the ability to direct for-profit CEOs using incentives, there is less reason to choose a for-profit CEO by cycling among different interest groups.[6]

The tendency to favor donors decreases with the innate wealth of the organization and rises with competition in the market for donations. If donations are forthcoming regardless of whether the donors are satisfied or if the organization has a large endowment, then the marginal benefits of satisfying the donor are less. This follows from the concavity of $f(.)$. Higher levels of innate income mean that the organization is already producing a significant amount of output and there is little need for more production. This will suggest that in early stages of the organization, when the endowment is low and the organization is really dependent on new donations,

6. Of course, different for-profit CEO styles may be appropriate at different times (see Bertrand and Schoar 2002), but in the case of an incentivized CEO there is less reason to cycle in order to take care of all of the interest groups.

donor preferences will be followed. However, as the wealth of the organization increases over time, the manager will find the pressure of his workforce more important than the desires of donors.

An innately lower value of $\underline{W}$ will act as an income shock, so organizations that have an innately cheaper workforce will be free not to accommodate donors. An example of an organization with access to particularly cheap labor might be the church. In a sense, faith-subsidized labor acts just like an endowment for religious organizations. Firms that hire workers at market wages will have to pay more attention to the needs of donors, and firms that have access to below market wage workers will not. Volunteer labor frees organizations from attending to donors' wishes.

Greater competition in the donation market, $d$, induces the organization to follow the wishes of donors more. Alternatively, $d$ might be low because donors are particularly motivated by a desire for prestige, as the Goetzman and Oster chapter in this volume emphasizes. Some nonprofits, because of their permanence and visibility, might provide an ideal way to signal wealth and altruism. If donors are presumably interested in having their names clearly attached to permanent things, such as buildings, but otherwise they do not really care about the internal functioning of the nonprofit (as long as it survives), then $d$ will be low.

Even if $d$ is high, nonprofits are likely to follow the desires of prospective donors, not past donors. The lack of legal controls means that unless the tastes of the new donors (or the CEO) line up well with the tastes of the "old" donors, old donors will have little sway. In practice, older donors tend to have influence on nonprofits in two ways: explicit legal arrangements that bind nonprofits and representation on the board.

One example of explicit legal restrictions is the actual mission statement of the nonprofit. In principle, if management strays too far from this mission statement, it can open itself up to legal action. A recent example includes the legal challenges that were considered a few years ago against the Lincoln Land Institute. The Lincoln Land Institute was set up by a philanthropist follower of Henry George. As national interest in the ideas of Henry George has waned, recent management has certainly put less emphasis on Georgist research and a group of Henry George-inspired individuals were considering legal action against the institute to push it toward its original orientation.

Other examples of explicit contracts binding nonprofits are more specific. Gifts often come with terms, i.e., a building for a particular type of medicine or a chair for Canadian studies. If the nonprofit grossly violates these terms, it leaves itself open to legal challenge. However, in most contexts, contractual incompleteness ensures that the nonprofit has a great deal of latitude in actually implementing the donor's wishes. An exception to this claim is that donors do seem to be effective at legally insuring that their name remains attached to the gift. The model suggests that a desire for new donations, not legal contracts, keeps nonprofits oriented toward the desires of donors.

When there are not effective, explicit, legal restrictions, board membership tends to be the best means of ensuring that a nonprofit will follow the wishes of a past donor. However, boards themselves may find it easier to control some aspects of nonprofits than others. Boards will find it easy to monitor cash outlays and to make decisions about big construction projects. As Jencks and Riesman (2002, 16) said, originally more than thirty years ago, "Mistaken judgments about bricks and mortar are more obvious to the lay trustees than most mistakes in academic policy or personnel." They will find it extremely difficult to actually monitor the nature of services. This predicts that donors will be good at controlling new buildings, and will be good at holding down salaries, but they will be bad at determining what is said during lectures. Indeed, a major trend over the twentieth century is the rise in faculty autonomy over research and teaching. Another major trend in universities is the decline in board (or CEO) control over hiring and firing decisions. This trend again should be seen as an example of increasing worker influence over an area that boards find it hard to monitor.

While the boards of for-profit firms are ultimately elected by shareholders, the boards of nonprofit organizations resemble self-perpetuating oligarchies. In some cases, particular groups (such as alumni) have the right to elect members of a nonprofit board.[7] In other cases, large donations will be "rewarded" with board membership. However, even if a board is initially made up of representatives of the nonprofit's major donors, eventually this board will be replaced. The CEO usually plays a large role in selecting the new board members. As such, if the CEO is an elite worker at the university, then the CEO will be able to influence the selection of new members of the board to match his or her own preferences. The history of nonprofit organizations is rife with examples of boards that at one time were filled with representatives of the original donor, but later moved in some other direction.

Even in cases where board membership is passed along within a family, a donor's descendants' preferences will often differ from those of the original donor.[8] As time goes by, the goals of management will tend to follow their own paths and rarely seem bound by the wishes of the original donors. Modern universities may be swayed by the desires of new donors or

7. For example, in the case of Harvard University, the board of overseers is elected by alumni, but the Harvard Corporation is a self-perpetuating organization that selects its own members.
8. There is some evidence to suggest that the preferences of the children (and grandchildren) of philanthropists like John MacArthur or John D. Rockefeller are not all that close to the preferences of their parents.

alumni, but no one can look at modern universities and think that the desires of the original donors, who generally wanted to endow training grounds for the clergy, are being ardently pursued.

The degree of institutional wealth and worker autonomy will impact the nature of donations. Because donor control over rich nonprofits is often weak, donors who really want their money to be spent in a specific manner will start their own foundations instead of giving to wealthy nonprofits. Donors whose preferences are in line with those of elite workers at the nonprofit will continue to give. As such, the original donors to Harvard might have been motivated by a desire to train clergy. More recent donors are presumably more motivated by a desire to fund research.

Many donors also appear to be more interested in broadcasting their own wealth and benevolence than in changing nonprofit behavior. These donors should be particularly attracted to the largest nonprofits. In some cases, nonprofit endowments will have increasing returns, as large endowments serve as a guarantee of future survival and tend to increase the publicity value of donations. These particularly wealthy nonprofits will tend to have a comparative advantage with "signaling" donors because (a) their wealth often means that they can broadcast the signal to a wider audience and (b) their wealth guarantees permanence. As such, we should expect donations to weak and poor nonprofits to be driven by a desire to change nonprofit behavior, and we should expect donations to wealthy, strong nonprofits to be driven by a desire to broadcast wealth and benevolence.

Managerial and worker power both determine and are determined by the composition of donors. If a nonprofit reaches the stage where it can generate a steady stream of donations based entirely on the desire for eternal fame or on the desire to fund workers, then it will be relatively free to follow its own objectives without interference from donor wishes. However, if donors are primarily involved altruists, then the wishes of donors will tend to be quite important in the decisions of nonprofits. The independence of some universities and art museums probably has as much to do with their ability to raise donations, motivated entirely by a desire for fame, as by their endowments themselves.

Changes in $B$—the extent to which workers care about the nature of the product—will impact the choice of $X$ only through the wage. As such, changes in $B$ will increase the organization's income if $X > 0$ and if $\sigma$ is high. Thus, the more that the organization favors workers, increases in the strength of workers' tastes will lead to decreases in the price of the wage bill and to increases to the extent that workers favor workers if the organization is already catering to those workers.

Finally, changes in $K$ and $P$ have two effects. First, an increase in $P$ or a decrease in $K$ raises the income available to the organization. This effect will tend to make the organization increase the value of $X$. Second, an increase in $P$ or a decrease in $K$ lowers the cost of output—this will tend to make it more attractive for the manager to increase output and this will increase the desire for more cash, thus the importance of donors. Of course, if we get to the point where $P > K$, then the manager will increase output purely for the sake of making money.

The following corollary to proposition 1 follows directly from the fact that wages equals the reservation utility plus $B$ times $X$.

COROLLARY TO PROPOSITION 2. *As long as $\sigma < 1$, then observed wages of workers in nonprofits will be less than if $P(|X - X_C|) = P$, and wages will be falling with C, D, and E and rising with d. The level of wages is falling with K and rising with P if and only if $f'(N) > -Nf''(N)$.*

This corollary implies that rich nonprofits may have low wages because workers are able to influence the organization's production processes. This result would change if the employees are also good at lobbying to get their nominal wage increased, but, as I have argued earlier, boards tend to be effective at limiting massive salary increases for workers. If workers can increase their wages, then there will be queues for jobs at particularly wealthy nonprofits. Indeed, any situation where $\sigma > 0$ will result in a situation where there are queues for entry into the organization because worker wages do not adjust fully to the higher level of amenities in nonprofits, we should expect to see workers getting some of the rents.[9]

I have so far discussed the ability of workers to influence managers during the everyday business of the managers' term of employment. It is also true that workers are able to influence the board to get managers who are friendly to their interests. As workers will generally serve on search committees, in part because their expertise is helpful in finding a new manager, they will also be able to get a manager with preferences close to their own.

The impact of the strength of the manager's preferences will depend on whether $X$ is above $X_M$, or below $X_M$, or in other words, if the nature of the nonprofit looks more like an average of managers' and workers' tastes or more like an average of managers' and donors' tastes.

PROPOSITION 3. *If second-order conditions hold, then an increase in the value of g will raise the value of X if and only if $X_M > X$.*

This proposition actually has some useful implications for the impact of a strong president. At a point in time where donors are particularly powerful (because $D$ and $E$ are small), $X$ is likely to be low or less than $X_M$. In that case, an increase in $g$—a powerful president—will be likely to raise the value of $X$, to make the nonprofit more into a workers' cooperative and less

---

9. It is possible that in some cases worker control will lead to higher nominal wages in nonprofit firms. However, management is likely to take at least some advantage of their ability to hire cheaper workers.

into a donors' organization. Alternatively, in spectacularly rich and long-standing organizations, the value of $X$ is likely to be high, and strong managers will find themselves fighting against workers, rather than supporting them. As such, in the early twentieth century, university presidents saw their goal as liberating the university from the control of the donors (in some cases, state governments). Men like Robert Maynard Hutchins at Chicago or Clark Kerr at Berkeley fought for their professors and generally opposed their donors and boards.

Today, presidents of well-endowed universities are often as likely to find themselves allied with their donors against their faculties. This does not occur because the views of the presidents have changed, but rather because the status quo value of $X$ is much closer to workers' interests than to donors' interests, i.e., the increasing wealth of universities has made them much closer to workers' cooperatives than to donors' playthings.

One exception to this claim tends to be state universities. In these places, probably because (a) legislators care more about the nature of the university (i.e., have a higher value of $d$) and (b) because endowments are smaller, the universities have stayed closer to the interests of the donors (i.e., the state legislatures) and further from the interests of the faculty. As such, $X$ is often below $X_M$, and strong university presidents find themselves trying to push the university toward more academic goals, rather than toward goals that are aligned with those of donors.

The influence of the idiosyncratic tastes of nonprofit CEOs implies that there will be much more variance in the methods and practices of nonprofits than is comparable for profit firms. The model implies that the level of $X$ in for-profits will be determined by the demands of consumers and partially of workers. In some cases, for-profits will differ in their services to fit different product niches. However, they should not change their patterns in response to the whims of their CEOs. As such, the model predicts more variation from firm to firm and within firms over time in response to different managers.

## Commercialism and Product Market Competition

I now turn to the topic of commercialism. The previous section dealt with the conflict between the goals of donors and those of workers. However, the interests of consumers also matter. When we think about nonprofits commercializing themselves, this tends to mean that they are taking the interests of consumers into account more strongly.

In the framework, these issues can be captured by different values of $X_C$. If $X_C$ is negative, then the preferences of consumers differ from the preference of both donors and workers. If $X_C$ is positive, then customers' tastes will lie somewhere between the tastes of workers and donors.

To simplify the analysis, I will analyze two cases which capture the intuition of the differing scenarios. First, I consider where customers want the value of $X$ to be as low as possible, and thus their interests are opposed to the interests of both donors and workers. This may well capture the reality in private hospitals, where commercialism tends to act against the wishes of both doctors and donors. Second, I will discuss the case where $X_C$ lies between zero and 1, and thus customers' tastes lie between the tastes of managers and donors.

For simplicity, we will also assume that the interests of workers and management are perfectly aligned, i.e., $X_M = 1$, so that we can focus on a three-way (rather than a four-way) conflict between workers, donors, and customers.

$$(1')\quad C + g = f'\left[\frac{E + D + \sigma BX - dX \cdot I(X > 0) - \underline{W}}{K - P(|X - X_C|)}\right]$$

$$\cdot \left[\frac{d \cdot I(X > 0) - \sigma B - P'(|X - X_C|) \cdot I(X > X_C)N}{K - P(|X - X_C|)}\right]$$

PROPOSITION 4. *If $P(|X - X_C|) = P_0 - P_1 X$, and if we assume that $-(C + g)(K - P_0 + P_1 X)f''(N) > 2P_1 f(N)^2$ so that second-order conditions hold, then*

1. The level of $X$ will rise with $E$ and $D$ and fall with $\underline{W}$.
2. The level of $X$ will rise with $C$ and $g$. The level of $X$ will rise with $B$ and $\sigma$ as long as $X$ is not too negative. If $X$ is not too negative, then the level of $X$ will fall with $d$ if and only if $X$ is positive.
3. The level of $X$ will rise with $P_0$ and fall with $K$ as long as $K > P_0 + P_1 X - 0.25$.
4. The value of $X$ will decline with $P_1$.

The intuition of the first result is that increases in wealth allow nonprofits to cater to their own preferences a little bit more. Technically, this occurs because income causes the number of units to rise and this decreases the marginal benefit per unit. As such, this predicts that decreases in wealth will tend to make nonprofit organizations more commercial.

Result (2) tells us that the desire to cater to customers will decrease when worker or manager preferences are stronger, or when workers have more influence over manager utility. This result is unsurprising and just suggests that noncommercial nonprofits will particularly appear when managerial or worker preferences are strong. The impact on donor preferences depends on whether $X$ is positive or not. In either case, increases in $d$ will make the nonprofit adhere more closely to donor preferences.

The third comparative static tells us that increases in the profit per unit sold will tend to make nonprofits less attentive to market demands. This effect works through the income effect discussed above. However, it is conceivable that increases in profitability can have another effect—they can increase the desire to produce more units. In this case, the nonprofit organization may cater to customers in order to raise income and increase the number of units produced.

Finally, the comparative static on $P_1$ is quite straightforward. I interpret higher values of $P_1$ as reflecting either stronger consumer preferences or greater product market competition. If the product market is particularly competitive or if customers are particularly interested in goods of a certain quality, then nonprofits are likely to cater to consumers' tastes. This helps us make sense of Barro's finding that university hospitals particularly took to advertising, a form of commercialism, in the 1990s. He argues that this can be understood because there was an increase in the marginal revenue from advertising for hospital nonprofits and less of an increase for other firms.

When $X_C$ lies between zero and 1, the situation gets somewhat murkier. In that case, the comparative statics depend on whether $X$ lies above or below $X_C$. Increases in wealth or increases in the strength of managerial or worker preferences will still cause $X$ to rise. Increases in donor preferences will cause $X$ to fall. Increases in the strength of consumer preferences will generally cause nonprofits to adhere more closely to the demands of consumers. As none of these results are all that surprising, I will omit a formal proposition.

This model has emphasized several points about nonprofits and the differences between nonprofits and profit-maximizing firms. First, nonprofits will be more oriented toward the desires of their elite workers than for-profit firms. In particular, nonprofits will cater to the workers who have direct contact with the CEO. This difference between nonprofits and for-profits will be most visible among the richest nonprofit organizations. As nonprofits become poorer, they will more closely resemble for-profit firms.

Second, nonprofits will offer lower wages than for-profit firms, unless worker control has cut off any labor market competition. These lower wages are compensating differentials for greater control over the working environment. Third, nonprofits will be less oriented toward the interests of consumers and their policies will be much less likely to shift with changes in consumer demand. This will depend on the degree to which there is profound product market competition. Four, nonprofits will on the other hand be much more likely to shift policies with changes in their CEO. Finally, nonprofit behavior is likely to show much more profound "income effects" than for-profit behavior.

### Conflicts in Nonprofit Organizations

In this section, I focus on four areas of nonprofit organizations and discuss some of the history of these sectors. My interest is only in certain episodes of donor-worker or customer-worker-donor conflict, and I am not trying to give even a thumbnail sketch of the history of these sectors.

The Rise of the Modern American Research University[10]

In this section, I discuss the conflict between donors and faculty in the wealthiest universities. These comments are irrelevant for the majority of the higher education sector which is not well endowed.

Writing in 1968, Jencks and Riesman (2002) describe an "academic revolution" where early nineteenth-century colleges, dominated by the preferences of founders, donors, and customers, evolved into twentieth-century universities, which increasingly were dominated by upper level administrators and faculty. This transformation follows exactly the logic of the model. Nineteenth-century colleges were poor and because "financial solvency was so precarious . . . colleges responded to even the smallest external pressures and had only the most limited ability to reshape the priorities established by their supporters" (Jencks and Riesman 2002, 6).

In the twentieth century, a few colleges became rich, in part because of the increasingly important role of education in the modern economy and in part because of the increasing value of some endowments. These richer universities reoriented themselves to the preferences of upper-level administrators and faculty. As Jencks and Riesman (2002, 17) write: "What is perhaps unusual about the academic world is the extent to which the top management, while nominally acting in the interests of the board, actually represents the interests of 'middle management' (i.e., the faculty)." Of course, I have argued that this orientation is not particular to academia, but it is a general feature of wealthy nonprofits.

The wealthiest nonprofit universities were founded in the colonial period. As Morison (1935) describes, Harvard was founded by the General Court of Massachusetts with an initial grant of 400 pounds. John Harvard's own bequest came in his will in 1638 and appears to have been somewhere between 200 and 800 pounds. Contemporary observers, such as Governor Winthrop and Thomas Shepard, appear to have thought that Nathaniel Eaton, Harvard's first professor, absconded with the funds. Thus, from the first, the funding of America's universities appears to have been used in the interests of faculty (see Morison 1935 for details).

While there was certainly substantial secular education at Harvard, as Morison writes, "we should miss the spirit of early Harvard if we supposed the founders' purpose to be secular" (1935, 250). The ultimate goal of the university was certainly to propagate the Puritan faith. Indeed, the religious orientation of college persisted for centuries. Jencks and Riesman begin their book by writing that "during the seventeenth, eighteenth, and early nineteenth centuries, American colleges were conceived and operated as pillars of the locally established church" (2002, 1). They were

10. As is obvious from my quotation practices, my view of the changes in the modern university has been primarily influenced by Jencks and Riesman (2002).

funded by a combination of private donations (often given at death) and public funding. New colleges were founded by local entrepreneurs who responded to some combination of their own idiosyncratic passions and local demand, and these entrepreneurs often provided strong, occasionally overwhelming leadership.

Jencks and Riesman describe the world of the nineteenth-century colleges as being characterized by "self-confident trustees [who] tended to intervene in college affairs far more often and more disastrously than is usual today" (2002, 6). They continue and write that "nineteenth-century college presidents also tended to be far more domineering than they are today, carrying the business of the college around in their brief cases or even in their heads, entrusting very little to committees of faculty members of lower-level bureaucrats, and imposing their personal stamp on the entire college" (Jencks and Riesman, 6). Of course, in many cases, powerful presidents, like the University of Chicago's William Rainey Harper, were powerful because they acted in concert with founding donors, such as John D. Rockefeller. As such, control of the nineteenth-century university was shared between donors, the CEO, and customers.

Over the course of the twentieth century, two major complementary trends occurred that transformed research universities into their more modern incarnations: The most prestigious universities grew in both complexity and wealth. The rise in complexity meant that CEOs could not micromanage the entire organization and as such had to trust in subordinates. Naturally, a greater reliance of subordinates meant that these subordinates were able to influence the direction of the university. The rise in income meant that universities were freed from catering to the customers and donors. The net result, again quoting Jencks and Riesman, was that "most university presidents see their primary responsibility as 'making the world safe for academicians,' however much the academicians resent the necessary (and unnecessary) compromises made on their behalf" (2002, 17). By the late twentieth century, the university was "more concerned with keeping the faculty happy than with placating any other single group" (Jencks and Riesman 2002, 18).

The importance of university wealth in the transformation from donors' universities to faculty universities is well illustrated in the remarkable career of Robert Maynard Hutchins, who ran the University of Chicago between 1929 and 1951. Hutchins was highly idiosyncratic and also fundamentally oriented toward faculty preferences. The most glaring example of Hutchins's faculty orientation was his decision to shut down Chicago's extremely successful football program (the original Monsters of the Midway) because it distracted from more academic pursuits. Hutchins also created his Great Books program and ardently pursued his vision of the university as a "community of scholars." Hutchins had the freedom to pursue this vision because of the vast wealth of the University of Chicago. Because of the generosity of the Rockefellers, the University of Chicago had the largest endowment in the country, and Hutchins could use it to pursue his own interests and those of his faculty. Of course, the downside of creating a true professors' paradise is the loss in donations that ultimately caused a massive reduction in the relative financial standing of the university.

Of course, the academic history of the late twentieth century also shows that university management is also vulnerable to the lobbying and influence of students. In the model, I assumed that only workers can punish the CEO. More realistic, I would have allowed current students to also cause pain to the administration. Indeed, the student riots of the 1960s and the current living wage sit-ins are examples of students exploiting their ability to cause pain to university administrators. These actions appear to be effective in influencing the behavior of nonprofit CEOs. It is hard to imagine that similar demonstrations would have been as effective in changing the behavior of General Steel or Exxon.[11] The weak incentives for nonprofit CEOs make them more vulnerable to this type of local influence.

Two examples of the power of faculty over the twentieth century are the institution of tenure and the rise of faculty research. The widespread existence of academic tenure only came in the mid-twentieth century. Appointments without fixed end dates existed before 1900, but in general, it was accepted that the president of the university could end these appointments virtually at will. In many cases, appointments were always explicitly for one year and reappointment was far from automatic. A hundred years ago, most colleges were sufficiently precarious that a lifetime commitment to a faculty member would have been a ridiculous encumbrance.

But faculty members, beginning at the turn of the century, made a concerted effort to get formal control over the dismissal process. For example, E. A. Ross, an economist, had been dismissed from Stanford because his left-wing views annoyed Jane Lathrop Stanford, the sole trustee of Stanford University at that time. When Ross was fired, he began a defamation campaign in the press against David Jordan, the president of Stanford (see Metzger 1973 for details). Ross's allies in the American Economic Association undertook an investigation of his dismissal. Jordan fought back, and Ross's dismissal was not reversed, but a concerted faculty effort certainly managed to impose pain on Jordan and on the university as a whole. During the early twentieth century, these types of tactics were regularly used by faculty members who were dismissed by their universities.

Eventually the faculty members won. In 1940, the American Association of University Professors (AAUP) and the American Association of Colleges agreed on a set of principles about tenure. By 1970, tenure was a

---

11. Of course, large-scale strikes can influence large corporations. But these strikes generally involve a large fraction of the workforce (often sit-ins are perpetrated by a tiny minority of the student body) and generally involve a focused change in workers' compensation.

fairly universal institution at four-year colleges. This was achieved through the actions of individual professors and through the power of the AAUP. As I have argued, the actions of unions and individual lobbying should be much more effective against nonprofits with weak incentives than against profit-maximizing firms. There is no major for-profit sector with an institution comparable to tenure.

Of course, the other ingredient that made tenure possible was growing university resources. As Metzger (1973) writes, "helped by enormous largesse from the states, steep rises in federal support, the seed millions of the Ford Foundation, the success of innumerable alumni fund drives, and public willingness to pay the tuition and other college attendance costs . . . the fortunes of judicial tenure rode high upon this arc." He continues: "wealthier institutions were able to consider the positive sides of tenure and not dwell on its alleged inefficiencies and money costs." Just as the model predicts, an increase in nonprofit wealth led to an increase in the orientation toward worker preferences.

Accompanying this change in status, professors also changed their work habits. The typical professor in an elite institution in the early twentieth century spent much more time teaching and much less time doing research than his late-twentieth-century counterpart. Then and now, professors in less well endowed institutions do more teaching, but there has been a significant change in the amount of time allocated to nonteaching activities. As Jencks and Riesman write,

> Until World War II even senior scholars at leading universities did a good deal of what they defined as scut work: teaching small groups of lower-level students, reading papers and examinations, and the like. . . . Today, however, few well-known scholars teach more than six hours a week, and in leading universities many bargain for less. Even fewer read undergraduate examinations and papers. (2002, 40)

Professors have been able to reshape their jobs to fit their own scholarly ideals.

Of course, some of this change reflects the growing market power of some professors, not lobbying for rents. However, teaching loads appear to be more closely correlated with the wealth of an institution than with the market power of the professor within that institution. The decline in teaching and the rise in research appear to have been shared among the faculty of wealthy institutions—these changes didn't just affect mobile faculty who were in demand. Ultimately, donors have been found to pay for at least some of this research, but in many cases, this seems more like an ex post adjustment to a new reality than a driver of change.

The story of twentieth-century universities appears to show that faculty members and elite administrators were able to exercise increasing control over increasingly wealthy institutions. A hundred years ago, universities were still generally dominated by powerful donors and occasionally auto-cratic presidents. Presidential power still matters, but the ability of donors to dictate university actions has fallen since the days when Mrs. Stanford could get a left-wing economist fired on a whim. Academics have instituted tenure and gotten control over hiring and firing decisions. In wealthy in-stitutions, they have managed to replace teaching with research. While boards have certainly stopped extreme looting of the university by its workers, it is hard not to be impressed with the general success that elite workers have had in taking control of nonprofit universities and colleges.

An alternative interpretation of the change in universities is that this was just a response to a changing market. In 1900, students did not care about having researchers as faculty members—in 2000, they do. While there may be some truth to this claim, ultimately it seems difficult to accept that the switch to research was really motivated by a desire to cater to students. In part, the best counterexample is the continuing success of teaching colleges throughout the United States.

Teaching colleges generally operate with significantly lower endow-ments and much less state aid than large research universities. Instead, they require much more from their teachers and allow them much less free time to do research. While it is true that the top universities are more popular than any teaching colleges, top teaching colleges, such as Amherst or Haverford, are able to compete easily with many research universities and to give many fewer perquisites to their professors. If research was such an important component of consumer demand, then students would always prefer the University of Rochester or the University of Chicago to Williams. They do not.

Indeed, the history of teaching colleges reminds us that there are cases where elite workers are not able to dominate schools. In places with smaller endowments, schools end up requiring much more from teachers and giv-ing them much less in terms of both amenities and income. The extreme ex-ample of this tends to be private high schools (at least those without large endowments). In these schools, teachers work for generally quite low sums. They have little control over the direction of the school, and donors and parents tend to dominate. Worker control is not inevitable in nonprofits, and greater financial need severely limits the ability of workers to reorient the institution's mission.

The Rise and Fall of the Doctor's Cooperative

The first half of the history of the hospital strongly echoes the history of the university. Between 1800 and 1950, hospitals evolved from being char-itable institutions dominated by their donors and oriented toward the poor into being the "physicians' cooperatives" described by Pauly and Redisch (1973). As Rosenberg (1987, 7) writes, "the perceptions, the values and rewards, the career patterns, and, increasingly the specific knowledge of physicians have structured this development [of the hospital]." Starr (1982, 146) agrees: "Authority over the conduct of the institution [the hospital] passed from the trustees to the physicians and administrators." In the case of hospitals, though, there is a second act where increasingly financial pressure has led to commercialism and to a decline in the autonomy of physicians and professional administrators.

Hospitals begin in America in the eighteenth and early nineteenth centuries as charitable institutions for the indigent. The early hospitals, such as Pennsylvania Hospital (founded in 1752) or Massachusetts General Hospital (1821), were "something Americans of the better sort did for their less fortunate countrymen" and where "the worthy poor would find an opportunity to recover outside the almshouse's demeaning walls" (Rosenberg 1987, 20). Starr (1982, 145) writes that "from their earliest origins in preindustrial societies, hospitals had been primarily religious and charitable institutions for tending the sick, rather than medical institutions for their cure." He also emphasizes that "in the nineteenth century, the trustees or managers entered directly into the detailed operation of hospitals, including decisions that now would be seen as strictly medical" (153). For example, in many hospitals, donors determined who would be admitted. Like early universities, early hospitals were dependent on donations, and, as a result, donors wielded a great deal of authority.

Even at this early stage, though, it was understood that hospitals served in part as educational institutions for physicians. Rosenberg writes that "education has always played a prominent role in the American hospital" (1987, 190). Some physicians volunteered to work in hospitals out of a combination of desire for experience and philanthropic impulses. Unlike teachers, who were unlikely to have the ability to subsidize hospitals, doctors were also donors and as such had some donor-like control even in the earliest hospitals.

But over time, the medical control of hospitals grew and ultimately changed the very nature of these institutions. Starr (1982, 145) evocatively writes that "in developing from places of dreaded impurity and exiled human wreckage into awesome citadels of science and bureaucratic order, they acquired a new moral identity, as well as new purposes and patients of higher status." By 1900, hospitals had focused on elite private patients. They were centers of elite medicine and were significantly involved in teaching and research. As Rosenberg (1987, 262) writes, by 1900, "the hospital had become easily recognizable to twentieth-century eyes."

For our purposes, the most striking shift is the degree of medical control over hospital operations. In 1825, the trustees of Massachusetts General had entrusted the management of their hospital to Nathan Gurney, a retired sea captain. As Rosenberg (1987, 262) writes, "the possibility of appointing a physician as superintendent was not even considered." Early trustees feared that doctors would put their professional objectives first and the preferences of patients second. This situation corresponds to the situation in the model where donors and customers are arrayed against elite workers. Over the nineteenth and twentieth centuries, the relative power of trustees and doctors shifted: "Admissions, appointments, and control of teaching were all areas of conflict between lay and medical authorities—and all areas in which laymen gradually retreated and left the field to their medical staff" (Rosenberg 1987, 263). The modern hospital is an outcome of the increasing power of doctors, who shaped the hospital toward their own interests.

Why did doctors come to control hospitals? Like universities, the rise in doctor-controlled hospitals had much to do with increasing wealth. However, the wealth of twentieth-century universities came primarily from the generosity of donors. The wealth of twentieth-century hospitals came more from commercial activity that became profitable because of changes in medical technology. These technological changes made doctors more effective and increased the medical value of hospitals. The biggest early innovations appear to have been improvements in avoiding infections during surgery. These improvements specifically favored specialized locations for surgery (as opposed to surgery at home) and came to increase demand for hospitals. The rise in specialization also favored hospitals where large medical staffs could share their expertise in caring for the sick. These changes increased the demand for medical care and the wealth of both hospitals and doctors. Given the more central role that doctors played in generating income for hospitals relative to faculty in universities, it is not surprising that they came to dominate these nonprofits at a somewhat earlier time period.

Doctors' control did not just reflect their financial muscle. They were able to influence the way that all of the hospital's financial resources were used, including those contributed by donors or the state. Because doctors actually handled the day-to-day operations and because they were the workers who interacted with the superintendent regularly, they naturally became able to exert influence. Moreover, the increasing specialization of medical knowledge meant that retired sea captains no longer had sufficient expertise to run large hospitals and that doctors and later professional administrators themselves became superintendents. As in the case of universities, the weak incentives present in nonprofits meant that the elite workers were able to redirect the institution toward their own goals.

Of course, doctors are not the only powerful hospital employees. Starr (1982, 178) argues, following Charles Perrow, that "medical domination of hospitals began to weaken in the thirties and forties, as challenges from administrators to the authority of physicians became more common." This again echoes the rise in power of the upper-level administrators in universities. Hospital administrators, like their university counterparts, became the workers who interacted most often with the CEO (often providing the CEO), and, unsurprisingly, they became an influential group of elite workers.

But the control of hospitals by doctors and administrators has eroded significantly since 1980, and the primary reason for change has again been wealth. Sloan (1998) describes the bevy of negative income shocks that have occurred during the past twenty years. Government payments for Medicare and Medicaid have become less lucrative. Health maintenance organizations have sprung up and replaced traditional fee-for-service insurance. As a result, hospitals have considerably less ability just to set their own fees. Skyrocketing costs associated with changing medical technology have also greatly increased the price of being a hospital. As a result, the amount of rents available to nonprofit hospitals has shrunk dramatically.

In some cases, this has led nonprofit hospitals to close. While Hansmann, Kessler, and McClellan's chapter shows that nonprofits are slower to shut their doors than for-profits, there has still been a significant reduction in many areas in the number of nonprofit hospital beds. Another trend has been the conversion of nonprofit hospital to for-profit status. This trend is investigated by Cutler and Horwitz (1999). This is surely the ultimate example of commercialism.

More subtle examples of commercialism in nonprofit hospitals also exist. Weisbrod (1998) describes a wide array of nonprofit hospital behavior that appears to mimic for-profit firms and that appears to be a response to decreasing profit margins. The doctors' cooperative, described by Pauly and Redisch (1973), can only exist if there are substantial rents to be directed by workers. As these rents disappear, hospitals have become more like for-profits firms and this is exactly what the simple model predicts.

## Connoisseurship in Art Museums

The case of art museums also fits the general patterns. The large museums began with large bequests from donors, who generally exercised a great deal of control over the collections. Over time, curators began to exercise an increasing amount of dominance in the running of museums. As museums became rich, curators got independence from their donors, and they began to orient collections toward their own objective—displaying their own curatorial competence. Still, museums probably look more like donor-run enterprises than do either universities or hospitals. The continuing power of donors comes from the relative simplicity of museum operations, which makes it easier for donors to give bequests that are bound by legal restrictions. The power of donors also stems from the extremely high ratio of physical to human capital and from the fact that nondonation museum revenues are extremely small relative to the nondonation revenues of hospitals and universities.

Art museums in the United States sprang from the wealth of the Gilded Age. Collectors, like J. P. Morgan, Andrew Mellon, and Isabella Stewart

Gardner, used their wealth to collect vast troves of European art. At first this art was in their own private collections. Then, motivated by some combination of a desire to elevate public tastes and to enhance their own prestige, they turned their collections into public museums. In many cases, their collections were turned over to museums when they died. These gifts enabled the collections to stay intact and free from the impact of estate taxes. As such, the wealth of museums, like the Metropolitan (which received a great deal of Morgan's magnificent collection) and the National Gallery (which relied on Mellon's paintings), came from socially elite art owners who wanted to preserve and show off their collections in perpetuity.

Occasionally, these gifts came with strong legally binding limitations that still impact the collections. Museums built around a single collection, such as the Frick Gallery in New York or the Barnes Foundation in Philadelphia, were the most restrained. In those cases, the donor had the most freedom to craft the bylaws of the foundation and the greatest ability to influence future actions of the museum. So for example, both the Frick Gallery and Barnes Foundation have restrictions that block the extent to which their art can travel. Both museums have severe restrictions that block the selling of existing paintings. In the case of the Frick, the gift of art was accompanied by a large cash endowment as well, so these restrictions have not been all that problematic. However, the Barnes endowment came with paintings but not enough cash to actually support the museum (at least in the manner that the Barnes' curators think that the museum should be run). As such, the restrictions placed on the paintings actually severely influence the operations of the museum.

In many cases, the private donors were also supported by some degree of direct governmental involvement as well. In the case of the National Gallery or the Metropolitan Museum, the government was involved in bequeathing either direct or indirect subsidies to the museums. In some cases, the government really directly runs museums as public enterprises. In other cases, universities run museums and have their own interests at play.

Over the course of the twentieth century, the power of curators generally increased. Figures, such as Thomas Hoving at the Metropolitan, used the increasing wealth of their museums to pursue their own agendas and were often at odds with their wealthy trustees. A classic example of rising curatorial independence was Hoving's show *Harlem on My Mind*. This exhibition showcased pictures of Harlem's architecture and focused on social conditions in the neighborhood. It was a flamboyant gesture with adverse political consequences that did little but cause pain to the museum's wealthy donors. This type of curatorial showboating was typical of Hoving's tenure. In a sense, he was the museum equivalent of Hutchins, who pushed his own agenda, which was deeply tinged by his curatorial ambitions, rather than the goals of the trustees.

A particularly frequent area of dispute between curators and donors is the organization of collections. Generally, curators like to design collections around historical periods and themes which can highlight their own vision. Donors, on the other hand, like to keep their collections intact. Presumably, their goal is also to highlight their own artistic vision. In most cases, the curators have won. Museums rarely highlight their donors' visions, except in extreme cases like the Frick and the Barnes. However, there are cases, such as the Lehman wing at the Metropolitan, where donors are able to keep their collections intact through an explicit legal contract with the museum.

Another area of conflict between donors, curators, and customers, which the Goetzman and Oster chapter in this volume highlights, is the degree of accessibility of the museum to the general public. Museum fees are one way that the museum controls the inflow of observers. However, fees may be far from the most important attribute of the museum. Collections can be designed in a particularly user-friendly manner in which the nature of the art is made accessible to a wide range of the public. Once again, Hoving was the aggressive pursuer of a more open vision of the museum.

Ultimately, museum attendance in some cases serves to provide nondonation revenues that can free curators from their reliance on donors. The extreme example of this is "blockbuster" exhibitions that have been designed in a very user-friendly manner and tend to attract a very large audience. These blockbusters are a relatively recent phenomenon, but the large revenues that they generate may be a portent of things to come. If museums can generate sufficient revenues from this source, it seems likely that they will end up being more curatorial in their orientation and less oriented toward donor demands.

All in all, museums show some of the same features as the other nonprofits. Generally, they have become oriented toward their elite workers and away from their donors over time. However, the extreme reliance of museums on donor financing means that museums are still much more dependent on their donors than other nonprofits, and, as such, donors continue to wield significant power.

## The Medieval Church

At this point, in the spirit of the Nelson and Zeckhauser chapter in this volume, I stray considerably from twentieth-century America to the rise of the medieval church. A thousand years before elite workers were able to wrest some degree of control over universities, hospitals, and art museums from lay donors, the clergy fought and won a battle with their lay sponsors. This battle has all of the trademark features that we see in these modern nonprofits. Increasing wealth in combination with the ability of elite workers to directly influence top management leads to a reorientation of the institution toward workers and away from donors.

The medieval church shares several elements with the nonprofits we have already discussed. Officially, the Catholic Church's CEO (the pope) was formally elected by the College of Cardinals, a self-perpetuating group of elite workers in the church, and, indeed, the Pope had some authority even at the turn of the last millennium. But 1,000 years ago, wealthy donors generally had significant say over appointments and indeed over church policy itself. Like hospital donors, who controlled admissions, and university trustees, who could dismiss professors, local kings and noblemen often had the right to appoint and, if necessary, dismiss local bishops and clergymen. Indeed, laymen generally appointed the pope throughout the tenth and most of the eleventh century. For example, in 1046, at the Synod of Suri, the Holy Roman Emperor Henry III removed the existing pope, Gregory VI.

At the end of the eleventh century, Gregory VII began an extremely bitter conflict with lay authorities to establish clerical control over the church. The most important area of controversy between cleric and donor was lay investiture—the appointment of bishops and other clergymen by lay authorities. This policy led to significant lay control over church policies. After all, if the emperor chose the bishops, then surely he controlled much of the course of the church. Lay investiture also led to a significant transfer of resources from clergymen to nobles. In general, nobles would charge the clergy for the right to be appointed. The unsurprising use of power to extract rents was condemned by the papacy as the sin of simony.

The opening salvo of the war between the pope and lay authorities occurred in 1075, when Gregory VII, in a remarkable display of papal autonomy, announced the end of lay investiture and defrocked clergymen who had paid for their offices. Gregory had a remarkable prepapal career as the reformer Bishop Hildebrand, and he was the first non-German pope since Henry III had started appointing popes in 1046.[12] The emperor, Henry IV, used his ability to influence German bishops to try and depose the pope. Ultimately, Henry would humble himself at Canossa, and accept some limits on investiture. The pope's victory was actually due to support from the Hohenstaufen's lay Saxon enemies who were eager to use this religious conflict as an excuse to depose the emperor.[13] Still, the emperor was powerful enough to exile the pope to Salerno, where he died.

The conflict over investiture would last for centuries, but ultimately the papacy would free the church from most lay authority.[14] While the conflict between pope and emperor was surely the most important early battle,

12. The fact that Henry III's son Henry IV became emperor while he was a child certainly contributed to the move toward papal independence.
13. Henry's Saxon opponents were Welfs, while Henry was a Hohenstaufen. The famous Florentine parties of the Guelfs and the Ghibellines are linguistic descendants of the Welfs and the Hohenstaufens.
14. However, it is worthwhile emphasizing that the Emperor's eventual heir, the Austrian emperor, was still seen as having veto power over the choice of pope as late as the twentieth century.

conflicts over investiture and clerical authority occurred in many countries. For example, the famous battle between Thomas á Becket and Henry II of England concerned secular authority over priests. In 1302, Boniface VIII faced off against Philip the Fair of France. After Boniface issued a papal bull announcing papal supremacy, Philip demanded his trial as a heretic. Ultimately, the French would at least temporarily win as they moved the papacy to Avignon.

But overall, the movement was toward increasing clerical control over the church. Popes, like Innocent III, managed to increase the wealth and authority of the papacy substantially. The land holdings of the church increased. By the fifteenth century, the time of the Nelson and Zeckhauser chapter, the papacy had moved back to Rome, and the church had finally gained some measure of independence from secular authorities. Under a succession of popes, starting with Martin V, the church became something like its modern, more independent form: Lay investiture disappeared, clerics achieved control over church policy, and ultimately the church became oriented toward the interests of priests, not kings and nobles.

Within the church, the Curia, the pope's court, came to dominate during this period. During the earlier medieval period, local bishops enjoyed a significant amount of autonomy. As the power of the pope increased, the powers of the clergy who were closest to the pope also increased. The result was that the Catholic Church became increasingly Roman. Theological unity, based generally on the opinions of Roman clerics, drove out previous diversity. A particularly strong example of this was the Albigensian crusade where Rome crushed the Catharist heretics in the South of France. Orders of mendicant friars, such as the Dominicans and Franciscans, who were obedient to Rome, not to local bishops, became increasingly important and further served to extend the reach of the Roman clergy throughout Europe.

Why did the papacy and the Roman bishops eventually win control? There are two obviously important factors that created independence. The first was the increasing wealth of the church. A rich variety of innovations and the growing wealth of Europe, generally, had increased the wealth of the Papacy. The sale of indulgences, taxes on clergy, and general levies imposed to fund the religious wars all filled the papal coffers. The crusades also were a source of papal funds. An increasingly competent papal bureaucracy was able to enforce these rent extractions.

The second factor was the ability of successive popes to play off European leaders. In a number of major political crises, the pope's support was seen as an important edge. Popes, such as Innocent III, were able to wring extractions from secular leaders in exchange for support. The rise of the nation state was accompanied by an increasing emphasis on legal forms and the appearance of legitimacy: While an eighth-century monarch generally relied only on his swords for dominance, thirteenth-century kings increasingly needed less bloody forms of support. Thus, political division and an increasing emphasis on quasi-legal institutions acted as an income shock to the papacy. Just as in hospitals and universities, clerics were able to take control of the church as the independent wealth of the church rose.

Of course, there is a striking postscript to the rise of clerical independence. Just as the papacy appeared to have control over the church, the Reformation tore Christendom in half. While there are certainly intellectual elements to the Reformation as well, much of the early political support for reformers came from secular rulers who were eager to take back the authority that they had lost to Rome. Henry VIII is the most obvious example of a ruler for whom the reformation was little more than a bald attempt to seize lost royal prerogatives, but the German princes who supported Martin Luther were probably no less selfish. Ultimately then, the Reformation stands as a warning to nonprofits who try to establish too much independence from their donors. It is likely that these donors will find alternative nonprofits to support.

The past 200 years have also seen many episodes of increasing worker power in a number of churches. Within the United States, the Catholic Church eliminated lay appointments in 1845. In the richly competitive world of the American churches, there actually appears to be something of a lifecycle. New faiths are open to lay preachers and the clergy is essentially powerless, as free entry and lack of organization prevents clerical rents. As churches grow, they acquire wealth, and the clergy organizes and manages to gain some degree of control. With this control comes barriers to entry into the priesthood, such as seminaries, that stop lay competitors. Furthermore, the churches often tend to reorient themselves away from their lay people toward clerical comfort.

## Papers in the Volume

The volume that follows explores the governance of nonprofit organizations. It contains seven chapters: two on art museums, three on hospitals, and two on nonprofits generally. The first two chapters in the volume concentrate on donor-worker interactions in nonprofits and the incentives of different actors. Hansmann, Kessler, and McClellan examine the closure decisions of different hospitals. As discussed above, one of the implications of the model is that nonprofits will continue to produce when there are negative profits. For-profits generally will not. This gap stems from the ability of nonprofits to subsidize production out of donations and endowment and from the occasional inclination of nonprofits to overproduce.

In particular, the decision to close seems likely to really matter to the workers at a nonprofit institution. Closures are almost surely going to include layoffs and a substantial loss of welfare to the workers. As such, if workers are able to influence management, we should expect management to be particularly influenced to fight closures. Furthermore, some closures are likely to include managers themselves losing their jobs—something managers are likely to oppose. As such, the closure decision is an area where we should really expect the weak governance of nonprofits to matter. Nonprofits with substantial endowments and weak governance are likely to cater to their workers and stay open when comparable for-profits are likely to close.

Hansmann, Kessler, and McClellan look at the responses of hospitals to changes in local demand. They look at exogenous shifts in an area's population of Medicare-eligible population. This population represents one of the more lucrative populations of potential hospital clients, and, in principle, hospitals should be expected to rein in capacity when this key population falls. Hansmann, Kessler, and McClellan compare different ownership groups: for-profit and nonprofit hospitals. They find that both types of hospitals respond equally to increase in demand, but decreases in demand create a greater decline in for-profit than in nonprofit hospitals.

They can then further distinguish between different types of nonprofit hospitals. Religious hospitals appear to contract more readily than secular nonprofit hospitals. This may occur because there is residual claimant in the case of religious hospitals (the church) that imposes some discipline on these hospitals. In the framework of the model, it might be that in the case of religious hospitals (presumably with the chief officers in the church), management ultimately is not nearly as strongly opposed to closures as top management in nonprofit hospitals. Cardinals will not lose their jobs if a hospital shuts down—chief executives of hospitals will. As such, the differences between secular and religious hospitals again emphasize the importance of weak governance in the decision making of nonprofit firms. Although donors who care about overall national health would presumably prefer it if the resources of a hospital in a declining area were used elsewhere, managers will tend to keep the hospital open.

Goetzmann and Oster examine the donor-management conflict in the area of art museums. They emphasize that art museums serve three constituencies: donors, curators, and the public. Donors, they argue, seek social prestige through the prominent placement of donated art. Art museum workers and managers are generally connoisseurs who care primarily about preservation and perhaps their own research. Presumably, the public is particularly interested in the entertainment value of the museum experience.

In their view, the relative power of these constituencies will tend to differ across museum types. Free-standing nonprofit museums will generally be the most oriented toward the interests of their donors. As the model suggests, though, this orientation will probably decline as the wealth of the museum rises. University museums are likely to be the most free from donors or any other concerns. Their managers will be beholden to the managers of the university, not to donors. Finally, public museums will have the most obligation to serve the voting public. As such, Goetzmann and Oster predict that university museums will be most engaged in connoisseurship activities, free-standing nonprofits will serve their donors, and public museums will charge low entrance fees and try to attract large audiences.

They are able to test this prediction using attendance data. They find that collection size and location influences attendance, but governance also matters. Public museums have significantly higher attendance levels than their private competitors. Free-standing nonprofits have the next highest attendance levels, and university museums have the least attendance. This exactly fits a model where university museums are the least oriented toward customers (and the most toward their elite workers) and public museums are the most customer oriented.

Importantly, they also find that the attendance elasticity with respect to the value of the museum collection is far less than 1 (about 0.26) across the entire sample. Perhaps this should be compared with an expected benchmark elasticity of 1—twice as many paintings, twice as many visitors. The model predicts that richer museums will be less oriented toward the public (and more toward workers). As such, we should expect attendance to rise with size of collection far less than one-to-one because the richer museums are less oriented toward catering to the public and more oriented toward the interests of their curators.

Interestingly, the university museums appear to have found an alternative source of funding that relies on their connoisseurship—traveling shows. While the real blockbusters are the product of wealthy free-standing nonprofits with the most important pieces, university museums appear to have a disproportionate share of the midlevel shows that are designed around important artistic themes. These shows are generally time intensive and serve the interests of the curators who design them. As such, we should probably not be surprised that it is the university museums that specialize in them.

The next two chapters examine different forms of "commercialism" in nonprofits. Barro looks at the rise of hospital advertising over the last ten years. There has been a striking rise in this particularly commercial form of activity among hospitals since the early 1980s. This rise appears to go against traditional medical biases against advertising, and it represents a striking, new attempt of hospitals to reach out to consumers.

The model, discussed above, suggests that this type of commercialism might tend to show up when hospitals are in trouble financially, but this is not what Barro finds—instead, it is the wealthiest, teaching hospitals. In particular, these hospitals are advertising in markets with big HMOs. It seems that this is meant to increase their bargaining power vis-à-vis HMOs. Thus, hospitals that do have high-quality doctors and facilities are trying to market themselves directly to consumers to eliminate some of the monopsony power held by large HMOs.

This chapter is interesting in that it helps us to understand this dramatic shift in nonprofit behavior, and it emphasizes that commercialism is not necessarily a response to poverty but sometimes a response to wealth. In this case, the teaching hospitals invested in quality, probably (as discussed above) because they were responding to the interests of their elite workers. However, this quality turns out to complement advertising, a "commercial" activity. The high-quality firms have a greater incentive to broadcast their quality than the low-quality firms. As such, large endowments may, in some cases, tend to make the firm ultimately more commercial (at least by some measures) than small endowments.

Erus and Weisbrod look explicitly at bonuses within nonprofit organizations. These are important because they directly look at the incentives being placed on nonprofit managers. Changes in bonuses over time, especially if those bonuses are related to organization profitability, can also be seen as increases in the level of commercialism.

Erus and Weisbrod find that bonuses became widespread in nonprofit hospitals over the 1990s. They were rarer in religious hospitals, which appear to follow a more classic pure-salary approach, but in nonprofit hospitals as a whole the prevalence of bonuses appears to rival the prevalence in for-profit hospitals. They suggest that this increase in bonuses may well be the result of increasingly tough market conditions in hospitals, which, just as the model above predicts, will tend to eliminate the freedom of managers to follow their own objectives and will instead reorient them toward profitability.

Nelson and Zeckhauser take us back to Renaissance Florence to understand the role that donor-church relationships played in the creation of some of the world's greatest art. They document that the building of churches in the Renaissance was a relatively decentralized affair. Local leaders, in combination with some members of the clergy, would decide to finance the public good of a local church. The bulk of this financing would be found by selling private chapels. These chapels were paid for entirely by private families who would both decorate the chapels and would pay for masses at the chapels that would be said for themselves. In general, these chapels would not be open to the public.

The architectural importance of this type of financing appears to be significant. By necessity, chapels needed to be ringed by private chapels to pay for the public aspects of the construction. As such, there was a division between private and public space in these churches. There was also a divergence from the simpler forms of design that were more common during the Romanesque period.

In a sense, the Nelson and Zeckhauser chapter reminds us of the fascinating ways in which nonprofits are able to induce donors to contribute to things to which donors have little personal attachment. Because the donors want the religious returns from chapels and the social prestige of a prominently placed chapel, the church is able to use their funding to subsidize a more general public worship space. The donors themselves appear to have little interest in the existence of that space directly, but they certainly appear to have valued the social prominence that a large, visible chapel created for them. In a place like Florence, where political institutions were fluid and dependent upon local prestige, prominent displays of wealth (and benevolence) could perhaps even finance themselves by providing a basis for political power.

By taking us to the roots of nonprofit organizations, Nelson and Zeckhauser may help us to see that the essence of many nonprofits lies in providing an opportunity for the wealthy to display their resources and benevolence. In a sense, the provided service may actually be pretty secondary and really only a way to get the public in the door. The key client of the nonprofit is the donor who is willing to provide large sums of cash as long as the money is tastefully displayed and as long as the donor is guaranteed that his generosity will be well observed. This characterization is perhaps extreme, but it does seem to fit many typical modern donor-financed nonprofits including art museums, universities, and some hospitals.

Malani, Philipson, and David present an overall synthesis of the approach to nonprofit organizations and stands, in a sense, as an apt conclusion to the volume. They divide the existing theories of nonprofit organizations into three categories: (a) the altruism model, (b) the worker cooperative model, and (c) the noncontractible quality model. The altruism model loosely follows Newhouse (1970) and Lakdawalla and Philipson (1998). It argues that nonprofit organizations can be characterized by preferences over quality and quantity of output and that generally nonprofits prefer more of both. This fits nicely with the governance model where the nonprofit managers care about both of these attributes.

Their second theory is the worker cooperative model, which clearly adheres most closely to the work of Pauly and Redisch (1973). According to this model, the organization maximizes net revenue per worker. While their model assumes that workers focus on "wages," this view is a close cousin of the model discussed above where workers are able to orient production toward their own needs and interests. The classic result of this model is that because worker cooperatives maximize average revenues instead of total revenues, they will have lower levels of employment and lower levels of production than for-profit firms.

The final theory is the noncontractible quality theory advanced by Hansmann (1980), Weisbrod (1988), and Glaeser and Shleifer (2001). This theory argues that nonprofits have an advantage because of the weak incentives that are inherent in the nondistribution constraint. As such, non-profit organizations are better at ensuring that they will not cheat on providing high-quality goods than are for-profit firms, and, in some cases, this will enable the nonprofits to be able to charge higher prices. Variations on this theory argue that nonprofits are also safer for their workers, or other investors in some cases, because they are less likely to have strong incentives to expropriate. As such, workers may be more willing to invest in firm-specific human capital with nonprofit organizations because they believe that it is less likely that the nonprofit will later expropriate their investment.

Malani, Philipson, and David present a simple model that integrates all of these views and then look at the different predictions of the different models about the differences between nonprofit and for-profit firms. While this approach has many advantages, it suffers from the fact that it is hard in industries that do not have both for-profit and nonprofit firms. Three examples of their approach give the style of this chapter.

First, they discuss the implications of the different theories for firm size. The noncontractible quality model tells us little about the expected firm size of the nonprofit, but the other two theories do indeed give us contrasting implications. The altruism model predicts larger firm sizes, at least holding quality constant, because the nonprofit organization directly cares about the scale of production. The workers' cooperative model predicts that there will be fewer workers and smaller firm size, at least holding capital constant, because the number of workers at which average revenue per worker is reached is less than the number of workers where total revenues is maximized. The existing studies appear to confirm that nonprofit hospitals and nursing homes tend to be bigger than their for-profit counterparts. This presents some evidence for the altruism model. This can fit into the discussion above where firm size might be larger in nonprofits because of the manager's preferences for size (which is exactly the same as the Newhouse 1970 model), even if adhering to workers' preferences leads to at least some drop in size (relative to a donor-controlled firm).

The different models also give different predictions about the quality of care. The noncontractible quality model predicts that nonprofits will have higher levels of nonverifiable quality. The altruism model predicts that non-profits will have higher levels of all forms of quality, because, after all, the managers directly care about the quality of care. Empirically, most studies find little difference in the quality of care across different ownership types. This evidence does not square all that well with any of the models.

A final example of their approach is their examination of pricing in nonprofit and for-profit firms. Here the models diverge again. The noncontractible quality model predicts that, holding observable quality constant, for-profit firms will generally charge more in recompense for their higher quality levels. Alternatively, the altruism model predicts that prices will be lower both as a result of altruism for customers and also to increase capacity utilization. The governance approach will also tend to predict lower prices, but in this case prices might be lower because low prices and queues make it easier for incumbent workers than trying to push the product hard at the true market wage. In the hospital context, the evidence on prices is limited but appears to be mixed. Some evidence suggests that once you adjust for quality, the nonprofits have a slight price premium that appears to be waning over time. Other evidence suggests that nonprofits charge a lower price in the health sector. Certainly, in the educational sector it is hard to argue with the view that nonprofits often charge below market rates and attract queues.

The final chapter, by Fisman and Hubbard, explores the endowment effect. In the model, I took endowment as fixed, but this is clearly a mistake. The level of initial giving will itself take into account the impact of that giving on later actions by the nonprofit.

Fisman and Hubbard explore the role of endowments. They emphasize that endowments have two roles. First, as discussed above, they lead nonprofit organizations to follow their own objectives instead of the objectives desired by donors. Second, endowments protect foundations from the winds of fate. As such, endowments create permanence in nonprofit organizations and make them more likely to survive. Hubbard and Fisman emphasize this trade-off between alleviating risk and governance.

Of course, this raises the question about who is determining the size of the endowment. If we think of endowments as the result of the management of nonprofits' saving, rather than spending, current earnings, then endowments will be attractive both because they insure against future shocks and because they give independence to nonprofit management. Presumably the cost of endowments, to managements, is that they represent forgoing current expenditure. As such, endowments should probably be seen as a classic form of savings.

If we think of endowments as being the result of donors' decisions to contribute to an endowment rather than to current spending, then the puzzle becomes a little more difficult. Why would a donor ever give money all at once rather than dribbling it out over time? Presumably, the donor always maintains more control by keeping the money in his or her own bank account rather than by giving to the nonprofit. Of course, endowment gifts at the time of death are presumably less puzzling. At that time, donors really have no option of continuing to keep control over the gift.

One possible explanation for donors giving to endowments all at once instead of giving a slow flow of gifts is that this type of gift represents a firm commitment to the nonprofit, which may attract other donors.[15] If the attraction of nonprofits is intimately linked to their permanence, perhaps be-

---

15. Of course, in many cases a larger endowment may reduce the flow of future donations because it reduces the marginal impact of any new donations (see Glaeser and Shleifer 2001).

cause of the selling immortality aspects of donations, then a large endowment may end up attracting other donors. As such, endowments are a commitment device by one donor to make the long-term viability of the organization more obvious to others and hopefully to elicit more donations.

While Fisman and Hubbard do not necessarily answer all of the questions about the determinants of nonprofits, they do give us two key empirical clues about endowments. First, they find that endowments are higher in sectors with more income volatility. This evidence strongly supports the precautionary savings view of endowments. Whether endowments are determined by nonprofit management or by donors (or by a combination of both), we should expect to see larger endowments in riskier areas, and that is what they find.

Their second finding documents a connection between measures of governance and the size of endowments. They find that in states where donors have more control over the actions of nonprofits, endowments tend to be larger. This result should probably be interpreted as meaning that donors understand that by endowing nonprofits they are ceding independence. As such, they will be more likely to give endowments if there are other checks on the actions of nonprofit organizations.

### Conclusion

Nonprofit organizations have governance problems that resemble the problems in for-profit firms, but are often far more extreme. In both nonprofit and for-profit firms, investors have trouble ensuring that the firm's decisions maximize the investors' welfare. However, the market for corporate control and the ultimately democratic nature of for-profits, gives investors in for-profit firms and shareholders much more power than donors. In nonprofits, the preferences of management end up being far more important and in most cases, nonprofits end up being quite independent of their original investors—the donors. This independence becomes particularly extreme in the wealthiest nonprofits that have large endowments with which to support the preferences of their managers. Poorer nonprofits find it more necessary to either cater to customers or to donors.

In the case of wealthy nonprofit organizations, the interests of the elite workers become quite powerful. The idiosyncrasies of the particular CEO matter a lot, but the CEO will also end up making choices that are close to the choices that are preferred by the most entrenched workers. One reason for this connection is that CEOs are usually chosen from among the group of elite workers. Hospitals are often run by doctors, universities are often run by professors, and museums are run by curators. After all, running a nonprofit often requires specific skills that only the elite workers have. A second reason for the power of the workers is that they interact with the CEO and have the ability to make his or her life more or less pleasant.

As such, it should not surprise that over time, nonprofits, which were originally dominated by donors, ultimately resemble workers' cooperatives. Hospitals, museums, and universities have all transformed from institutions that maximized donors' interests to institutions that generally maximize the interests of their elite workers, making some exception for the continuing power of some boards and the idiosyncrasies of individual CEOs. To the extent that wages are free to adjust, the power of workers to push the nonprofits explains why there are lower wages in the nonprofit sector.

As much as I am convinced that there are serious governance issues within nonprofits, I also remain convinced that most nonprofits ultimately do a reasonable job of attending to their core function. The absence of powerful instruments of corporate control allows workers and managers a fair amount of latitude, but ultimately the sector still works. To some degree this may stem from the altruistic objectives of workers or managers, but in many cases, this probably comes from the need for nonprofits to compete in product markets and in the market for donations. Just as the model suggests, competition proves to be a powerful check on managerial whimsy. Ultimately, the lesson of nonprofits is that competition tends to keep organizations in line, even if their governance structure is weak. Perhaps this is ultimately the virtue of delegating social services to the nonprofit sector instead of having these services provided by the government.

# Appendix

## Proofs of Propositions

PROOF OF PROPOSITION 1. In the nonprofit firm, production is set so that $K'(N) = P(|X - X_C|) + f'(N)/\lambda$. In the for-profit firm production is set so that $K'(N) = P(0)$. From the convexity of $K(.)$, the proposition immediately follows.

PROOF OF PROPOSITION 2. First, we can immediately note that since $X_M > 0$, it is impossible for the optimal $X$ to be negative. If $X$ were negative, then an increase in $X$ would please workers, donors, and the manager and there is (by assumption) no impact on price.

I will use the notation that $a = D + E - \underline{W}$, $b = d - \sigma B$, and $c = K - P$, so $N = (a - bx)/c$, and I denote the overall maximization problem of the manager as $V(X, a, b, c, C, g)$. The value of $(\partial V)/(\partial X)$ equals $g \cdot I(X < X_M) + C - f'([a - bx]/c)(b/c)$. Standard differentiation tells us that for any parameter $Z$, $(\partial X)/(\partial Z) = ([\partial^2 V]/[\partial XZ])/([\partial^2 V]/[\partial X^2])$ and the value of $(\partial^2 V)/(\partial X^2)$ equals $f''(N)([d - \sigma B]/[K - P])^2$ which is negative, so the sign of $(\partial X)/(\partial Z)$ is the same as the sign of $(\partial^2 V)/(\partial XZ)$.

The value of $(\partial^2 V)/(\partial X \partial C) = 1 > 0$ so $X$ increases with $C$, and differentiation yields

(A1)
$$\frac{\partial^2 V}{\partial X \partial D} = \frac{\partial^2 V}{\partial X \partial E} = -\frac{\partial^2 V}{\partial X \partial \underline{W}} = \frac{\partial^2 V}{\partial X \partial a} = -f''(N)\frac{b}{c^2} > 0,$$

and

(A2)
$$\frac{\partial^2 V}{\partial X \partial b} = \frac{\partial^2 V}{\partial X \partial d} = -\frac{1}{B} \cdot \frac{\partial^2 V}{\partial X \partial \sigma}$$

$$= -\frac{1}{\sigma} \cdot \frac{\partial^2 V}{\partial X \partial B} = -\frac{f'(N)}{c} + f''(N)\frac{bX}{c^2} < 0$$

and

(A3)
$$\frac{\partial^2 V}{\partial X \partial c} = \frac{\partial^2 V}{\partial X \partial K} = -\frac{\partial^2 V}{\partial X \partial P} = \frac{f'(N)b}{c^2} + f''(N)\left(\frac{bN}{c^2}\right),$$

which is certainly negative if and only if $f'(N) > -Nf''(N)$. Differentiation also yields.

PROOF OF COROLLARY 1. The proof of corollary 1 follows immediately from proposition 1, and the fact that wages equal $\underline{W} - \sigma BX$.

PROOF OF PROPOSITION 3. We assume that $(\partial^2 V)/(\partial X^2)$ is negative and $(\partial^2 V)/(\partial X \partial g) = -I(X > X_M)$, which is negative if and only if $X$ is greater than $X_M$, so the proposition holds.

PROOF OF PROPOSITION 4. Adjusting the notation of the previous section, I now let $z = C + g$, $a = D + E - \underline{W}$, $b = d \cdot I(X > 0) - \sigma B$, and $c = K - P_0$, so $(\partial V)/(\partial X)$ equals $z - f'([a - bX]/[c + P_1 X])/([bc + aP_1]/[c + P_1 X]^2)$. Differentiating again produces $(\partial^2 V)/(\partial X^2) = ([bc + aP_1]/[c + P_1 X]^3)$ $([\{bc + aP_1\}/\{c + P_1 X\}]f''[N] + 2P_1 f'[N])$, which is negative if and only if $-([bc + aP_1]/[c + P_1 X])f''(N) > 2P_1 f'(N)$, or $-(C + g)(K - P_0 + P_1 X)f''(N) > 2P_1 f(N)^2$, which we assume is negative, and so again, the sign of $(\partial X)/(\partial Z)$ is the same as the sign of $(\partial^2 V)/(\partial XZ)$. Differentiation gives us that

(A4)
$$\frac{\partial^2 V}{\partial X \partial z} = \frac{\partial^2 V}{\partial X \partial g} = \frac{\partial^2 V}{\partial X \partial C} = 1 > 0,$$

and

(A5)
$$\frac{\partial^2 V}{\partial X \partial D} = \frac{\partial^2 V}{\partial X \partial E} = -\frac{\partial^2 V}{\partial X \partial \underline{W}} = \frac{\partial^2 V}{\partial X \partial a}$$

$$= -f''(N)\frac{(bc + aP_1)}{(c + P_1 X)^3} - f'(N)\frac{P_1}{(c + P_1 X)^2},$$

and this is positive if $-f''(N)bc + aP_1/c + P_1 X > P_1 f'(N)$, which follows from the assumption that $-([bc + aP_1]/[c + P_1 X])f''(N) > 2P_1 f'(N)$. Further differentiation yields

$$(A6) \quad \frac{\partial^2 V}{\partial X \partial b} = \frac{\partial^2 V}{\partial X \partial d} \cdot I(X > 0) = -\frac{1}{B} \cdot \frac{\partial^2 V}{\partial X \partial \sigma}$$

$$= -\frac{1}{\sigma} \cdot \frac{\partial^2 V}{\partial X \partial B} = f''(N) \frac{(bc + aP_1)X}{(c + P_1 X)^3} - f'(N) \frac{c}{(c + P_1 X)^2}.$$

This is negative as long as $X$ is positive or close to zero. Further differentiation yields $z - f'([a - bX]/[c + P_1 X])([bc + aP_1]/[c + P_1 X])$.

$$(A7) \quad \frac{\partial^2 V}{\partial X \partial c} = \frac{\partial^2 V}{\partial X \partial K} = -\frac{\partial^2 V}{\partial X \partial P_0}$$

$$= 2f''(N) \frac{(a - bX)(bc + aP_1)}{(c + P_1 X)^4} + P_1 f'(N) \frac{a - bX}{(c + P_1 X)^4},$$

which is negative if $-2f''(N)(bc + aP_1) > P_1 f'(N)$; and this follows from $-([bc + aP_1]/[c + P_1 X])f''(N) > 2P_1 f'(N)$ as long as $4 > 1/(c + P_1 X)$. Differentiation again yields

$$(A8) \quad \frac{\partial^2 V}{\partial X \partial P_1} = f''(N) \frac{(a - bX)(bc + aP_1)X}{(c + P_1 X)^4} - 2cf'(N) \frac{a - bX}{(c + P_1 X)^4},$$

which is certainly negative.

# References

Bertrand, M., and A. Schoar. 2002. Managing with style. University of Chicago, Department of Economics. Unpublished manuscript.

Cutler, D., and J. Horwitz. 1999. Converting hospitals from not-for-profit to for-profit status: Why and what effects? In *The changing hospital industry: Comparing for-profit and not-for-profit hospitals,* ed. D. Cutler, 45–79. Chicago: University of Chicago Press.

Duggan, M. G. 2000. Hospital ownership and public medical spending. *Quarterly Journal of Economics* 115 (4): 1343–73.

Glaeser, E., and A. Shleifer. 2001. Not-for-profit entrepreneurs. *Journal of Public Economics* 81 (1): 99–115.

Hansmann, H. 1980. The role of the nonprofit enterprise. *Yale Law Journal* 89:835–901.

Hansmann, H. 1996. *The ownership of enterprise.* Cambridge: Harvard University Press.

Jencks, C., and D. Riesman. 2002. *The academic revolution.* New Brunswick, N.J.: Transaction Publishers.

Lakdawalla, Darius, and Tomas Philipson. 1998. The nonprofit sector and industry performance. NBER Working Paper no. 6377. Cambridge, Mass.: National Bureau of Economic Research, January.

Metzger, Walter P. 1973. Academic tenure in America: A historical essay. In *Faculty Tenure,* ed. W. R. Keast and J. W. Macy Jr., 111–16. San Francisco: Jossey-Bass Publishers.

McCormick, R. E., and R. E. Meiners. 1988. University governance: A property rights perspective. *Journal of Law and Economics* 31 (3): 423–42.

Morison, S. 1935. *The founding of Harvard College.* Cambridge: Harvard University Press.

Newhouse, Joseph P. 1970. Toward a Theory of nonprofit institutions: An economic model of a hospital. *American Economic Review* 60 (1): 64–74.

Pauly, M., and M. Redisch. 1973. The not-for-profit hospital as a physicians' co-operative. *American Economic Review* 63 (1): 87–99.

Rosenberg, C. 1987. *The care of strangers: The rise of America's hospital system.* New York: Basic Books.

Sloan, F. 1998. Commercialism in nonprofit hospitals. In *To profit or not to profit: The commercial transformation of the nonprofit section,* ed. B. Weisbrod, 151–68. Cambridge: Cambridge University Press.

Starr, P. 1982. *The social transformation of American medicine.* New York: Basic Books.

Weisbrod, B. 1988. *The nonprofit economy.* Cambridge: Harvard University Press.

Weisbrod, B. 1998. *To profit or not to profit: The commercial transformation of the nonprofit section.* Cambridge: Cambridge University Press.

# Ownership Form and Trapped Capital in the Hospital Industry

Henry Hansmann, Daniel Kessler, and Mark McClellan

## 1.1 Introduction

Hospital care is the most prominent of several important service industries—concentrated heavily in health care, education, and the arts—in which nonprofit firms account for a substantial share of total production. Nonprofit firms do not, however, provide all of the nation's hospital care; the industry is also heavily populated with both for-profit and governmental firms. The mix of ownership forms in this industry has fed a long-standing debate among economists, sociologists, and legal scholars about the patient and social welfare implications of ownership, with particular attention to differences between nonprofit and for-profit institutions. In this vein, several studies (reviewed in Kessler and McClellan 2002) have examined the effects of ownership on quality of care, operating efficiency, prices, costs, and the volume of charity care. We explore here a different but related issue: the effects of ownership on the rapidity of exit in the face of declining demand.

In recent years, hospital care in the United States has been characterized by rapidly falling demand, likely due in large part to technological ad-

Henry Hansmann is the Sam Harris Professor of Law at Yale Law School. Daniel Kessler is associate professor of economics, law, and policy at Stanford University, a research fellow of the Hoover Institution, and a research associate of the National Bureau of Economic Research. Mark McClellan is associate professor of economics at Stanford University and a research associate of the National Bureau of Economic Research.

We would like to thank Alex Whalley and Arran Shearer for exceptional research assistance, and David Cutler, Ed Glaeser, and conference participants for many helpful suggestions. Funding from the U.S. National Institutes on Aging through the National Bureau of Economic Research and from the Center for Social Innovation at the Stanford Graduate School of Business is greatly appreciated. The views expressed herein are those of the authors and not necessarily those of the U.S. government or any of their affiliated institutions.

vances in medical procedures and to managed care (Cutler 2000). Between 1980 and 1999, inpatient nonfederal days in short-stay hospitals in the United States fell from 293,830,162 to 160,560,460, or 45.4 percent (National Center for Health Statistics 2001, tables 1, 91). Capacity, however, has declined significantly less rapidly. The number of nonfederal hospital beds fell from 1,247,188 to 938,746 over this period, or 24.7 percent (National Center for Health Statistics, table 108).

The preponderance of the nonprofit form in the hospital industry may largely explain this divergence between the rate of decline in demand and the rate of contraction of capacity. The managers of nonprofit hospitals, lacking a class of owners to whom they are accountable, face no external pressure to maximize profits, or even (like a public utility) to produce at least a market rate of return on the firm's invested capital. Rather, when cash flow is positive, they are free to reinvest all of it, expanding capacity to the point where net revenues (and hence the marginal rate of return on existing investments) is zero. And, even if cash flow is negative, they are free to maintain capacity by drawing down on accumulated net assets (which, among nonprofit hospitals, are often substantial). Indeed, managers of nonprofit hospitals may even feel it is their duty to behave in this fashion, believing in good faith that all of the firm's revenues and net assets must be dedicated to providing the maximum amount of hospital care possible.

A natural and potentially more efficient alternative would be for the hospital to return its (potential) free cash flow, beyond what can be reinvested with an appropriately high social rate of return, to patients in the form of lower prices. But for hospital managers this alternative is rendered even less morally salient than it might otherwise be by the fact that the bulk of hospital revenue today comes, not directly from patients, but rather from third-party insurers. (Another alternative would be to donate net revenues or assets to other charities with greater social need, as is sometimes done with the proceeds from conversion from nonprofit to for-profit form.) Reluctance to reduce capacity is likely to be strongly reinforced, moreover, by pressure from a hospital's affiliated staff physicians, whose income may be threatened by reduction or elimination of the hospital's facilities (Pauly and Redisch 1973).

To be sure, the managers of for-profit firms, and particularly of broadly held business corporations, also have at times both the incentive and the opportunity to engage in empire building. But the market for corporate control acts as an ultimate check on such tendencies, as demonstrated by the numerous hostile takeovers of the 1980s, which were in part directed at reducing overcapacity and excessive reinvestment (Jensen 1988). No similar check exists for nonprofit firms, which cannot be the subject of a hostile takeover.

It follows that a nonprofit firm not only can, but might well be expected to, maintain capacity and even expand in circumstances where its for-profit competitors choose to contract or exit the market entirely. And this can remain true even if for-profit firms are significantly more cost efficient, and even if the nonprofit firm receives no special subsidies (Hansmann 1996a). In short, nonprofit firms have a tendency to act as capital traps, in which capital remains strongly embedded over long periods.

The social welfare implications of such behavior are theoretically indeterminate. On one hand, "slow" adjustment of capacity to demand may be optimal. Altering the level of a factor of production whose costs are as sunk as those of a hospital bed is socially costly. On the other hand, "slow" adjustment may be socially wasteful. Maintaining a hospital bed is costly, in both financial and nonfinancial terms. Substantial research, starting with Roemer (1961), has suggested that high levels of bed capacity per patient lead to longer lengths of stay and higher costs. More recent research indicates that hospitals that treat relatively few cases of any particular type of patient—a potential consequence of high capacity—may deliver lower-quality care. Kessler and McClellan (2000), for example, find that elderly heart attack patients from markets with high levels of capacity per unit cardiac patient experience both generally higher levels of Medicare expenditures and higher mortality rates (although somewhat lower rates of cardiac complications).

Thus, it is important to understand how ownership affects capacity choice. If ownership forms respond differently to changes in demand, then public policies that favor one ownership form over another may affect welfare not just by altering the mix of ownership forms itself, but also by affecting the aggregate level of industry capacity. Moreover, identifying differences in the response of capacity to demand by ownership type can help distinguish among competing general models of nonprofit firm behavior.

Despite the importance of the subject, little empirical work has focused on the impact of ownership form on capacity choice. Two studies have examined the differential supply response of nonprofit and for-profit firms, and of hospitals in particular, to rapid increases in demand. Both studies found that the market share of for-profit as opposed to nonprofit firms was significantly higher in areas that had recently experienced rapid growth in population (Steinwald and Neuhauser 1970; Hansmann 1987). These studies concluded that this pattern is explained, in important part, by the difficulties that nonprofit firms face in obtaining rapid access to capital.[1] The long-term pattern of development in the hospital industry, prior to the implementation of Medicare and Medicaid in 1966, was that the ratio of for-profit to nonprofit firms increased during periods of rapidly increasing demand and then fell—owing, in part, to conversions from for-profit to

1. See Lakdawalla and Philipson (1998) for related work on other constraints on nonprofits' ability to expand.

nonprofit form—as demand growth slackened (Steinwald and Neuhauser 1970). The sluggish nonprofit supply response to increasing demand was thus largely a short-term phenomenon.

The principal problem facing the hospital industry today, however, may not be to hasten capacity expansion to meet growing demand, but just the opposite: to hasten the elimination of excess capacity already in place. Moreover, the problem is not peculiar to the hospital industry. The nonprofit form frequently performs a transitional role in the early stages of a service industry's development, serving as an important source of production until adequate demand-side financing is organized and the service is sufficiently standardized or regulated to permit for-profit firms to serve as efficient providers. After that, the nonprofit firms lose their special raison d'etre, yet retain a substantial market share owing to trapped capital. Savings banking is a conspicuous example from the past (Hansmann 1996b), health insurance and health maintenance organizations are contemporary examples, and higher education may be an example in the future (Hansmann 1996a). The problem of trapped capital is generic in the nonprofit sector.

We have spoken so far of the effects of nonprofit versus for-profit ownership on the rate of capacity adjustment, but the underlying model of behavior described above can explain other differences in capacity choice between ownership forms. Hospital care, like some other important services such as education, is also provided in substantial part by governmental institutions. Supply response in general, and trapped capital in particular, may be less of a problem for these public firms than it is for nonprofit firms. A public hospital is not a nonprofit entity but rather a proprietary entity with the government as the owner, and the government has other pressing uses for its funds besides providing hospital care. Consequently, when the private sector becomes capable of providing services formerly provided by the government, governments may face political incentives to exit. Consistent with this logic, after Medicare and Medicaid relieved much of the need for public and nonprofit hospitals to provide uncompensated care, there was substantial exit by public institutions, whose share of total beds dropped from roughly 31 percent to 24 percent between 1971 and 1992, while for-profit hospitals simultaneously increased their market share from 6 percent to 12 percent. In striking comparison, nonprofit hospitals, rather than exiting in large numbers like the public institutions, actually increased their market share slightly during that period, from 63 percent to 64 percent (Hansmann 1996a).

For similar reasons, one might expect nonprofit hospitals to differ among themselves in terms of supply response. The most conspicuous divide in this respect is between religiously affiliated and nonreligious hospitals. Like public hospitals, religiously affiliated hospitals often have an owner of sorts, if not in the formal legal sense, then at least in the functional sense that they are commonly associated with another entity, the church, that both exercises substantial control over them and stands to benefit from economics achieved in the hospitals' operations (and can serve as a source of funds and act as entrepreneur when expansion or entry is called for). By this reasoning, religiously affiliated hospitals would show greater supply response than nonreligious nonprofit hospitals.

In this paper we seek to test whether rates of exit from the hospital industry differ significantly across the different forms of ownership and especially whether secular nonprofit hospitals, which supply the majority of industry capacity, are much slower to reduce capacity than are other types of hospitals. We examine the relative responsiveness of the different types of hospitals to changes in demand for hospital services, using changes in the size of the elderly population as a proxy for changes in demand. We present estimates of the effect of population changes at the zip code level between 1985 and 1994 on changes in the capacity of for-profit, secular nonprofit, religious nonprofit, and public hospitals over the same period, holding constant metropolitan statistical area (MSA) fixed effects and other 1985 baseline characteristics of residential zip codes. We decompose the effect on each ownership form's capacity of population into four mutually exclusive and exhaustive sources: changes due to opens and closes of hospitals, changes due to conversions, changes due to mergers and spin-offs, and changes due to changes in hospitals' bed size. We also investigate whether the responsiveness of different ownership forms' capacity to population differ according to zip codes' baseline 1985 hospital market characteristics.

Sections 1.2 through 1.4 present the statistical models, the sources of data, and the empirical results. Section 1.5 concludes with some observations about the implications of our results for the hypothesized model of nonprofit firms' behavior described above, and for economic efficiency in sectors dominated by nonprofit firms.

## 1.2  Models

For every residential zip code $z = 1, \ldots, Z$ in an MSA in 1985 and 1994, we construct a measure of the hospital capacity serving that zip code. We assume that $z$ is served by every nonfederal, general medical or surgical hospital $j = 1, \ldots, J_z$ within 35 miles of the patient's residence with at least five heart attack (AMI) admissions and every large, nonfederal, general medical or surgical teaching hospital within 100 miles of the patient's residence with at least five AMI admissions.[2] We allocate a hospital's beds $B_j$

---

2. We explain the reason for these a priori constraints in Kessler and McClellan (2000): Because markets for cardiac care are generally much smaller than the constraints, they are not restrictive.

to $z$ in inverse proportion to the distance between the hospital and the center of $z$, such that the capacity of $z$ in 1985 is defined as

$$C_{z,85} = \sum_{j=1}^{J_z} \frac{B_{j,85}}{D_{jz} \sum_{z=1}^{Z_j} \left(\frac{1}{D_{jz}}\right)},$$

where $D_{jz}$ is the distance from $j$ to $z$ for every $z = 1, \ldots, Z_j$ that is served by $j$. We define $C_{z,94}$ analogously, and the log growth of capacity in zip code $z$ as dln $C_z = \ln(C_{z,94}) - \ln(C_{z,85})$. The normalizing factor

$$\frac{1}{\sum_{z=1}^{Z_j} \left(\frac{1}{D_{jz}}\right)}$$

assures that for any hospital the sum across the zip codes that it serves of the weights allocating its capacity equals 1, i.e.,

$$\sum_{z=1}^{Z_j} \frac{1}{D_{jz}} \cdot \frac{1}{\sum_{z=1}^{Z_j} \left(\frac{1}{D_{jz}}\right)} = 1.$$

We decompose capacity in two ways to explore whether market conditions and changes in demand for hospital services have different effects on the capacity provided by hospitals of different ownership types. First, we decompose each residential area's capacity by its form of ownership. We define the secular nonprofit capacity of $z$, $C_z^{SNP}$, as

$$C_{z,85}^{SNP} = \sum_{j=1}^{J_z} \frac{B_{j,85} \cdot SNP_{j,85}}{D_{jz} \sum_{z=1}^{Z_j} \left(\frac{1}{D_{jz}}\right)},$$

where $SNP_j = 1$ if $j$ is a secular nonprofit hospital. We define for-profit capacity $C_{z,85}^{FP}$, religious nonprofit capacity $C_{z,85}^{RNP}$, and public capacity $C_{z,85}^{P}$ (and their associated growth rates) analogously. Estimates of the effect of market conditions and changes in demand on each ownership form's capacity will show how different types of organizations respond to exogenous shocks.

Second, we decompose each area's change in capacity by the source of the change. We categorize changes in total capacity and changes in each ownership form's capacity as due to one or more of four exhaustive and mutually exclusive causes: opens and closes of new hospitals, conversions (i.e., changes in ownership status), mergers and demergers, and changes in bed size for hospitals not experiencing any of the three changes above. We construct an area's (counterfactual) change in capacity due to, for example, opens and closes as follows. Define each hospital's 1985 capacity $B_{j,85}$ as its actual 1985 capacity; define each hospital's 1994 capacity $B_{j,94} = B_{j,85}$, unless the hospital opened or closed, in which case define $B_{j,94} = B_{j,94}$. Then, recalculate each area's capacity and change in capacity using these counterfactual hospital capacities.

We model area changes in capacity as a function of 1985–94 changes in a zip code's Medicare enrollee population (to proxy for changes in demand for hospital services), the 1985 demographic characteristics of each zip code, the 1985 hospital market characteristics of each zip code, and MSA fixed effects. Thus, our effects are identified from within–MSA changes in population and within–MSA differences in market characteristics. We allow hospital capacity to respond asymmetrically to population increases and decreases. Our basic models specify the log change in residential zip code $z$'s capacity of ownership form $k$ as a linear function of these factors:

$$(1) \qquad \text{dln } C_z^k = \alpha_k + \beta^+ \text{dln } P_z^+ + \beta^- \text{dln } P_z^- + X_z \phi + M_z \gamma + \varepsilon_z,$$

where $\alpha_k$ is an MSA–specific constant term; dln $P_z^+$ is $z$'s log change in population if $z$'s population expanded, zero otherwise; dln $P_z^-$ is $z$'s log change in population if $z$'s population contracted, zero otherwise; $X_z$ is a vector of six variables denoting the proportion of $z$'s population in 1985 who were female, black, aged seventy to seventy-four, seventy-five to seventy-nine, eighty to eighty-nine, and ninety to ninety-nine (omitted group is the proportion of population that were white males aged sixty-five to sixty-nine; $M_z$ is a vector of six variables denoting whether $z$ in 1985 was in a highly concentrated hospital market (in the top quartile of the distribution of Hirschman-Herfindahl indexes) and whether $z$ in 1985 had above-the-median density of patients admitted to large hospitals, teaching hospitals, hospitals that were members of multihospital systems, for-profit versus nonprofit hospitals, and public versus nonprofit hospitals;[3] and $\varepsilon_z$ is an independently distributed error term, with $E(\varepsilon_z | \text{dln } P_z, X_z, M_z) = 0$. We weight each observation by the number of beds of ownership type $k$ in zip code $z$, $C_z^k$.

We reestimate equation (1) including controls for baseline 1985 beds per capita as a control variable, to investigate the extent to which our results are sensitive to differences in baseline capacity that are correlated with ownership status across areas:

$$(2) \quad \text{dln } C_z^k = \alpha_k + \beta^+ \text{dln } P_z^+ + \beta^- \text{dln } P_z^- + X_z \phi + M_z \gamma + \theta \ln C_{z,85} + \varepsilon_z.$$

We also estimate two expanded models to investigate whether the responsiveness of capacity to population shifts varies by 1985 baseline characteristics of hospital markets. First, we estimate models that interact ln $C_z$

---

3. See Kessler and McClellan (2000, 2002) for a detailed description of how these variables were constructed.

with dln $P$ in order to investigate the extent to which capacity is differentially responsive to demand in high- versus low-capacity areas:

$$(3) \quad \text{dln } C_z = \alpha_k + \beta^+ \text{dln } P_z^+ + \beta^- \text{dln } P_z^- + \delta^+ \ln C_{z,85} \cdot \text{dln } P_z^+$$
$$+ \delta^- \ln C_{z,85} \cdot \text{dln } P_z^- + \theta \ln C_{z,85} + X_z\phi + M_z\gamma + \varepsilon_z$$

Second, we estimate models that interact $M_z$ with dln $P_z$:

$$(4) \quad \text{dln } C_z = \alpha_k + \beta^+ \text{dln } P_z^+ + \beta^- \text{dln } P_z^- + \delta^+ M_z \cdot \text{dln } P_z^+$$
$$+ \delta^- M_z \cdot \text{dln } P_z^- + X_z\phi + M_z\gamma + \varepsilon_z$$

Estimates from this model will show, for example, the extent to which capacity of different ownership forms responds differently to demand in more- versus less-competitive markets.

## 1.3   Data

We use data from four sources. First, we use data on U.S. hospital characteristics collected by the American Hospital Association (AHA). The response rate of hospitals to the AHA survey is greater than 90 percent, with response rates above 95 percent for large hospitals (>300 beds). We exclude rural hospitals and hospitals owned by the federal government (primarily Veterans' Administration hospitals) because the process governing capacity decisions for these hospitals may differ from those for other hospitals. We analyze the capacity of only those hospitals that ever reported providing general medical or surgical services (e.g., we exclude psychiatric and rehabilitation hospitals from analysis). To assess hospital size and bed capacity per patient, we use total general medical/surgical beds set up and staffed, including intensive care unit (ICU), critical care unit (CCU), and emergency beds. We classify hospitals as teaching hospitals if they report at least twenty full-time residents.

Second, we use a hospital system database constructed from multiple sources (see Madison 2001 for a detailed discussion). The AHA survey contains extensive year-by-year information on hospital system membership status. Our validity checking indicated that the universe of systems and system hospitals and the timing of hospitals' system membership, as defined by AHA, did not conform to discussion of hospital systems in the trade press, such as *Modern Healthcare*. We therefore created our own system database based on a combination of the AHA and other sources. We classify hospitals as for-profit, secular nonprofit, religious nonprofit, or publicly owned. We classify all public hospitals as nonsystem hospitals because system membership of public hospitals in our data did not reliably reflect actual transfer of control to an outside entity.

Third, we use Medicare enrollment data to calculate the size and the age, gender, and race distribution of each nonrural zip code's elderly population. The Health Care Financing Administration's Health Insurance Skeleton Eligibility Write-off (HISKEW) enrollment files include demographic information on virtually all elderly Americans, including those enrolled in Medicare health management organizations (HMOs), because of the extremely high rate of take-up in the Medicare program.

Fourth, we use comprehensive Medicare claims data on the hospital choices of virtually all elderly Medicare beneficiaries with heart attack in 1985, matched with the three data sources described above, to estimate a model of patients' demand for hospital services as a function of travel distances between patients and hospitals, the characteristics of patients, and the characteristics of hospitals. With these estimates, we construct measures of patient flows to hospitals of different broad types (ownership status, size, teaching status, system membership status) that are based only on the arguably exogenous factors described above. Then we calculate a vector of six indicator variables describing the hospital market characteristics of each zip code in 1985 as described above (see Kessler and McClellan 2000, 2002, for a detailed discussion).

Table 1.1 describes how hospital capacity under different ownership forms has changed over the 1985–94 period and the sources of those changes. Table 1.1 decomposes changes in the number of hospital beds (and the facilities experiencing changes in beds) into four exhaustive and mutually exclusive categories: changes due to conversions (changes in ownership status), changes due to opens and closes, changes due to mergers and spinoffs, and changes due to changes in bed size (absent a conversion, an open or close, or a merger or spinoff). The most salient feature of the hospital industry during our study period was a massive contraction in capacity.

In percentage terms, religious nonprofit hospitals experienced the greatest contraction in bed capacity (32.5 percent), with public hospitals close behind (29.6 percent). For-profit beds contracted by 21.4 percent, while nonreligious nonprofit beds contracted the least, by 20 percent. These simple percentages do not give a clear picture of relative supply response, however, because the environments in which these four forms of ownership are found tend to differ. In particular, at the beginning of the study period, nonprofit hospitals, in comparison with for-profit hospitals, tended to be concentrated in areas with unusually high levels of capacity, where the need for reduction in capacity was presumably greatest. In results not presented in table 1.1, the correlation coefficient between $M_z^5$ ($=1$ if the concentration of for-profit/nonprofit admissions in the zip code were above the median, zero otherwise) and log(capacity per person in 1985) is 0.062, $p < 0.01$, and the correlation coefficient between $M_z^6$ ($=1$ if the concentration of public/nonprofit admissions in the zip code were above the median, zero otherwise) and log(capacity per person in 1985) is 0.025, $p < 0.01$.

In recent years, much attention has been focused on conversions of non-

**Table 1.1**     Sources of Change in Hospital Capacity, 1985–1994

| | Beds | | | | | Facilities | | | | |
| --- | --- | --- | --- | --- | --- | --- | --- | --- | --- | --- |
| | | | Nonprofit | | | | | Nonprofit | | |
| | Total | For-Profit | Secular | Religious | Public | Total | For-Profit | Secular | Religious | Public |
| 1985 total | 546,321 | 63,276 | 296,650 | 116,134 | 70,261 | 2,684 | 449 | 1,401 | 445 | 389 |
| 1994 total | 414,716 | 49,711 | 237,232 | 78,339 | 49,434 | 2,363 | 383 | 1,284 | 388 | 308 |
| Net change | -131,605 | -13,565 | -59,418 | -37,795 | -20,827 | -321 | -66 | -117 | -57 | -81 |
| Proportion of 1985 total | -24.1% | -21.4% | -20.0% | -32.5% | -29.6% | -12.0% | -14.7% | -8.4% | -12.8% | -20.8% |
| *1985–1994 opens and closes* | | | | | | | | | | |
| Gross gains | 13,524 | 4,091 | 7,231 | 1,022 | 1,180 | 110 | 39 | 50 | 12 | 9 |
| Gross losses | 42,325 | 9,313 | 20,495 | 5,843 | 6,674 | 343 | 99 | 158 | 36 | 50 |
| Net change | -28,801 | -5,222 | -13,264 | -4,821 | -5,494 | -233 | -60 | -108 | -24 | -41 |
| Proportion of 1985 total | -5.3% | -8.3% | -4.5% | -4.2% | -7.8% | -8.7% | -13.4% | -7.7% | -5.4% | -10.5% |
| *1985–1994 conversions* | | | | | | | | | | |
| Gross gains | 38,257 | 5,757 | 22,359 | 7,011 | 3,130 | 242 | 51 | 125 | 46 | 20 |
| Gross losses | 50,177 | 4,718 | 17,746 | 17,494 | 10,219 | 242 | 32 | 89 | 65 | 56 |
| Net change | -11,920 | 1,039 | 4,613 | -10,483 | -7,089 | 0 | 19 | 36 | -19 | -36 |
| Proportion of 1985 total | -2.2% | 1.6% | 1.6% | -9.0% | -10.1% | 0.0% | 4.2% | 2.6% | -4.3% | -9.3% |
| *1985–1994 mergers and spinoffs* | | | | | | | | | | |
| Gross gains | 36,367 | 3,795 | 21,678 | 8,078 | 2,816 | 137 | 22 | 81 | 26 | 8 |
| Gross losses | 48,644 | 6,370 | 28,572 | 10,602 | 3,100 | 225 | 47 | 126 | 40 | 12 |
| Net change | -12,277 | -2,575 | -6,894 | -2,524 | -284 | -88 | -25 | -45 | -14 | -4 |
| Proportion of 1985 total | -2.2% | -4.1% | -2.3% | -2.2% | -0.4% | -3.3% | -5.6% | -3.2% | -3.1% | -1.0% |
| *1985–1994 changes in bed size* | | | | | | | | | | |
| Gross gains | 7,597 | 1,581 | 3,481 | 1,546 | 989 | 306 | 54 | 155 | 40 | 57 |
| Gross losses | 86,504 | 8,388 | 47,654 | 21,513 | 8,949 | 1,474 | 196 | 816 | 258 | 204 |
| Net change | -78,907 | -6,807 | -44,173 | -19,967 | -7,960 | -1,168 | -142 | -661 | -218 | -147 |
| Proportion of 1985 total | -14.4% | -10.8% | -14.9% | -17.2% | -11.3% | -43.5% | -31.6% | -47.2% | -49.0% | -37.8% |
| Facilities without changes | | | | | | | 21 | 62 | 6 | 10 |

*Notes:* Includes only nonrural, nonfederal hospitals that ever reported providing general medical or surgical services. The 1994 total facilities = 1985 total facilities + net change due to opens and closes + net change due to conversions + net change due to mergers and spinoffs. 1985 total facilities = gross losses due to opens and closes + gross losses due to conversions + gross losses due to mergers and spinoffs + facilities experiencing gross gains in bed size + facilities experiencing gross losses due to changes in bed size + facilities without changes.

**Table 1.2**             **Sources and Products of Hospital Conversions, 1985–1994**

| Ownership Status in 1985 | Ownership Status in 1994 | | | | |
| --- | --- | --- | --- | --- | --- |
| | Nonprofit Secular | Nonprofit Religious | For-Profit | Public | Total |
| Nonprofit secular | | 38 | 37 | 14 | 89 |
| Nonprofit religious | 56 | | 8 | 1 | 65 |
| For-profit | 22 | 5 | | 5 | 32 |
| Public | 47 | 3 | 6 | | 56 |
| Total | 125 | 46 | 51 | 20 | |

profit hospitals to for-profit form—attention that has been due, in part, to concerns about the private profiteering accompanying some of these conversions (see e.g., Sloan, Taylor, and Conover 2000). Table 1.1 suggests that the pattern of conversion activity is not well described, however, as an overall shift of capacity from nonprofit to for-profit form. Rather, table 1.1 shows that conversions were in fact a net source of *increase* in secular nonprofit hospital beds between 1985 and 1994, and it further shows that, in aggregate, net conversion activity in that period moved out of both public and religious nonprofit hospitals and into both for-profit and secular nonprofit hospitals.

To provide a more refined view of conversion activity, table 1.2 tabulates the conversions in our data according to the ownership status of the hospitals involved both before and after the conversion. Those data show that, while there is a substantial number of conversions directly from secular nonprofit to for-profit form, there are also nearly two-thirds as many conversions in the reverse direction—likely as a response to declining profitability. The principal net conversion activity across ownership forms is, instead, from public hospitals to secular nonprofit hospitals, which accounts for nearly all of the overall net increase in secular nonprofit hospitals through conversion during the period in question.[4]

Table 1.3 shows how residential zip codes' hospital capacity responds to changes in population, according to the size of the zip codes' MSA, and previews the results of our regression models. Table 1.3 reports the 1985–94 percentage change in the four hospital ownership types' capacity by MSA size for fast-growing versus slow-growing MSAs. Specifically, table 1.3 groups zip codes according to the quartile of the zip codes' urban 1985 elderly population, with eighty MSAs in each quartile. Then, within each population quartile, each of the eighty MSAs is classified into one of two groups of forty MSAs, depending on its 1985–94 growth in elderly population.

4. There is, however, an important caveat to be added here. We do not count as a conversion the potentially important phenomenon of nonprofit hospitals' contracting out management of its facility to a for-profit firm.

Table 1.3    Percentage Change in Hospital Capacity in Fast- and Slow-Growing MSAs, by MSA Size and Ownership Status, 1985–1994

| | All MSAs | | Least Populous MSAs | | MSAs in 2nd Population Quartile | | MSAs in 3rd Population Quartile | | Most Populous MSAs | |
|---|---|---|---|---|---|---|---|---|---|---|
| | Fast-Growing | Slow-Growing | Fast-Growing | Slow-Growing | Fast-Growing | Slow-Growing | Fast-Growing | Slow-Growing | Fast-Growing | Slow-Growing |
| All ownership forms | −23.7 | −25.7 | −18.9 | −33.0 | −23.1 | −27.9 | −20.1 | −25.7 | −25.4 | −25.0 |
| For-profit | −24.2 | −25.9 | −6.1 | 155.0 | −26.8 | −37.8 | −7.4 | −35.8 | −30.4 | −26.3 |
| Nonprofit secular | −20.9 | −20.8 | 7.1 | −34.8 | −24.3 | −18.0 | −23.2 | −16.2 | −21.2 | −20.9 |
| Nonprofit religious | −25.0 | −35.3 | −41.0 | −43.4 | −13.6 | −39.9 | −25.7 | −33.6 | −26.0 | −34.5 |
| Public | −29.2 | −34.4 | −33.2 | −43.0 | −29.3 | −46.2 | −15.0 | −37.5 | −32.6 | −31.6 |
| Number of MSAs | 160 | 160 | 40 | 40 | 40 | 40 | 40 | 40 | 40 | 40 |

*Notes:* Population quartile cutpoints are based on elderly Medicare beneficiary enrollments of 15,005; 27,387; and 63,867. Fast-growing/slow-growing cutpoints are 17.0 percent for the least populous MSAs, 14.7 percent for 2nd quartile, and 15.3 percent for 3rd quartile, and 12.3 percent for the most populous MSAs.

Table 1.3 shows that, in the 2nd and 3rd population quartiles, variation across MSAs in supply response is consistent with the predictions that follow from the organizational incentives discussed in section 1.1. Capacity for all ownership types decreased in each group of MSAs, as one would expect in an industry generally characterized by substantial overcapacity. For all ownership types except secular nonprofits, moreover, the percentage reduction in capacity is markedly greater in the slow-growing MSAs than in the fast-growing MSAs. For example, for-profit capacity in areas in the 2nd population quartile shrank by 26.8 percent in fast-growing MSAs, but by 37.8 percent slow-growing MSAs. For secular nonprofit hospitals, however, not only is the relative rate of capacity reduction in fast- versus slow-growing MSAs much smaller than the relative rate of contraction for the other three ownership forms, but the absolute rate of contraction in fast-growing MSAs is actually higher than the rate of contraction in slow-growing MSAs.

The rates of capacity change in the most and least populous MSA quartiles present a more complex pattern. In particular, table 1.3 shows that, among the most populous MSAs, for-profit hospitals exited the faster-growing MSAs at a slightly faster rate than they exited slower-growing MSAs. At the same time, for-profit hospitals actually *expanded* capacity in the slowest growing MSAs in the least populous quartile. Both these results are consistent with a wholesale shift by for-profit hospitals from the largest urban areas to smaller MSAs, regardless of expected trends in demand. The figures for the least populous quartile of MSAs, including particularly the large percentage increase in for-profit capacity that appears there, are also affected by the small number of institutions from which the figures are computed: The quartile of least populous MSAs contains dramatically fewer hospital beds than does the quartile containing the most populous MSAs.

The fact that the response to changing demand of hospitals of different ownership types differs depending on the characteristics of the cities in which they are located motivates our regression models. Those models identify the effects of changing demand on capacity based on within-MSA variation in population rather than on variation across MSAs to control for such unobserved differences in hospitals' strategies. Specifically, we estimate the effect, on zip-code-level measures of changes in capacity, of zip code changes in demand and zip code hospital market characteristics, holding constant MSA fixed effects. Descriptive statistics of all of the variables used in the regression analysis appear in table 1.4.

## 1.4   Results

Table 1.5 presents estimates of the effect of population changes and base-year hospital market characteristics on changes in differently owned forms of hospital capacity from equation (1). For hospitals overall, and for

Table 1.4          Characteristics of Zip Codes Used in Regression Analysis

| Variable | N | Mean | Standard Deviation | Minimum | Maximum |
|---|---|---|---|---|---|
| Capacity, 1985 | 12,753 | 24.754 | 19.274 | 0.420 | 275.842 |
| Secular nonprofit capacity | 12,753 | 13.877 | 12.846 | 0.000 | 127.115 |
| Religious nonprofit capacity | 12,753 | 5.018 | 7.114 | 0.000 | 148.047 |
| For-profit capacity | 12,753 | 2.787 | 5.970 | 0.000 | 63.160 |
| Public capacity | 12,753 | 3.071 | 5.286 | 0.000 | 77.473 |
| Log change in capacity | | | | | |
| 1985–1994 | 12,753 | −0.298 | 0.277 | −4.465 | 4.041 |
| Secular nonprofit capacity | 12,253 | −0.242 | 0.518 | −5.795 | 4.502 |
| Religious nonprofit capacity | 11,010 | −0.375 | 0.636 | −6.010 | 6.194 |
| For-profit capacity | 6,178 | −0.277 | 0.655 | −3.747 | 4.795 |
| Public capacity | 10,020 | −0.411 | 0.769 | −5.600 | 4.711 |
| Log change in population, | | | | | |
| 1985–1994 | 12,753 | 0.176 | 0.517 | −4.736 | 6.581 |
| Ln(beds per capita in 1985) | 12,753 | −1.921 | 1.420 | −6.137 | 4.500 |
| Very concentrated hospital | | | | | |
| market | 12,753 | 0.371 | 0.483 | 0.000 | 1.000 |
| Above-median density of | | | | | |
| for-profit/nonprofit | 12,753 | 0.441 | 0.497 | 0.000 | 1.000 |
| Above-median density of | | | | | |
| public/nonprofit | 12,753 | 0.479 | 0.500 | 0.000 | 1.000 |
| Above-median density of large | | | | | |
| hospitals | 12,753 | 0.400 | 0.490 | 0.000 | 1.000 |
| Above-median density of | | | | | |
| teaching hospitals | 12,753 | 0.410 | 0.492 | 0.000 | 1.000 |
| Above-median density of | | | | | |
| system hospitals | 12,753 | 0.484 | 0.500 | 0.000 | 1.000 |

each individual ownership type, responsiveness to increases in demand, as proxied by population increases, is lower than responsiveness to decreases in demand, controlling for other market characteristics. A 1 percent increase in population leads to a 0.017 percent increase in overall capacity, holding other factors constant, while a 1 percent population decrease leads to a 0.095 percent decrease in overall capacity. This is what one would expect in an industry generally characterized by overcapacity.

Comparing the second through fifth columns of the first row of table 1.5 shows that responsiveness to increases in demand of secular nonprofits is similar to that of religious nonprofit and for-profit hospitals and rather lower than that of public institutions. This is perhaps because the expansionary incentives facing (the managers of) secular nonprofits, which—as we have suggested above—are arguably greater than those present in the other three ownership types, are counterbalanced by the greater difficulty that secular nonprofits face in obtaining rapid access to capital.

Of primary interest to us here, however, is the relative responsiveness to *decreases* in demand exhibited by hospitals under different forms of own-

Table 1.5     **Effect of Increases and Decreases in Population and 1985 Hospital-Market Characteristics on Changes in Hospital Bed Capacity, 1985–1994**

|  | All Ownership Types | Nonprofit | | For-Profit | Public |
|---|---|---|---|---|---|
|  |  | Secular | Religious |  |  |
| Dln(pop), increases | 0.017** | 0.023** | 0.017 | 0.033** | 0.053** |
|  | (0.005) | (0.008) | (0.011) | (0.012) | (0.016) |
| Dln(pop), decreases | 0.095** | 0.043** | 0.109** | 0.146** | 0.110** |
|  | (0.006) | (0.009) | (0.012) | (0.014) | (0.014) |
| | *Characteristics of hospital market in 1985* | | | | |
| Very concentrated | −0.014** | 0.000 | −0.023 | −0.124** | −0.117** |
|   hospital market | (0.007) | (0.009) | (0.014) | (0.024) | (0.020) |
| Above-median density | −0.010 | 0.056** | 0.013 | −0.332** | −0.233** |
|   of for-profit/nonprofit | (0.008) | (0.011) | (0.017) | (0.039) | (0.026) |
| Above-median density | −0.021** | 0.054** | −0.044** | −0.062** | −0.261** |
|   of public/nonprofit | (0.006) | (0.009) | (0.013) | (0.019) | (0.024) |
| Above-median density | 0.029** | 0.047** | 0.032** | 0.015 | 0.059** |
|   of large hospitals | (0.005) | (0.008) | (0.012) | (0.014) | (0.019) |
| Above-median density | 0.010* | 0.029** | 0.001 | 0.019 | 0.125** |
|   teaching hospitals | (0.006) | (0.009) | (0.013) | (0.017) | (0.020) |
| Above-median density | −0.003 | 0.021** | −0.008 | −0.133** | 0.004 |
|   of system hospitals | (0.006) | (0.009) | (0.011) | (0.018) | (0.018) |

*Notes:* Dependent variable is zip-code-level ln(1994 capacity) − ln(1985 capacity). Standard errors are in parentheses. Number of zips with nonmissing change in capacity for all ownership types is 12,753; for secular nonprofit, 12,252; for religious nonprofit, 11,010; for for-profit, 6,178; and for public, 10,020.
**Significant at the 5 percent level.
*Significant at the 10 percent level.

ership. Here, the results in table 1.5 follow precisely the pattern that our theoretical discussion would predict. For-profit capacity is most responsive to decreases in demand. The next most responsive are public capacity and religious nonprofit capacity, for which the estimated coefficients are nearly identical. Secular nonprofit capacity is distinctly the least responsive to decreases in demand, with a coefficient that is less than half the coefficient for public and religious nonprofit capacity and only one-third of the coefficient for the responsiveness of for-profit capacity.

Tables 1.6 and 1.7 present estimates of equations (2) and (3), respectively. Estimates of equation (2) from table 1.6 differ from the estimates of equation (1) from table 1.5 in that the former are calculated controlling baseline (1985) total hospital capacity per elderly Medicare beneficiary. Estimates of equation (3) from table 1.7 differ from the estimates of equation (1) in table 1.5 in that the former are calculated controlling for baseline hospital capacity plus baseline capacity interacted with the two population change variables, producing estimates of the effect of demand responsiveness that vary with the level of baseline capacity.

Table 1.6 shows that, especially for both forms of nonprofit capacity, the

Table 1.6    Effect of Increases and Decreases in Population and 1985 Hospital-Market Characteristics on Changes in Hospital Bed Capacity, 1985–1994, Including Controls for Baseline 1985 Capacity

| | All Ownership Types | Nonprofit | | For-Profit | Public |
|---|---|---|---|---|---|
| | | Secular | Religious | | |
| Dln(pop), increases | 0.026** | 0.036** | 0.044** | 0.049** | 0.056** |
| | (0.006) | (0.009) | (0.012) | (0.013) | (0.017) |
| Dln(pop), decreases | 0.091** | 0.037** | 0.096** | 0.142** | 0.109** |
| | (0.006) | (0.010) | (0.012) | (0.015) | (0.014) |
| | *Characteristics of hospital market in 1985* | | | | |
| Ln(beds per capita in | −0.006** | −0.008** | −0.017** | −0.010** | −0.002 |
| 1985) | (0.001) | (0.002) | (0.003) | (0.004) | (0.004) |
| Very concentrated | −0.014** | 0.000 | −0.022 | −0.126** | −0.117** |
| hospital market | (0.007) | (0.009) | (0.014) | (0.024) | (0.020) |
| Above-median density | −0.011 | 0.055** | 0.010 | −0.336** | −0.234** |
| of for-profit/nonprofit | (0.008) | (0.011) | (0.017) | (0.039) | (0.026) |
| Above-median density | −0.021** | 0.054** | −0.043** | −0.061** | −0.261** |
| of public/nonprofit | (0.006) | (0.009) | (0.013) | (0.019) | (0.024) |
| Above-median density | 0.029** | 0.046** | 0.031** | 0.018 | −0.059** |
| of large hospitals | (0.005) | (0.008) | (0.012) | (0.014) | (0.019) |
| Above-median density | 0.010 | 0.029** | 0.001 | 0.018 | 0.124** |
| teaching hospitals | (0.006) | (0.009) | (0.013) | (0.017) | (0.020) |
| Above-median density | −0.003 | 0.021** | −0.008 | −0.133** | 0.004 |
| of system hospitals | (0.006) | (0.009) | (0.011) | (0.018) | (0.018) |

*Notes:* See notes to table 1.5. Dependent variable is zip-code-level ln(1994 capacity) − ln(1985 capacity).
**Significant at the 5 percent level.
*Significant at the 10 percent level.

estimated responsiveness of capacity to increases in population grows larger once baseline capacity is held constant. The results are similar for the alternative specification in table 1.7. In both tables 1.6 and 1.7, this increase in responsiveness is offset by a significant negative effect of high baseline capacity on the rate of growth in capacity. These are the results one would expect: There is less need to expand capacity to meet growing demand when the capacity in place is already unusually large.

The estimated responsiveness of capacity to population decreases remains essentially unchanged from table 1.5 to table 1.6 for all forms of ownership, even though baseline capacity is statistically significantly correlated with population decreases, just as it is with population increases (from analysis not in the table, $\rho = 0.106$ and $\rho = -0.047$, respectively). One possible interpretation is that areas with declining population are already marked by sufficient overcapacity, that they are contracting as rapidly as feasible (given organizational constraints), and that the added stimulus of yet further overcapacity has no important effect on the rate of contraction. In table 1.7, the responsiveness of capacity to decreases in population drops substantially for all ownership types. High-capacity areas are less re-

**Table 1.7**     **Effect of Increases and Decreases in Population and 1985 Hospital-Market Characteristics on Changes in Hospital Bed Capacity, 1985–1994, Including Controls for Baseline 1985 Capacity and Capacity/Population Interactions**

| | All Ownership Types | Nonprofit | | For-Profit | Public |
| --- | --- | --- | --- | --- | --- |
| | | Secular | Religious | | |
| Dln(pop), increases | 0.039** | 0.046** | 0.051** | 0.068** | 0.062** |
| | (0.006) | (0.009) | (0.012) | (0.013) | (0.017) |
| Dln(pop), decreases | 0.034** | 0.004 | 0.087** | 0.034 | 0.059** |
| | (0.007) | (0.012) | (0.015) | (0.021) | (0.019) |
| *Interactions between ln(population) and ln(beds per capita) in 1985* | | | | | |
| Dln(pop), increases* | −0.017** | −0.016** | −0.025** | −0.022** | −0.026** |
| Ln(beds/cap in 1985) | (0.002) | (0.004) | (0.005) | (0.005) | (0.008) |
| Dln(pop), decreases* | −0.035** | −0.024** | −0.004 | −0.049** | −0.026** |
| Ln(beds/cap in 1985) | (0.003) | (0.005) | (0.007) | (0.007) | (0.007) |
| *Characteristics of hospital market in 1985* | | | | | |
| Ln(beds per capita in | −0.007** | −0.007** | −0.011** | −0.012** | 0.000 |
| 1985) | (0.002) | (0.002) | (0.003) | (0.004) | (0.005) |
| Very concentrated | −0.010 | 0.003 | −0.018 | −0.121** | −0.111** |
| hospital market | (0.007) | (0.009) | (0.014) | (0.023) | (0.020) |
| Above-median density | −0.010 | 0.056** | 0.010 | −0.334** | −0.231** |
| of for-profit/nonprofit | (0.008) | (0.011) | (0.016) | (0.038) | (0.026) |
| Above-median density | −0.022** | 0.053** | −0.044** | −0.057** | −0.261** |
| of public/nonprofit | (0.006) | (0.009) | (0.013) | (0.018) | (0.024) |
| Above-median density | 0.031** | 0.048** | 0.033** | 0.016 | −0.055** |
| of large hospitals | (0.005) | (0.008) | (0.012) | (0.014) | (0.019) |
| Above-median density | 0.012* | 0.030** | 0.005 | 0.023 | 0.128** |
| teaching hospitals | (0.006) | (0.009) | (0.013) | (0.017) | (0.020) |
| Above-median density | −0.005 | 0.019** | −0.010 | −0.136** | 0.000 |
| of system hospitals | (0.006) | (0.009) | (0.011) | (0.018) | (0.018) |

*Notes:* See notes to table 1.5. Dependent variable is zip-code-level ln(1994 capacity) − ln(1985 capacity). **Significant at the 5 percent level.

sponsive to decreases in demand than are low-capacity areas, likely due to the same factors—not captured in these models—that were responsible for the high capacity to begin with.

Table 1.8 presents estimates of equation (4), which allows the effects on capacity of increases and decreases in population to vary by hospital market characteristics. For-profit hospitals adjust to demand contractions much more rapidly when the market is concentrated, as do religious nonprofits (to a much lesser extent). Secular nonprofit hospitals, in contrast, do not respond differently to demand contractions in concentrated versus unconcentrated markets.[5] One possible interpretation is that individual in-

5. In results not presented in the table, we also reestimated equation (4) with controls for baseline 1985 capacity per capita (as we did for equation [1], with results in table 1.5), which had no substantial effect on this finding.

Table 1.8    Differential Effects of Increases and Decreases in Population on Changes in Hospital Bed Capacity, 1985–1994, by Characteristics of Hospital Market in 1985

| | All Ownership Types | Nonprofit | | For-Profit | Public |
|---|---|---|---|---|---|
| | | Secular | Religious | | |
| Dln(pop), increases | 0.022 | 0.002 | 0.107** | −0.216** | −0.006 |
| | (0.014) | (0.021) | (0.028) | (0.070) | (0.055) |
| Dln(pop), decreases | 0.126** | 0.169** | 0.034 | 0.116 | 0.054 |
| | (0.020) | (0.030) | (0.043) | (0.105) | (0.082) |
| *Interactions between ln(population) and characteristics of hospital market in 1985* | | | | | |
| Very concentrated mkt · | 0.044** | −0.010 | −0.123** | 0.131** | 0.086** |
| ln(population increase) | (0.013) | (0.021) | (0.026) | (0.032) | (0.034) |
| Very concentrated mkt · | 0.124** | −0.037 | 0.078** | 0.682** | 0.023 |
| ln(population decrease) | (0.016) | (0.028) | (0.039) | (0.048) | (0.038) |
| High for-profit/nonprofit · | −0.032** | −0.013 | −0.056** | 0.097 | 0.001 |
| ln(population increase) | (0.012) | (0.019) | (0.023) | (0.066) | (0.036) |
| High for-profit/nonprofit · | 0.083** | 0.085** | −0.022 | −0.254** | 0.132** |
| ln(population decrease) | (0.015) | (0.024) | (0.030) | (0.105) | (0.042) |
| High public/nonprofit · | −0.001 | 0.012 | 0.035 | 0.096** | −0.005 |
| ln(population increase) | (0.010) | (0.016) | (0.021) | (0.025) | (0.047) |
| High public/nonprofit · | −0.075** | −0.088** | 0.106** | 0.035 | −0.041 |
| ln(population decrease) | (0.015) | (0.023) | (0.029) | (0.046) | (0.074) |
| High density of large · | −0.026** | 0.024 | −0.023 | −0.116** | −0.052* |
| ln(population increase) | (0.011) | (0.018) | (0.022) | (0.024) | (0.031) |
| High density of large · | −0.036** | −0.054** | 0.111** | −0.084** | 0.091** |
| ln(population decrease) | (0.014) | (0.022) | (0.033) | (0.033) | (0.035) |
| High density of teaching · | −0.009 | −0.004 | −0.084** | 0.058* | 0.027 |
| ln(population increase) | (0.012) | (0.020) | (0.024) | (0.032) | (0.036) |
| High density of teaching · | −0.067** | −0.123** | −0.053 | 0.171** | −0.084** |
| ln(population decrease) | (0.016) | (0.026) | (0.037) | (0.037) | (0.042) |
| High density of system · | 0.027** | 0.025 | −0.003 | 0.133** | 0.085** |
| ln(population increase) | (0.011) | (0.017) | (0.023) | (0.030) | (0.032) |
| High density of system · | −0.019 | −0.013 | −0.042* | 0.195** | −0.089** |
| ln(population decrease) | (0.012) | (0.019) | (0.025) | (0.035) | (0.033) |

*Note:* See notes to table 1.5. Dependent variable is zip-code-level ln(1994 capacity) – ln(1985 capacity).
**Significant at the 5 percent level.
*Significant at the 10 percent level.

stitutions internalize more of the gains from capacity reduction when they have a larger market share—and thus have a stronger incentive to eliminate excess capacity in such circumstances—but only if the institutions value profitability above size and survival, which is presumably true of for-profit hospitals but may not be true of secular nonprofits. Differences by owner-ship status in the response of capacity to population increases in concentrated versus unconcentrated markets follow a different pattern. For-profit and public hospitals adjust to demand increases statistically significantly more rapidly in concentrated markets, whereas religious nonprofits adjust to demand increases statistically significantly less rapidly, reflecting the

Table 1.9          Effect of Increases and Decreases in Population and 1985 Hospital-Market
                   Characteristics on Changes in Total Hospital Bed Capacity, 1985–1994

| | Cause of Change in Dependent Variable | | | |
| | Opens/ Closes (1) | Conversions (2) | Mergers/ Spinoffs (3) | Changes in Bed Size (4) |
|---|---|---|---|---|
| Dln(pop), increases | 0.007** | 0.001 | 0.002 | 0.004 |
| | (0.002) | (0.002) | (0.002) | (0.004) |
| Dln(pop), decreases | 0.000 | 0.001 | −0.002 | 0.089** |
| | (0.002) | (0.002) | (0.002) | (0.005) |
| *Characteristics of hospital market in 1985* | | | | |
| Very concentrated | 0.004** | 0.000 | 0.005** | −0.027** |
| hospital market | (0.002) | (0.002) | (0.002) | (0.005) |
| Above-median density of | −0.007** | −0.012** | 0.011** | 0.000 |
| for-profit/nonprofit | (0.003) | (0.002) | (0.003) | (0.006) |
| Above-median density of | −0.004** | −0.008** | 0.007** | −0.013** |
| public/nonprofit | (0.002) | (0.002) | (0.002) | (0.005) |
| Above-median density of | 0.010** | −0.001 | −0.002 | 0.017** |
| large hospitals | (0.002) | (0.002) | (0.002) | (0.004) |
| Above-median density | −0.011** | 0.002 | 0.015** | 0.003 |
| teaching hospitals | (0.002) | (0.002) | (0.002) | (0.005) |
| Above-median density of | −0.005** | 0.000 | −0.014** | 0.015** |
| system hospitals | (0.002) | (0.002) | (0.002) | (0.005) |

*Notes:* See notes to table 1.5. Dependent variable is zip-code-level change in ln(capacity) due to the listed cause of change.
**Significant at the 5 percent level.

conflicting incentives for and constraints on expansion of hospitals of different ownership statuses discussed above.

Tables 1.9 through 1.13 present estimates of equation (1) analogous to those in table 1.4, but decomposed by the source of the change in capacity. Each table decomposes the changes in a single ownership form's capacity into four exhaustive and mutually exclusive sources: opens and closes, conversions, mergers and spinoffs, and changes in bed size.[6] Table 1.9 gives results for hospital capacity in aggregate. The exhaustive and exclusive nature of the decomposition is reflected in the fact that the coefficients across columns in table 1.9 add to approximately the coefficients in the first column of table 1.2. Tables 1.10 through 1.13 give results for each ownership form taken separately.

Table 1.9 indicates that, as means of responding to both increases and decreases in demand, neither conversions nor mergers and spinoffs are sig-

6. The effects of population (and other covariates) on changes in an ownership form's capacity due to different causes do not necessarily average to the total effects on that ownership form because a zip code's percentage change in the (counterfactually constructed) capacity due to the four causes does not necessarily average to a zip code's total percentage change in capacity.

Table 1.10          Effect of Increases and Decreases in Population and 1985 Hospital-Market
                    Characteristics on Changes in Nonprofit Secular Hospital Bed Capacity, 1985–1994

| | Cause of Change in Dependent Variable | | | |
| | Opens/ Closes (1) | Conversions (2) | Mergers/ Spinoffs (3) | Changes in Bed Size (4) |
|---|---|---|---|---|
| Dln(pop), increases | 0.006** | 0.003 | 0.003 | 0.009* |
| | (0.002) | (0.004) | (0.003) | (0.005) |
| Dln(pop), decreases | 0.005** | 0.001 | −0.011 | 0.079** |
| | (0.002) | (0.005) | (0.003) | (0.006) |
| *Characteristics of hospital market in 1985* | | | | |
| Very concentrated | 0.006** | 0.012** | 0.001 | −0.021** |
| hospital market | (0.002) | (0.005) | (0.003) | (0.006) |
| Above-median density of | −0.003 | 0.020** | 0.015** | −0.018** |
| for-profit/nonprofit | (0.002) | (0.006) | (0.004) | (0.007) |
| Above-median density of | 0.004** | 0.028** | 0.001 | −0.016** |
| public/nonprofit | (0.002) | (0.005) | (0.003) | (0.006) |
| Above-median density of | 0.005** | 0.026** | −0.013** | 0.020** |
| large hospitals | (0.002) | (0.004) | (0.003) | (0.005) |
| Above-median density | −0.009** | −0.010** | 0.020** | 0.017** |
| teaching hospitals | (0.002) | (0.005) | (0.003) | (0.006) |
| Above-median density of | 0.001 | −0.015** | −0.010** | 0.025** |
| system hospitals | (0.002) | (0.005) | (0.003) | (0.006) |

*Notes:* See notes to table 1.5. Dependent variable is zip-code-level change in ln(capacity) due to the listed cause of change.
**Significant at the 5 percent level.
*Significant at the 10 percent level.

nificant vehicles for all forms of ownership in aggregate. This is not surprising since those transactions do not in themselves lead to any change in aggregate capacity, although they can be the occasion for change. More interesting is the result that opens and closes, but not changes in bed size, are significant means of responding to increases in demand. One reason for this pattern may be that areas with increasing population are often newly developed sections of MSAs that are far from existing facilities and hence not easily served by expanding those facilities; rather, new facilities must be built to serve those areas. Another reason may be that, with changes in technology, it is often easier to build an entirely new facility than to expand an existing one.

The most surprising result in table 1.8, however, is that only changes in bed size, not opens and closes, are a significant means of reducing aggregate hospital capacity in response to decreases in demand. This result is due to the fact (as seen in tables 1.9 and 1.10) that both secular and religious nonprofit hospitals use reductions in bed capacity much more than closure of facilities to respond to decreasing demand, consistent with the

Table 1.11     **Effect of Increases and Decreases in Population and 1985 Hospital-Market Characteristics on Changes in Nonprofit Religious Hospital Bed Capacity, 1985–1994**

|  | Cause of Change in Dependent Variable | | | |
|---|---|---|---|---|
|  | Opens/ Closes (1) | Conversions (2) | Mergers/ Spinoffs (3) | Changes in Bed Size (4) |
| Dln(pop), increases | 0.004** | −0.003 | 0.011** | 0.004 |
|  | (0.002) | (0.007) | (0.004) | (0.006) |
| Dln(pop), decreases | 0.002 | 0.007 | 0.018** | 0.087** |
|  | (0.002) | (0.007) | (0.004) | (0.007) |
| | *Characteristics of hospital market in 1985* | | | |
| Very concentrated | 0.004** | −0.013 | 0.034** | −0.049** |
| hospital market | (0.002) | (0.009) | (0.005) | (0.008) |
| Above-median density of | 0.010** | −0.067** | 0.008 | 0.049** |
| for-profit/nonprofit | (0.002) | (0.010) | (0.006) | (0.009) |
| Above-median density of | −0.011** | −0.043** | 0.048** | −0.010 |
| public/nonprofit | (0.002) | (0.008) | (0.005) | (0.007) |
| Above-median density of | 0.006** | −0.011 | 0.012** | −0.007 |
| large hospitals | (0.002) | (0.007) | (0.004) | (0.007) |
| Above-median density | −0.020** | 0.000 | 0.023** | −0.003 |
| teaching hospitals | (0.002) | (0.008) | (0.005) | (0.007) |
| Above-median density of | 0.016** | −0.007 | −0.022** | 0.010 |
| system hospitals | (0.002) | (0.007) | (0.004) | (0.006) |

*Notes:* See notes to table 1.5. Dependent variable is zip-code-level change in ln(capacity) due to the listed cause of change.

**Significant at the 5 percent level.

*Significant at the 10 percent level.

strong managerialist bias against complete exit that theory suggests we would find at least among secular nonprofits.

At first glance, tables 1.10–1.13 appear to suggest that conversions are not used to transform the ownership structure of beds in response to demand changes: The values in column (2), in the first and second rows of tables 1.10–1.13, are small and statistically insignificant. However, this may be an artifact of our limited definition of conversion (i.e., same name and AHA identifier in 1985 and 1994, but with a different ownership status), which may exclude some changes in control that were de facto conversions. Tables 1.10–1.13 hint that this may be the case. In areas of decreasing population, nonprofit capacity contracts through opens and closes, while for-profit and public hospitals actually *expand* capacity significantly through opens and closes, suggesting that some of the closes and opens involved may actually be conversions. This finding underscores one potential limitation of the analysis of tables 1.10–1.13: Any classification of changes in capacities into mutually exclusive categories necessarily in-

Table 1.12          Effect of Increases and Decreases in Population and 1985 Hospital-Market
                    Characteristics on Changes in For-Profit Hospital Bed Capacity, 1985–1994

| | Cause of Change in Dependent Variable | | | |
|---|---|---|---|---|
| | Opens/ Closes (1) | Conversions (2) | Mergers/ Spinoffs (3) | Changes in Bed Size (4) |
| Dln(pop), increases | 0.015** | −0.010 | 0.004 | 0.020** |
| | (0.003) | (0.007) | (0.005) | (0.007) |
| Dln(pop), decreases | −−0.017** | −0.006 | 0.003 | 0.145** |
| | (0.004) | (0.008) | (0.006) | (0.008) |
| | *Characteristics of hospital market in 1985* | | | |
| Very concentrated | −0.009 | −0.049** | −0.048** | 0.000 |
| hospital market | (0.007) | (0.013) | (0.010) | (0.013) |
| Above-median density of | 0.000 | −0.161** | −0.005 | −0.003 |
| for-profit/nonprofit | (0.010) | (0.020) | (0.015) | (0.020) |
| Above-median density of | −0.003 | −0.010 | −0.007 | −0.035** |
| public/nonprofit | (0.005) | (0.010) | (0.008) | (0.011) |
| Above-median density of | −0.005 | −0.028** | 0.031** | 0.030** |
| large hospitals | (0.004) | (0.008) | (0.006) | (0.008) |
| Above-median density | −0.021** | 0.016* | 0.032** | −0.006 |
| teaching hospitals | (0.005) | (0.010) | (0.007) | (0.010) |
| Above-median density of | −0.031** | 0.012 | −0.088** | −0.025** |
| system hospitals | (0.005) | (0.010) | (0.008) | (0.010) |

*Notes:* See notes to table 1.5. Dependent variable is zip-code-level change in ln(capacity) due to the listed cause of change.

**Significant at the 5 percent level.

*Significant at the 10 percent level.

volves some arbitrary decisions that may not reflect the complex realities of the changing structure of the hospital industry.

## 1.5   Conclusion

Numerous empirical studies have sought to identify how differences in the incentives facing managers of nonprofit and for-profit firms lead to differences in economic performance.[7] Many of these studies have taken the hospital industry as their focus. Depending on the dimension of performance examined, these studies have reported both similarities and differences across ownership forms.[8] We have focused here on a largely neg-

7. See Scott-Morton, Podolny, and Podolny (2001) for work on the related question: how differences in the incentives of hobbyist versus professional managers lead to differences in price and quality in the California wine industry.

8. Compare, for example, Kessler and McClellan (2002?), who find that areas with a presence of for-profit hospitals have lower levels of hospital expenditures but virtually the same patient health outcomes, to Duggan (2000), who finds that nonprofit firms responded as strongly as for-profit firms to a California program that greatly increased immediate financial incentives to treat the indigent.

Table 1.13     **Effect of Increases and Decreases in Population and 1985 Hospital-Market Characteristics on Changes in Public Hospital Bed Capacity, 1985–1994**

| | Cause of Change in Dependent Variable | | | |
| --- | --- | --- | --- | --- |
| | Opens/ Closes (1) | Conversions (2) | Mergers/ Spinoffs (3) | Changes in Bed Size (4) |
| Dln(pop), increases | 0.008* | 0.041** | −0.004 | −0.003 |
| | (0.004) | (0.011) | (0.003) | (0.008) |
| Dln(pop), decreases | −0.008* | −0.019* | 0.000 | 0.106** |
| | (0.004) | (0.011) | (0.003) | (0.008) |
| | *Characteristics of hospital market in 1985* | | | |
| Very concentrated | 0.044** | −0.101** | 0.011** | −0.018 |
| hospital market | (0.006) | (0.015) | (0.005) | (0.011) |
| Above-median density of | −0.019** | −0.105** | 0.007 | −0.063** |
| for-profit/nonprofit | (0.008) | (0.020) | (0.006) | (0.015) |
| Above-median density of | −0.029** | −0.155** | −0.018** | 0.006 |
| public/nonprofit | (0.007) | (0.018) | (0.005) | (0.013) |
| Above-median density of | 0.044** | −0.070** | −0.040** | 0.047** |
| large hospitals | (0.006) | (0.014) | (0.004) | (0.010) |
| Above-median density | 0.029** | 0.088** | 0.013** | −0.083** |
| teaching hospitals | (0.006) | (0.015) | (0.005) | (0.011) |
| Above-median density of | 0.018** | 0.001 | 0.003 | −0.015 |
| system hospitals | (0.005) | (0.013) | (0.004) | (0.010) |

*Notes:* See notes to table 1.5. Dependent variable is zip-code-level change in ln(capacity) due to the listed cause of change.
**Significant at the 5 percent level.
*Significant at the 10 percent level.

lected aspect of performance—rapidity of exit—where differences in behavior between nonprofit and for-profit hospitals seem likely to be unusually pronounced and where those differences may have important implications for the overall structure and performance of the industry.

Managers of for-profit hospitals and, to a lesser degree, also managers of public hospitals and of religiously affiliated nonprofit hospitals may have incentives to minimize costs of service and hence to eliminate unused or underused capacity. Managers of unaffiliated nonprofit institutions, in contrast, may not feel such an incentive so long as net cash flow does not become negative. Consequently, it is a plausible hypothesis that such nonprofit hospitals adjust capacity much more slowly than do for-profit firms in response to reductions in demand, effectively serving as capital traps.

The results presented here provide strong support for that hypothesis. For-profit hospitals are the most responsive to reductions in demand, followed in turn by public and religiously affiliated nonprofit hospitals, while secular nonprofits are distinctly the least responsive of the four ownership types. Our results do not support the hypothesis that bureaucratic inertia and multiple stakeholders make public hospitals uniformly less responsive to market forces than their nonprofit counterparts.

It follows that if excess capacity is a continuing social problem in the hospital sector, then the high density of nonprofit firms, which are the legacy of a very different era of hospital technology and financing, may be in large part responsible. This suggests, in turn, that encouraging exit by nonprofit institutions, particularly by secular nonprofits, may enhance efficiency. For example, the withdrawal of federal, state, and local tax exemption from nonprofit hospitals, or at least from those that do not provide substantial amounts of uncompensated care, much as federal tax exemption was withdrawn from nonprofit health insurance companies in 1986, could lead to a reallocation of assets to more productive uses. Alternatively, facilitating conversion to more cost-sensitive forms of organization by altering the corporate law fiduciary duties of nonprofit directors to deny them the right to "just say no" to acquisition offers from other firms, and particularly from for-profit firms (Hansmann 1996a, 2000), could accomplish the same goal. The latter reform would restrict the defensive tactics available to the managers of nonprofit corporations even more severely than those available to the managers of business corporations. Given, however, that nonprofit institutions by their nature are relatively insensitive to market pressures for exit, more expansive legally imposed fiduciary duties may be socially optimal.

# References

Cutler, David. 2000. Introduction. In *The changing hospital industry: Comparing not-for-profit and for-profit institutions,* ed. David Cutler. Chicago: University of Chicago Press.

Duggan, Mark. 2000. Hospital ownership and public medical spending. *Quarterly Journal of Economics* 140:1343–73.

Hansmann, Henry. 1987. The effect of tax exemption and other factors on the market share of nonprofit versus for-profit firms. *National Tax Journal* 40:71–82.

———. 1996a. The changing roles of public, private, and nonprofit enterprise in education, health care, and other human services. Chapter 9 in *Individual and social responsibility: Child care, education, medical care, and long-term care in America,* ed. Victor Fuchs. Chicago: University of Chicago Press.

———. 1996b. *The ownership of enterprise.* Cambridge: Harvard University Press.

Jensen, Michael. 1988. Takeovers: Their causes and consequences. *Journal of Economic Perspectives* 2:21–48.

Kessler, Daniel P., and Mark B. McClellan. 2000. Is hospital competition socially wasteful? *Quarterly Journal of Economics* 115:577–615.

———. 2002. The effects of hospital ownership on medical productivity. *RAND Journal of Economics* 33 (Autumn): 488–506.

Lakdawalla, Darius, and Tomas Philipson. 1998. Nonprofit production and competition. NBER Working Paper no. 6377. Cambridge, Mass.: National Bureau of Economic Research.

Madison, Kristin. 2001. The relationship between multihospital system membership and treatments, costs, and outcomes of Medicare patients with acute myocardial infarction. Ph.D. diss. Stanford University, Department of Economics.

National Center for Health Statistics. 2001. *Health United States 2001, with urban and rural chartbook.* Hyattsville, Md.: National Center for Health Statistics.

Pauly, Mark, and Michael Redisch. 1973. The not-for-profit hospital as a physician's cooperative. *American Economic Review* 63:87–99.

Roemer, M. 1961. Bed supply and hospital utilization: A natural experiment. *Hospitals* 35:36–42.

Scott-Morton, Fiona Podolny, and Joel Podolny. 2001. Love or money? The effect of motivation in the California wine industry. Yale University, School of Business and Stanford University, Graduate School of Business. Unpublished manuscript, draft.

Sloan, Frank A., Donald H. Taylor Jr., and Christopher J. Conover. 2000. Hospital conversions: Is the purchase price too low? Chapter 1 in *The changing hospital industry: Comparing not-for-profit and for-profit institutions,* ed. David Cutler. Chicago: University of Chicago Press.

Steinwald, Bruce, and Duncan Neuhauser. 1970. The role of the proprietary hospital. *Law and Contemporary Problems* 35:817–38.

# Does Governance Matter?
# The Case of Art Museums

Sharon Oster and William N. Goetzmann

## 2.1 Introduction

Art museums provide a classic example of organizations operating with multiple objectives. On the one hand, many American museums take as their central function the education of the populace. At the same time, there is a long tradition in museum management of conservation and appeal to the narrower elite. In the past decade, the balance between these objectives seems to have tilted in favor of the broader populace. In writing of this change, one museum activist, Kenneth Hudson, has argued: "The most fundamental change that has affected museums is the now almost universal conviction that they exist in order to serve the public" (Kotler and Kotler 2001, 171). Sociologists have explored this tension at some length. D'Harnoncourt et al. (1991), for example, describe the movement of art museums from secluded temples of culture to the present-day more public institutions. Grana (1971) similarly contrasts patron-oriented museums, focused on "men of leisure from the upper classes," with public-oriented ones.

This paper uses cross-sectional and time-series data on U.S. museum finances and operating characteristics to explore the effect of governance structure on performance. We are particularly interested in whether the ownership structure of a museum influences the balance it strikes among competing constituents. Increasingly, economists have come to appreciate

Sharon Oster is the Frederic D. Wolfe Professor of Management and Entrepreneurship and faculty director of the Partnership on Nonprofit Ventures at the Yale School of Management. William N. Goetzmann is the Edwin J. Beinecke Professor of Finance and Management Studies and director of the International Center for Finance at the Yale School of Management.

We thank Cathy Shu for collecting the data. We thank the numerous museums who shared their data with us. We thank workshop participants for their suggestions.

the role played by governance structures on decision making in organizations, and the differentiated structure of the industry makes museums an excellent case study.

## 2.2  The Role of Museums

We begin our discussion by considering the objective function of the typical museum. In the literature, there are three oft-cited museum goals: art preservation, education of the populace, and the providing of a social signal for the elite of a community. The first two of these goals appear frequently in the mission statements of museums. The mission statement of the Portland Art Museum in Oregon is typical: "The mission of the Portland Art Museum is to serve the public by providing access to art of enduring quality, by educating a diverse audience about art and by collecting and presenting a wide range of art for the enrichment of present and future generations." The opening lines of the mission statement of the Boston Museum of Fine Arts strike a similar theme: "The Museum of Fine Arts houses and preserves preeminent collections and aspires to serve a wide variety of people through direct encounters with works of art."[1] The interest in both art preservation and education for the public are clear.

The role of museums in reinforcing a social elite within a city is less often articulated in mission statements. Yet, until well into the twentieth century, most American museums depended on private philanthropic dollars for their support (Anheier and Toepler 1998, 235). Indeed, wealthy industrialists, to whom Dimaggio refers as "cultural capitalists," founded many of our most well-known museums (1986). Dimaggio describes in some detail the way that these industrialists, in cities like Boston, used art institutions to build cultural boundaries separating themselves from the rest of society. As Temin suggests, displaying one's art validates both a patron's possessions and his or her position in society (1991). Consequently, one might expect that the more affluent the society, the greater the need to signal taste through support and display of the arts.

The growth of art museums was thus based not only on an aesthetic tradition in American society, but upon a philanthropic one. John Ingham (1997) and Ruth Krueger Meyer and Madeleine Fidell Beaufort (1997), in an exhibition catalogue to a major exhibition, *Collection in the Gilded Age: Art and Patronage in Pittsburgh: 1890–1910,* describe the art-collecting and philanthropic activities of Gilded-Age Pittsburgh through the lenses of class and society. Wealthy Pittsburgh families vied with each other to create spectacular collections of European art and also, in many cases, made gifts of these collections to the public. Andrew Carnegie, the city's (and perhaps the nation's) wealthiest citizen at the time, led by example in do-

---

1. See the Web mission statement at http://207.127.106.123/mission.

## Distribution of Museum Founding Dates

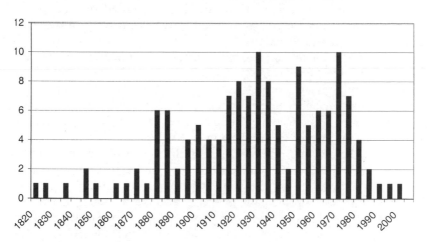

**Fig. 2.1    The distribution of founding dates for museums in the 1989 and 1999 AAMD sample**

*Sample:* 1989 and 1999 AAMD with reported founding information

*Note:* Founding dates were collected from annual AAMD directories, as available.

nating much of his wealth in order to improve the access of Pittsburgh's citizens to higher arts and education (Ingham; Meyer and Beaufort). Subsequent gifts by leading Pittsburgh citizens enriched the artistic horizon of the nation as a whole. For example, Andrew Mellon's collection became the core of the National Gallery of Art, and Henry Clay Frick founded the Frick Collection of New York.

While the Gilded Age was an important period for museum founding and support, patronage of the arts through museum foundation has continued vigorously since. Figure 2.1 is a chart of museum-founding dates from the sample we study in this paper. It suggests that the most active periods for museum founding appear to have been the two decades preceding and the two decades following the Second World War. In fact, this probably understates the contributions of the most recent era. The figure shows a tailing-off at the end of the sample period that is most likely due to younger museums' not reporting statistical information to the Association of Art Museum Directors (AAMD) as commonly as more established institutions. Not only was the "birth process" of museums sustained through the last century, but the social context of arts patronage has also continued to be an important factor in museum management. Museums today, as in the past, rely upon gifts for collection development and operations support, and wealthy donors and founders remain key constituents of American art museums. The continuation of the philanthropic tradition—founded on the Gilded-Age sense of civic duty and, to some extent, maintenance of social position through public giving—is an important economic foundation for art museums. Indeed, in this paper, we test the extent to which urban concentrations of wealth are related to institutional reliance upon gifts and donations.

Consider now the role of governance structure in determining how museums pursue their varied objectives and balance the interests of their constituents. Approximately one-third of the art museums in the United States are public institutions. These public museums were most typically founded with service to the public in mind and are likely to emphasize public attendance as an objective. The remaining two-thirds of American museums are overwhelmingly nonprofit, but within this pool there are institutional differences, such as between university-based museums and free-standing nonprofits. University art museums, which emerged largely in the nineteenth century, were principally intended to serve the students and academic staffs of their own institutions (Boylan 1999). While many university museums have clearly broadened their reach to serve the general public, one might well expect some residual focus on the less popular end of the art spectrum and on curatorial and educational functions as opposed to mass appeal. Thus, we hypothesize that public museums will service the general public the most and university museums the least as they go about their respective businesses.

In pursuing these three objectives, museums have a number of instruments available. To the extent that public museums emphasize public access, one would expect them to maintain low prices, focus collection efforts on broadly accessible art and programs, and emphasize more popular exhibitions. University-based museums would be expected to focus on more sophisticated art and programs and be less concerned with keeping admission prices low for the general public, although free student access might well be important. Free-standing nonprofits, operating without other support, might be expected to charge higher prices and pay more attention to the interests of elite donors.

Unfortunately, it is difficult to gather data directly on many of these strategic variables. Locating pricing data is, for example, quite problematic. Many museums characterize admissions fees as "suggestions," where the suggestion carries varying levels of force at different museums. Hence, while the broad-brush data do support our hypotheses in that low or zero price levels are correlated with public ownership, it is hard to go much further simply looking at this variable. Assessing the collection efforts of museums on the spectrum of popular versus more esoteric is also difficult, although we have some relevant evidence in section 2.2.3, where we examine the special exhibits of the various museums.

Two elements of museums operations, space utilization and financing, afford some perspective on the objective functions of museums. Some measure of the emphasis that a museum places on the various elements of its mission may be revealed by the proportion of space it gives to education versus exhibitions, for example. The structure of a museum's financing may also affect the way it pursues various objectives. Finally, we use the attendance levels at museums with different ownership structures as an index of how vigorously these museums are pursuing public education and entertainment over their alternative goals.

### 2.2.1 Space and Money

The empirical work described in this section of the paper is based on 1999 data collected by the AAMD, the principal art museum membership organization, consisting of just over 200 museums located in the United States and Canada. The AAMD conducts annual surveys of its members, covering a wide range of information about finances, operations, and museum collections. While the survey data generally are not publicly available, we were given access to the data for 1989 and 1999. For the analysis of space utilization and financing in this section of the paper we have used the 1999 data. In a later analysis of attendance, we use both survey years.

In the full sample, there are 148 U.S. museums in 1989 and 140 in 1999 with substantial institutional overlap between the two years, although many of the museums have at least some missing data. The museums surveyed are quite diverse, ranging in size, for example, from the Metropolitan Museum of Art in New York, with 1,835 full-time employees in 1999, to the California State University Art Museum, with only 4 full-time employees. There is a similarly large range in the attendance figures. The National Gallery of Art in Washington, D.C. and the Metropolitan Museum of Art in New York both attract more than 5 million annual visitors, while the Yale University Art Gallery has a more modest 50,000. The summary statistics on the sample used in this paper are given in table 2.1.

**Table 2.1**       **Summary of Variables**

| | Full Sample | | Endowment Sample | |
|---|---|---|---|---|
| | Mean | Range | Mean | Range |
| Collection expenditures | $1,487,422 | $2,055–30,800,000 | $1,681,048 | $2,055–30,800,000 |
| Attendance | 379,003 | 25,000–6,500,000 | 507,7228 | 25,000–6,500,000 |
| Type of collection | | | | |
|   Survey | 72% | | 76% | |
|   Modern | 8% | | 6% | |
|   American | 10% | | 8% | |
| Governance | | | | |
|   College | 19% | | 16% | |
|   Public | 26% | | 24% | |
|   Other nonprofit | 55% | | 60% | |
|   Endowment | | | $46,400,000 | $114,885–1,020,000,000 |
| Observations | 190 | | 166 | |

Table 2.2          **Museum Space Utilization, 1999 Association of Art Museum Directors Survey**

|  | | Statistically Different? | | | |
|---|---|---|---|---|---|
|  | Mean | From Combined | From Public | From Nonprofit Not University | From University Nonprofit |
| *Exhibition space/all space* | | | | | |
| Public museums | .331 | No | | No | No |
| Nonprofits, not university | .342 | No | No | | No |
| University nonprofit | .345 | No | No | No | |
| *Educational space/all space* | | | | | |
| Public museums | .043 | Yes | | Yes | No |
| Nonprofit, not university | .074 | No | Yes | | No |
| University nonprofit | .065 | No | No | No | |
| *Museum store space/all space* | | | | | |
| Public | .018 | No | | No | No |
| Nonprofit/not university | .020 | No | No | | No |
| University/nonprofit | .016 | No | No | No | |

The first question we explore using the AAMD data is the way in which different museums use their space. The survey itself distinguishes a number of space categories. For this analysis, we have focused on three: space for exhibitions, space designated for educational use, and museum storage space. Our particular question is whether university-based museums have more educational space and less storage space than their public or general nonprofit peers.

As we see from table 2.2, just over one-third of the space for the museums in our sample is used in permanent exhibition space, while a more modest area is used for either education or the museum store. There is no difference by governance type either in exhibition space or in storage space. Simple regressions holding overall museum size and age constant confirm the results of table 2.2, revealing no influence from governance. The data do suggest that nonprofit museums are devoting significantly more space to educational uses than are the public museums.

In table 2.3 we compare revenue sources for the three museum types. The four major revenue streams of museums are considered: gross earned revenues, which include admission fees (suggested and otherwise), exhibition fees, museum store sales, and rentals; private philanthropic support, including corporate, individual, and foundation; government support; and finally, endowment support.

Considerable differences in the funding patterns of museums by governance types are clearly revealed in table 2.3. Nonprofit, nonuniversity museums are most dependent on earned income and private support. Public museums, not surprisingly, depend principally on public support. University museums, with access to university support, are less dependent on any

**Table 2.3** **Revenue Shares by Governance Structure, 1999 Association of Art Museum Directors Survey**

| | | Statistically Different? | | | |
|---|---|---|---|---|---|
| | Mean | From Both Combined | From Public | From Nonprofit Not University | From University Nonprofit |
| *Gross earned revenues/all revenues* | | | | | |
| Public | .20 | No | | Yes | Yes |
| Nonprofit, not university | .25 | Yes | Yes | | Yes |
| University | .11 | Yes | Yes | Yes | |
| *Private support/all revenues* | | | | | |
| Public | .21 | Yes | | Yes | No |
| Nonprofit, not university | .33 | Yes | Yes | | Yes |
| University | .21 | Yes | No | Yes | |
| *Government support/all revenues* | | | | | |
| Public | .41 | Yes | | Yes | Yes |
| Nonprofit, not university | .12 | Yes | Yes | | No |
| University | .08 | Yes | Yes | No | |
| *Endowment support/all revenues* | | | | | |
| Public | .08 | Yes | | Yes | No |
| Nonprofit, not university | .19 | Yes | Yes | | Yes |
| University | .12 | No | No | Yes | |

of the three constituent-based revenue sources than are public or general nonprofit museums.

We explore some of the consequences of these different financing patterns in the next two sections of the paper as we look at museum attendance and special exhibitions.

### 2.2.2 Attendance

Attendance levels are one of the traditional output measures used by many museums. We now consider how attendance may be influenced by governance. While governance is expected to influence the aggressiveness with which museums pursue audiences, characteristics of the collection itself likely affect its inherent attractiveness to the public. Finally, since museums deliver their output on site, we expect the city characteristics to help determine demand. Here we ask: Are museums like Wal-Mart, where all that really matters for attracting customers is the organization's location? Or will a museum attract its own audience despite location-specific features?

Before we turn to the econometrics, the raw data suggest something of the governance-attendance relationship. Consider the ratio of attendance to museum exhibition space as one (admittedly crude) measure of the "productivity" of a museum. By this measure, university-based museums are heavily overrepresented in the list of the twenty least productive museums.

Thirty-five percent of the museums on this list are university affiliates, as compared to a population of 23 percent. Among the twenty most space-productive museums, there is only one university affiliate. Similarly, public museums are overrepresented in the productive class and underrepresented in the underperformers.

In order to explore these differences across museums more thoroughly, we estimate a simple model of museum attendance. The attendance levels at museums are modeled as a production function, where the inputs include museum and city characteristics. In particular, we estimate a production function for museum attendance as follows:

$$(1) \qquad A_{it} = \alpha + \beta X_{it} + \delta Z_{it} + \phi G$$

where $A_{it}$ is the attendance at museum $i$ at time $t$, $X_{it}$ is a vector of characteristics associated with the collection of museum $i$ at time $t$, $Z_{it}$ is a vector of characteristics at time $t$ of the city in which museum $i$ is located, and $G$ is an indicator for governance structure.

Data on attendance levels and collection characteristics come from the 1989 and 1999 AAMD surveys. The survey data are not without problems, some of which are described by Rosett (1991) for the earlier 1989 data. From our point of view, the collection data are most problematic. Ideally, we would like a measure of the value of the museum collection to use as one element of the $X$ vector. In the more usual industrial-production-function context, this would be equivalent to a capital stock figure. As is well known, however, museum collections are not valued in the financial statements of museums; indeed, the standard procedure is to list the value of art assets at $1. In the AAMD survey, there are some data provided on the total value of a museum's collection based on insurance coverage.[2] These data are problematic both because insurance readjustments are likely to be sticky and because many of the museums self-insure and thus drop out of the sample when we measure collection value this way. Moreover, the censored museums are not representative since it is many of the large public museums that self-insure.

An alternative measure of collection value is the current expenditures on the collection. While we may presume that acquisitions are a major component of this category, expenditures on the collection may also include restoration, framing, and other expenses. Nevertheless, this measure has the advantage of being "real" data, and is also available for a broader set of museums. Clearly what we are measuring here is a flow (analogous to investment) rather than the preferable asset value, although the flow and stock values do appear to be highly correlated. Using current expenditures

---

2. Museum directors were asked to provide information on both the payoff of the insurance and the fraction of the collection covered. These two figures were then used to generate a total value figure.

on the collection may also create an endogeneity problem. Increased attendance at a museum typically contributes to the earned income of a museum, through either admissions fees or concession revenue, and thus may increase funds available for collections. To deal with this issue, we provide an alternative estimate of the attendance regression, instrumenting for collection expenditures using the market value of the endowment at the end of the prior period. Endowment value should be both independent of attendance and correlated with collection expenditures. Since a number of the museums in the sample do not report endowment values, instrumenting in this way reduces the sample size somewhat.

In addition to the variable measuring collection value, we also identify each collection by type. Narrative summaries of each museum provided by the AAMD were used to categorize each museum as either survey, modern, American, or other. We are interested here in whether there is any evidence of a type bias in American museum goers.

The $Z$ vector contains a set of variables describing the characteristics of the site of the museum. The typical museum attracts both residents and tourists. To capture local demand, we used the size of the local population and the percentage of the population with a college degree. Prior work (Dimaggio 1987) suggests that educational level is a better predictor of local demand than income. We used two measures of tourist demand: hotel expenditures per capita and mean January temperature. High January temperatures are intended to capture substitution possibilities for tourists and local residents alike. We expect that, holding tourism levels constant, museums do better in climates with cold winters.

Finally, we use dummies to capture governance type, distinguishing public, university-based, and other nonprofit museums. The public museums include those run by city, state, and federal governments. The set of independent variables used and the means of the data are given in table 2.1. We note that the problem of missing observations reduces the overall sample considerably, essentially halving the population of 300 museums we started with.

Table 2.4 reports the results of the estimation. In the estimation, all variables were transformed to logs, given the expected nonlinear relationship between attendance and museum and city characteristics. Thus, in this specification, we can think of the coefficient estimates as elasticities. The results in table 2.4 suggest that both museum and city characteristics matter for a museum's ability to draw an audience. Collection expenditures exert a large, positive, and highly significant effect on attendance. A 10 percent increase in the expenditures on collections increases current attendance by 2.5 percent to 4.0 percent, which seems to be a relatively large effect given the durable nature of collection expenditures. There is some evidence that survey collections have more drawing power than other collection types.

In fundamental terms, these results suggest that art matters. Our results

**Table 2.4**            **Attendance Regressions**

| Independent Variable | OLS | IV |
|---|---|---|
| Log collection expenditures | .258 | .414 |
| | (8.92)** | (6.68)** |
| Type | | |
| Survey | .501 | .454 |
| | (2.78)** | (2.00)* |
| American | .145 | .080 |
| | (.226) | (.27) |
| Modern | .296 | .408 |
| | (1.4) | (1.65) |
| MSA population (log) | .205 | .124 |
| | (4.53)** | (2.00)* |
| Percent of population with bachelor's degree (log) | .183 | .179 |
| | (1.22) | (1.04) |
| Hotel expenditures per capita (log) | .240 | .156 |
| | (3.46)** | (1.88) |
| January mean temperature (log) | −.442 | −.32 |
| | (−2.47)** | (1.53) |
| Governance | | |
| College | Omitted | Omitted |
| Public | .804 | .863 |
| | (4.61)** | (4.05)** |
| Other nonprofit | .539 | .552 |
| | (5.52)* | (3.03)** |
| Constant | 6.34 | 4.98 |
| | (5.56)** | (3.59)** |
| Observations | 190 | 166 |
| $R^2$ | .60 | .56 |

*Note:* MSA = metropolitan statistical area. OLS = ordinary least squares. IV = instrumental variables.
**Significant at the .01 level.
*Significant at the .05 level.

are consistent with the hypothesis that collections function as economic assets, with larger collections drawing more customers. In fact, we can go further and use the coefficient estimates to answer the question of what the economic impact of an increase in collection expenditures would have on the museum. The data in table 2.1 suggest that in our sample the mean annual collection expenditure is about $1.5 million, while average attendance in the sample is about 379,000. If we apply the lower elasticity figure of 0.25 generated in table 2.4, we see that an increased expenditure on the collection of $150,000 (10 percent) would yield approximately 9,500 more museum attendees each year. For this to pay off in strictly a one-year economic impact, each new attendee would have to spend $16 in a visit, which is likely high. Of course, one would not expect art investment to pay off this quickly for a museum or else they would be doing more of it!

In terms of location, all of the variables are of the right signs in both regressions, although only the population variable passes the usual significance tests in both specifications. We note again the truncated sample in the instrumental variable (IV) regressions. The tourist-related variables suggest that the ideal museum location from an attendance perspective is a tourist location in a cold area. For Tom Krens' new Guggenheim museum branch in Las Vegas, the regression gives a mixed prediction: Based on tourist beds, Las Vegas looks like a good site; based on January temperature, Krens may have a failure on his hands.

The results further suggest that governance type matters a good deal in terms of audience attraction. Public museums strongly outdraw nonprofit museums of either type, and university-based museums clearly deliver the smallest audiences. These results are consistent with the view that public museums stress public education, while college museums in particular may focus more on higher education, connoisseurship, and other aspects of the museum mission. These results further support Hansmann's (1981) observations on the differences in the focus on attendance by performance arts organizations. We turn now to look directly at the role of special exhibits in museums of varying ownership types.

### 2.2.3    The Role of Traveling Exhibitions

Special exhibitions play two important roles for museums. In some cases, these exhibitions are mounted by a museum's own curators and represent the historical vision of that curator, expressing a particular point of view about a body of work. Thus, at one level, special exhibitions represent a curatorial research product. On the other hand, some special exhibitions—the blockbusters—serve in large measure as a way to attract large, new audiences to a museum. Attracting large audiences has financial benefits as well. Even those museums that charge no admission fees benefit through their concession and museum shops from increases in visitorship. Indeed, for the average museum, revenues from audience-related concessions exceed admissions fees (AAMD Survey 1999).

The traveling special exhibition is particularly interesting in terms of function. In many cases, exhibitions travel from one museum to another and provide a way to expose a local audience to new work. For moderate sized art museums, some reliance on traveling exhibitions is common. The St. Louis Art Museum, for example, had thirty-five special exhibits in the 1990s, 35 percent of which were organized outside of the museum itself, including most of the very high-attendance shows. As such, traveling exhibitions are a way of temporarily augmenting a museum collection through, in effect, leasing more-valuable works from major museums. Much of the discussion by critics on the changed role of the museum has focused particularly on the use of the special exhibition as a crowd pleaser. By mounting a recent exhibit of guitars, the Museum of Fine Arts in Boston was described as "turning itself into a gigantic Hard Rock Café" (Leo 2001). Of New York's Guggenheim, which is well known for its unusual exhibits, Heather Macdonald opined that "the Giorgio Armani show at the Guggenheim reminds us that 'art' in an art museum these days is optional" (Leo).

There is a tension, then, between the smaller-scale special exhibit, which principally serves a research or educational function, and the audience-generating, revenue-producing blockbuster. In line with our earlier discussion, we expect to see different museum types specializing in each of these forms. In particular, university-based museums are likely to be overrepresented among museums mounting specialized exhibits, while public and nonprofit museums, lured by both revenues and audience, will focus on the blockbuster segment.

Before we can consider the different production of special exhibits by different museums, it is useful to touch briefly on the economics of exhibition production more generally. From the point of view of an industrial-organization economist and a finance professor, it is a curious process indeed.

Producing special exhibits requires essentially two inputs: curatorial time and art objects. While museums can and do use visiting curators, the ability to regularly mount a diverse group of special exhibits requires a substantial curatorial staff. In the modern blockbuster age, a staff of exhibit designers has become increasingly important (Silver 1982), further increasing the fixed costs burden for the smaller museum.

A more important barrier to mounting major exhibits by the small museums is created by the economics of art-object lending. The typical special exhibit relies on both a museum's own objects and borrowed objects. It is the custom in the museum business that these loans are made without a fee, although it is usual for the borrowing museum to pay for travel and insurance costs. Even objects from private collections are borrowed rather than rented, although there is, at times, some restoration work serving as a quid pro quo. Initially, one might think that the borrowing tradition would make it easier for smaller museums to mount exhibits, by lowering costs. We would argue, however, that this system may discriminate against the smaller museums. In the barter system used, the smaller museum may find itself with few objects of any appreciable "trade" value and thus more often find its requests for loans refused. Similarly, private exhibitors likely prefer lending to big-name museums. As with many barter systems, this one may create an inefficiency by reducing the ability of the creative curator in the smaller museum to exploit his or her skill. As we will shortly argue, however, the university museum—even the relatively small one—is in a somewhat advantaged position in the borrowing business.

The evidence suggests that production of traveling exhibitions among art museums is indeed a highly concentrated business. One way to measure concentration is to look at participation fees earned by museums. In 1999,

| Table 2.5 | Exhibit Census |
|---|---|
| Exhibit | Originating Museum |
| *Blockbusters in 1998, 1999 (attendance >400,000 at one museum)* | |
| Monet in the Twentieth Century | Boston MFA |
| The Private Collection of Degas | Metropolitan Museum |
| Van Gogh's Van Gogh | National Gallery |
| Mary Cassatt: Modern Woman | Art Institute, Chicago |
| Pierre Bonnard | MOMA |
| Cézanne to Van Gogh: Dr. Gachet | Metropolitan Museum |
| John Singer Sargent | National Gallery |
| Renoir's Portraits | Art Institute, Chicago |
| *Mini-blockbuster (attendance >200,000 and <400,000)* | |
| Monet: Portrait of Giverny | Walters Art Gallery |
| Alexander Calder | National Gallery |
| A Collector's Cabinet | National Gallery |
| Manet, Monet, and Gare St. Lazere | National Gallery |
| Degas at the Races | National Gallery |
| Collecting Impressionism | High and Seattle |
| Picasso and the War Years | Guggenheim |
| From Van Eyck to Brueghel | Metropolitan Museum |
| Picasso: Painter and Sculptor in Clay | Metropolitan Museum |
| Hans Hoffman in the Metropolitan | Metropolitan Museum |
| Jackson Pollock | MOMA |
| Delacroix: The Late Work | Philadelphia Museum |
| Portraits by Ingres | National Gallery |

*Notes:* MFA = Museum of Fine Arts. MOMA = Museum of Modern Art.

for example, the AAMD data indicate that the top four museums providing data on participation fees earned 55 percent of the total fees earned.[3] A decade earlier, in 1989, this figure was slightly lower. There are no university museums among this top list.

Another way to estimate concentration is to look at the originating museum for recent large exhibits. This allows us to look at some museums that do not provide AAMD survey data. This information is provided in table 2.5. Of the twenty-one exhibits we identified in the 1998–99 period with attendance levels over 200,000 in a single museum, the National Gallery had one-third and the Metropolitan one-fourth of the exhibits. Again, high concentration is clearly in evidence, public and nonprofit museums are represented in proportion to their place in the pool, and no university museums are present. One might also notice that almost all of the blockbuster shows are of Impressionist painters.

The 1999 AAMD list of museums with the highest earned income from

3. This figure is based on the approximately two-thirds of the museums responding to this question.

participation fees is principally dominated by the very largest museums. Interestingly, the smaller museums earning participation fees are dispro-portionately university-based museums. Here we see the importance of the more specialized traveling exhibition to the research life of the university museum. In 1999, the Harvard University Art Museums were among the top ten in participation fees among reporting institutions. These fees ap-pear to be the result of a show mounted in 1998, *Inside Out: the New Chi-nese Art,* which traveled throughout the country in 1999 and 2000 and was mounted in cooperation with the San Francisco Museum of Modern Art. Williams College, Smith College, and Yale University all earn more from participation fees than you might expect from their operating budgets. The Harvard and Yale art galleries routinely mount special exhibitions that travel to other museums. The university museum may well have cost ad-vantages in mounting these exhibits, as well as enhanced mission-driven reasons to support such activity. Here we see some of the advantages of the university museum in terms of ability to use curatorial talents outside the museum budget, in the quality of their history of art departments, and in terms of their ability to borrow, particularly from affiliated collectors. Col-leges with well-endowed alumni may be able to call on these alumni to lend art to their museum exhibitions and in this way are less hampered by the borrowing culture of the art world than their similarly sized cohorts.

### 2.3   Museums as Social Institutions

We have thus far explored the way in which museum ownership and gov-ernance structure may influence the emphasis it places on audience attrac-tion. We turn now to look more directly at the role of a museum vis-à-vis the social elite in a city.

Founding a museum, sitting on the board of a local arts institution, and contributing conspicuously to a public museum have long been an avenue into society. The role of the single philanthropist in founding museums like the Guggenheim and the Whitney in New York is well known, but the pat-tern is common in the rest of the country as well. In Minneapolis, T. B. Walker, who made his fortune in lumber, started the Walker Art Center in the mid-nineteenth century. The Center for British Art at Yale University is the gift of philanthropist and collector Paul Mellon. In Chicago, the Terra Museum of American Art was founded, funded, and named by its principal donor, Daniel Terra.

What has happened to the museum's role as a validator of social posi-tion? As we suggested earlier, the typical museum in the last several decades has attempted to broaden its public appeal in part to attract new audiences for revenue reasons. As museums have become democratized in their exhibitions, there is some question about whether they have lost their role as promoters of the social elite.

As part of their required Form 990 filings with the Internal Revenue Service, museums are asked a series of questions pertaining to their "public support" basis for tax exemption. As part of this set of questions, museums are required to indicate funds raised from individuals who have contributed over the past four years an amount in excess of 2 percent of the museum's total funds. We use this information as one measure of the "elite focus" of the museum's funds.

As table 2.6 suggests, there is considerable variation in the reliance of museums on very large contributions. Some museums report having no patron who, in the period 1994–97, contributed more than 2 percent of museum support, while several museums receive almost half of their private support from this source. Among the museums with substantial reliance on the large gift are included several very large, high-profile museums (e.g., the Whitney Museum and the San Francisco Museum of Modern Art [MOMA]), as well as a number of smaller, less well-known museums, including the Arkansas Art Center and the Akron Art Museum.

In table 2.7, we report the results of a simple regression intended to tease out some of the determinants of museum dependence on concentrated donors. The dependent variable is the ratio of donations raised from donors contributing each in excess of 2 percent of the pool to the total support pool. As independent variables, we consider two city characteristics: percentage of the city population in the top income group (>$150,000 in 1990), and population stability (percentage of the population living in the same county between 1985 and 1990). Our expectation is that a museum's reliance on high-end donors will be positively related to both measures, the intuition being that the social elites supporting museums have historically been high-income and stable in residence. In addition, we look at the museum's age, recognizing that in early stages museums are often the product of a few wealthy benefactors, and that through a museum's life cycle, the donor pool will tend to spread. While all variables are of the expected sign, only the income variable is statistically significant. The significance of the high-income variable is consistent with the conspicuous consumption function of museums. The greater the density of affluent citizens, the greater the need to signal social status through support of the arts.

It is also interesting to consider the way in which the importance of the big donor to museums may have changed over time. In panels A and B of table 2.8, we have briefly summarized the history of the museums listed in the AAMD survey founded in two historical periods: before 1920, a period in which many of the premier U.S. museums were founded, and since 1960. We note first that the ownership structure in these newer museums parallels those of the earlier museums: Two-thirds of the new museums are nonprofits, and one-third, public. There is no indication of an evolutionary trend toward one "ideal" museum form, the way we have seen in other areas of nonprofit management. A somewhat higher than expected fraction

| Table 2.6 | Museum Reliance on Large Donors |
|---|---|

| Museum | Proportion of Funds from Large Donors |
|---|---|
| 1. Akron Art Museum | .1899962 |
| 2. Albright-Knox Art Gallery | 0 |
| 3. Allentown Art Museum | .0012145 |
| 4. Arkansas Arts Center | .4329223 |
| 5. Asia Society and Museum | .1664267 |
| 6. Butler Institute of American Art | .056930 |
| 7. Boston Museum of Fine Art | 0 |
| 8. Chrysler Museum | 0 |
| 9. Columbus Museum of Art | .0743780 |
| 10. Columbus Museum | .1177242 |
| 11. Contemporary Arts Center | 0 |
| 12. Cummer Museum of Art | .0296322 |
| 13. Currier Gallery of Art | .0756367 |
| 14. Dallas Museum of Art | .0680886 |
| 15. Dayton Art Institute | .0931211 |
| 16. Detroit Institute of Arts | .0431507 |
| 17. Dia Center for the Arts | .3419761 |
| 18. Flint Institute of Arts | .0997698 |
| 19. Honolulu Academy of Arts | .1077176 |
| 20. Huntington Library and Art Gallery | .1057051 |
| 21. Huntington Museum of Art | .0330222 |
| 22. Huntsville Museum of Art | 0 |
| 23. Indianapolis Museum of Art | .1308966 |
| 24. International Center of Photography | .0312683 |
| 25. Isabella Stewart Gardner Museum | .0789347 |
| 26. JB Speed Art Museum | 0 |
| 27. Jewish Museum | .0891177 |
| 28. Joslyn Art Museum | 0 |
| 29. Long Beach Museum of Art | .0056818 |
| 30. Marion Koogler McNay Art Museum | .1067609 |
| 31. Metropolitan Museum of Art | .0564407 |
| 32. Milwaukee Art Museum | .0731025 |
| 33. Mint Museum of Art | .0057806 |
| 34. Museum of Contemporary Art | 0 |
| 35. Neuberger Museum of Art | .2936345 |
| 36. New Museum of Contemporary Art | 0 |
| 37. New Orleans Museum of Art | .0376919 |
| 38. Newark Museum | .0036008 |
| 39. North Carolina Museum of Art | .1515550 |
| 40. Palm Springs Desert Museum | .1635293 |
| 41. Parrish Art Museum | .0595174 |
| 42. Philadelphia Museum of Art | .0298572 |
| 43. Philbrook Museum of Art | .1342124 |
| 44. Phoenix Art Museum | .2005516 |
| 45. Pierpont Morgan Library | .2166278 |
| 46. Portland Art Museum | .1950636 |
| 47. San Antonio Museum of Art | .0700298 |
| 48. San Diego Museum of Art | .0187342 |

Table 2.6          (continued)

| Museum | Proportion of Funds from Large Donors |
|---|---|
| 49. San Francisco Museum of Modern Art | .3304738 |
| 50. San Jose Museum of Art | .0114623 |
| 51. Santa Barbara Museum of Art | .1068513 |
| 52. Seattle Art Museum | .0058311 |
| 53. Southeastern Center | .3356010 |
| 54. Studio Museum in Harlem | 0 |
| 55. Tampa Museum of Art | 0 |
| 56. Telfair Museum of Art | 0 |
| 57. Textile Museum | .1806287 |
| 58. Toledo Museum of Art | .3462301 |
| 59. Wadsworth Atheneum | .0241641 |
| 60. Walker Art Center | .0260312 |
| 61. Whitney Museum of American Art | .2245290 |
| 62. Winterthur Museum | .0056559 |
| 63. Worchester Art Museum | .0281015 |

Table 2.7          **Determinants of High Donor Funding**

| Independent Variable | Coefficient | $T$-statistic |
|---|---|---|
| Constant | −.045 | (−.30) |
| High-income | .961 | (2.31)* |
| Population stability | .002 | (.82) |
| Museum age | −.0002 | (−.41) |
| $R^2$ | .11 | |
| $N$ | 63 | |

*Significant at the .05 level.

of the new museums do, however, appear to be university based. Most significantly, nearly every one of the new museums—including those associated with universities—was founded by a large gift of money or a gift of art by a major donor. Indeed, the role of the single major donor appears, if anything, to have increased over time. Interestingly, many of the new donors come from the same industry bases as those in the earlier period manufacturing, oil, and transportation. Our evidence suggests remarkable stability in the prevalence of founding donors and the profile of those donors in the museum world.

## 2.4    Museums as Aesthetic Institutions

In the analyses thus far, we have emphasized the ways in which serving popular audiences and serving a narrower elite group compete for museum attention. While recent scholarship has underscored the contrasts in these

**Table 2.8    U.S. Museum, by Year Founded and Donor**

| Museum | Year | Donor (industry) |
|---|---|---|
| *A. Founded Since 1960* | | |
| Amon Carter Museum | 1961 | Amon Carter (publishing) |
| Asian Art Museum of San Francisco | 1966 | Avery Brundage (construction) |
| Brandywine River Museum | 1971 | DuPont (chemicals) |
| Contemporary Arts Center | 1976 | State |
| David and Alfred Smart Museum of Art (University of Chicago) | 1974 | Smarts (publishing) |
| Dia Center for the Arts | 1974 | DeMenil (oil and banking) |
| Elvehjem Museum of Art (University of Wisconsin) | 1962 | Faculty idea: no money |
| Georgia O'Keefe Museum | 1997 | Anne and John Marion (former Sotheby's head) |
| Hirshhorn Museum and Sculpture Garden | 1966 | Hirshhorn (finance, mining) |
| Huntsville Museum of Art | 1970 | City |
| Herbert F. Johnson Museum of Art (Cornell University) | 1973 | Johnson (manufacturing) |
| Jack S. Blanton Museum of Art (University of Texas) | 1963 | Blanton (oil) |
| Jane Voorhees Zimmerli Art Museum (Rutgers) | 1966 | Voorhees-Zimmerli (finance) |
| Krannert Art Museum (University of Illinois) | 1961 | Herman Krannert (box manufacturing) |
| Museum of Contemporary Art | 1967 | Daniel Brenner |
| National Museum of African Art | 1964 | Government |
| National Portrait Gallery | 1962 | Government |
| Neuberger Museum of Art (SUNY Purchase) | 1974 | Roy Neuberger (finance) |
| New Museum of Contemporary Art | 1977 | City |
| Salvador Dali Museum | 1971 | A. R. Morse (industry) |
| Samuel Harn Museum | 1981 | Samuel Harn (manufacturing) |
| San Antonio Museum of Art | 1981 | City |
| San Jose Museum of Art | 1969 | City |
| St. Petersburg Museum of Fine Arts | 1961 | M. Acheson Stuart (publishing) |
| Studio Museum in Harlem | 1967 | Volunteer founders |
| Tampa Museum of Art | 1967 | DeMenils (oil and banking) |
| UCLA Hammer Museum | 1994 | Hammer (chemicals) |
| University of California, Berkeley, Art Museum | 1970 | Hans Hoffmann (artist) |
| University of Iowa Museum of Art | 1967 | Owen and Leone Elliot |
| Wexner Center for the Arts | 1989 | Wexner (retail) |
| Yale Center for British Art | 1977 | Andrew Mellon (transport and aluminum) |
| *B. Founded before 1920* | | |
| Albright-Knox Art Gallery | 1826 | John Albright (steel) |
| Art Institute of Chicago | 1879 | Group of businessmen |
| Baltimore Museum of Art | 1914 | M. Carey Thomas (president of Bryn Mawr; railroad money inherited) |
| Brooklyn Museum of Art | 1823 | Community group |
| Butler Institute of American Art | 1919 | Joseph Butler (manufacturing) |
| Carnegie Museum of Art | 1896 | Andrew Carnegie (steel) |
| Cincinnati Art Museum | 1896 | Citizen group |

**Table 2.8**  (continued)

| Museum | Year | Donor (industry) |
|---|---|---|
| Cleveland Museum of Art | 1913 | Huntington (oil); Kelley (development); Hurlburt (banks) |
| Cooper-Hewitt National Design Muscum | 1887 | Cooper grandchildren (railroads) |
| Corcoran Gallery of Art | 1869 | William Corcoran (banking) |
| Crocker Art Museum | 1885 | Edwin Crocker (railroads) |
| Currier Gallery of Art | 1919 | Moody Currier (banking) |
| Dallas Museum of Art | 1903 | Citizen group |
| Davis Museum | 1889 | Wellesley College |
| Dayton Art Institute | 1919 | Julia Paterson Carnell (National Cash Register) |
| Delaware Art Museum | 1912 | Citizen group |
| Denver Art Museum | 1883 | Municipal |
| Detroit Institute of Arts | 1885 | Brearly (journalism) |
| Fine Arts Museums of San Francisco | 1894 | DeYoung (publishing) |
| Freer Gallery of Art | 1916 | Charles Freer (railroads) |
| Frick Collection | 1920 | Henry Frick (steel) |
| Harvard University Art Museums (Fogg) | 1895 | William Hayes Fogg (China trade) |
| Henry Art Gallery | 1917 | Horace Henry (railroads) |
| Huntington Library and Art Gallery | 1919 | Henry Huntington (railroads) |
| Indianapolis Museum of Art | 1883 | John Herron |
| Isabella Stewart Gardner Museum | 1903 | Isabella Gardner (commerce) |
| Los Angeles County Museum of Art | 1910 | City |
| Memory Art Gallery of Rochester | 1913 | Mrs. J. S. Watson (telegraph) |
| Metropolitan Museum of Art | 1870 | Group of businessmen |
| Michael C. Carlos Museum | 1876 | Emory; Carlos (alcohol distributor) |
| Milwaukee Art Museum | 1888 | |
| Minneapolis Institute of Arts | 1915 | |
| Mississippi Museum of Art | 1911 | Citizen association |
| Munson-Williams-Proctor Arts Institute | 1919 | Munson (banking); Williams (politics); Proctor (manufacture) |
| Museum of Fine Arts, Boston | 1870 | Group of citizens (Henry Kidder, finance; W. Endicott, dry goods; Charles Eliot, Harvard president) |
| New Orleans Museum of Art | 1911 | Isaac Delgado (sugar) |
| Newark Museum | 1909 | Louis Bamberger (retail) |
| Parrish Art Museum | 1898 | Samuel Parrish |
| Philadelphia Museum of Art | 1876 | Group: Centennial related |
| Phillips Collection | 1897 | Duncan Phillips (steel) |
| Portland (Maine) Museum of Art | 1883 | Margaret deMedici Sweat (retail) |
| Portland (Oregon) Art Museum | 1892 | Henry Corbett (bands) |
| Saint Louis Art Museum | 1892 | Group: St. Louis Fair |
| Seattle Art Museum | 1917 | Russell Fuller (medicine) |
| Telfair Museum of Art | 1875 | Alexander Telfair (trade; agriculture) |
| Toledo Museum of Art | 1901 | Edward Libbey (glass) |
| Wadsworth Atheneum | 1842 | D. Wadsworth (insurance) |
| Walker Art Center | 1879 | T. Walker (lumber) |
| Walters Art Museum | 1908 | William Walters (railroads) |
| Worcester Art Museum | 1896 | Stephen Salisbury (trade) |
| Yale University Art Gallery | 1832 | John Trumbull (artist) |

*Note:* Includes all museums listed in the AAMD directory.

two objectives, it is worth considering the commonalities as well. An art museum is, for the most part, a spatial technology for facilitating the personal experience of art. While connoisseurship might be the elite extreme of the aesthetic experience, and art education the populist extreme, they can be expected to share some common kernel or at least to be connected by a continuum of personal experience. Are there cultural commonalities in the "high" and "low" experience of art? Can a single institution serve both extremes? To explore the question of whether common and elite artistic tastes are connected, we used time-series analysis of art prices and attendance at museums.

Clearly, art serves in some measure as an investment good, and thus its price will reflect other forces in investment markets. This has been the direction of most of the prior literature. For example, Goetzmann and Spiegel (1995) take art as a fixed percentage of wealth and show how this may explain the covariation of art with equity markets. More recently, Ait-Sahalia, Parker, and Yogo (2001) show how this covariation between luxury goods like art might account for the magnitude of the equity premium. To date, however, there has been little theoretical work that links a social-pecking-order framework to the prices of the luxury goods and the aesthetic experience directly. On the other hand, such frameworks are common in other parts of the finance literature. For example, "keeping up with the Joneses" models in the asset pricing literature, such as Bakshi and Chen (1996) and Campbell and Cochrane (2001), show how competitive, socially determined preferences may affect security prices. A natural question to ask is whether local social competition determines the demand for conspicuous consumption as well and what role museums might play in this competition.

Economists have long debated the issue of whether art provides a fair rate of return to investors. The natural presumption is that some component of the return to art investment is the aesthetic dividend that accrues to the owner—the private benefits enjoyed by viewing the work. Neglecting expectations about future resale, the entire value of owning a painting would be the capitalized stream of the aesthetic dividends. Given the evidence on the social role of art institutions presented above, one could conceivably substitute "social" for "aesthetic," however. Museums deliver a flow of these nonmonetary dividends to participants: The aesthetic dividends are delivered through viewership, the social dividends are delivered through board association, membership, and attendance. To the extent that there are common tastes and desires for social signaling, we might expect that measures of the dividend flow and its capitalized value to covary. Indeed, our cross-sectional regressions found a relationship between attendance—i.e., the demand for the flow—and the value of the stock. We also might expect art prices to covary with attendance. By the same token, the existence of common aesthetic tastes and demand for social signaling should be associated with correlations in museum attendance. In this section, we test these two propositions with time-series data on museum attendance and the returns to art investment.

### 2.4.1   Data

It is surprisingly difficult to obtain time-series data on museum attendance. The AAMD was unwilling to provide us access to their annual survey for multiple years. As an alternative, we contacted the top fifty art museums in the country and asked for their annual attendance numbers. Many had to reconstruct this information specifically for us. In total, we were able to obtain annual attendance figures for twenty-six museums for different intervals of time. Table 2.9 reports this time-series data. In order to test hypotheses about the covariation in art prices and museum attendance, we construct an equal-weighted index of annual percentage changes in museum attendance from this data. As table 2.9 suggests, the composition of this changes as museums enter and exit the sample, but it provides the best measure we can get of the annual fluctuations in national art museum attendance. Table 2.10 reports the statistical characteristics of the index for different subperiods of the data.

For our measure of returns to investment in art, we use the Mei and Moses (2002) art price indexes. These are estimated from repeated sales of art works auctioned at major houses from 1875 to the present. The technology is similar to Goetzmann (1993)—it calculates pretax and precommission investment returns based upon the auction-to-auction price relative, conditional upon resale. Hence, those works that did not sell after once appearing at auction have no influence on the estimation of the time series of returns. For our purposes, we are chiefly interested in the intertemporal variation in art prices. In small sample, repeat-sales estimators may induce negative serial correlation in the series estimates. However the Mei and Moses data set is large, and thus we may take their index estimation as a fairly accurate representation of the trends in art prices over the past forty years.

### 2.4.2   Do Art Returns Explain Museum Attendance?

If art prices and museum attendance both reflect fluctuations in the common component of demand for the aesthetic or social dividend, we should expect to find some correlation between attendance and the art index. Figure 2.2 plots the cumulated growth in art prices and in museum attendance for the equal-weighed index and for a few representative cities. From 1961 to 2000, art prices appreciated at a considerably higher rate than the growth rate in attendance at art museums. The plot suggests little relationship between attendance and art prices, however. Art prices spiked in the late 1980s and 1990, while the attendance graph shows no such trend.

To more formally examine the relationship between art prices and attendance trends, we regress the equal-weighted index of annual percentage

Table 2.9    Museum Attendance Data

| Year | Asia | Baltimore | Dallas | DeCordova | Georgia | Johnson | Huntington | Illinois | Indianapolis | Getty | Kimbell | L.A. County | Memorial |
|---|---|---|---|---|---|---|---|---|---|---|---|---|---|
| 1. 1960 | n.a. | n.a. | n.a. | n.a. | n.a. | n.a. | n.a. | n.a. | n.a. | n.a. | n.a. | n.a. | n.a. |
| 2. 1961 | n.a. | n.a. | n.a. | n.a. | n.a. | n.a. | n.a. | n.a. | n.a. | n.a. | n.a. | n.a. | n.a. |
| 3. 1962 | n.a. | n.a. | n.a. | n.a. | n.a. | n.a. | n.a. | n.a. | n.a. | n.a. | n.a. | n.a. | n.a. |
| 4. 1963 | n.a. | n.a. | n.a. | n.a. | n.a. | n.a. | n.a. | n.a. | n.a. | n.a. | n.a. | n.a. | n.a. |
| 5. 1964 | n.a. | n.a. | n.a. | n.a. | n.a. | n.a. | n.a. | n.a. | n.a. | n.a. | n.a. | n.a. | n.a. |
| 6. 1965 | n.a. | n.a. | n.a. | n.a. | n.a. | n.a. | n.a. | n.a. | n.a. | n.a. | n.a. | n.a. | n.a. |
| 7. 1966 | n.a. | n.a. | n.a. | n.a. | n.a. | n.a. | n.a. | n.a. | n.a. | n.a. | n.a. | 2,665,388 | n.a. |
| 8. 1967 | n.a. | n.a. | n.a. | n.a. | n.a. | n.a. | n.a. | n.a. | n.a. | n.a. | n.a. | 1,887,135 | n.a. |
| 9. 1968 | n.a. | n.a. | n.a. | n.a. | n.a. | n.a. | n.a. | n.a. | n.a. | n.a. | n.a. | 1,174,674 | n.a. |
| 10. 1969 | n.a. | n.a. | n.a. | n.a. | n.a. | n.a. | n.a. | n.a. | n.a. | n.a. | n.a. | 1,133,870 | n.a. |
| 11. 1970 | n.a. | n.a. | n.a. | n.a. | n.a. | n.a. | 610,102 | n.a. | n.a. | n.a. | n.a. | 1,384,448 | n.a. |
| 12. 1971 | n.a. | n.a. | n.a. | n.a. | n.a. | n.a. | 487,753 | n.a. | n.a. | n.a. | n.a. | 1,185,741 | n.a. |
| 13. 1972 | n.a. | n.a. | n.a. | n.a. | n.a. | n.a. | 450,817 | n.a. | n.a. | n.a. | n.a. | 1,203,999 | n.a. |
| 14. 1973 | n.a. | n.a. | n.a. | n.a. | n.a. | n.a. | 450,000 | n.a. | n.a. | n.a. | n.a. | 1,124,870 | n.a. |
| 15. 1974 | n.a. | n.a. | n.a. | n.a. | n.a. | n.a. | 486,847 | n.a. | n.a. | n.a. | n.a. | 1,204,857 | n.a. |
| 16. 1975 | n.a. | n.a. | n.a. | n.a. | n.a. | n.a. | 552,299 | n.a. | n.a. | n.a. | n.a. | 1,026,918 | n.a. |
| 17. 1976 | n.a. | n.a. | n.a. | n.a. | n.a. | n.a. | 596,419 | n.a. | n.a. | n.a. | n.a. | 1,425,704 | n.a. |
| 18. 1977 | n.a. | n.a. | n.a. | n.a. | n.a. | n.a. | 590,075 | n.a. | n.a. | n.a. | n.a. | 1,350,302 | n.a. |
| 19. 1978 | n.a. | n.a. | n.a. | n.a. | n.a. | n.a. | 541,557 | n.a. | n.a. | n.a. | n.a. | 2,750,039 | n.a. |
| 20. 1979 | n.a. | n.a. | n.a. | n.a. | n.a. | n.a. | 444,094 | n.a. | n.a. | n.a. | n.a. | 357,577 | n.a. |
| 21. 1980 | n.a. | n.a. | n.a. | n.a. | n.a. | n.a. | 379,096 | n.a. | 545,152 | n.a. | n.a. | 506,956 | n.a. |
| 22. 1981 | n.a. | n.a. | n.a. | n.a. | n.a. | n.a. | 396,695 | n.a. | 596,223 | n.a. | n.a. | 586,587 | n.a. |
| 23. 1982 | n.a. | n.a. | n.a. | n.a. | n.a. | n.a. | 489,917 | n.a. | n.a. | n.a. | n.a. | 372,182 | n.a. |
| 24. 1983 | n.a. | n.a. | n.a. | n.a. | n.a. | n.a. | 502,635 | n.a. | n.a. | n.a. | n.a. | 415,000 | n.a. |
| 25. 1984 | n.a. | n.a. | n.a. | n.a. | n.a. | 63,591 | 470,692 | n.a. | n.a. | n.a. | n.a. | 579,569 | n.a. |
| 26. 1985 | n.a. | n.a. | n.a. | n.a. | n.a. | 73,993 | 509,292 | n.a. | n.a. | n.a. | n.a. | 914,978 | n.a. |
| 27. 1986 | n.a. | n.a. | n.a. | n.a. | n.a. | 71,701 | 456,824 | n.a. | n.a. | n.a. | n.a. | 421,296 | n.a. |
| 28. 1987 | n.a. | n.a. | n.a. | n.a. | n.a. | 83,762 | 515,058 | n.a. | n.a. | n.a. | n.a. | 1,099,440 | n.a. |
| 29. 1988 | n.a. | n.a. | n.a. | n.a. | n.a. | 73,665 | 483,964 | n.a. | n.a. | n.a. | n.a. | 860,689 | 85,333 |
| 30. 1989 | n.a. | n.a. | 291,100 | n.a. | n.a. | 77,656 | 442,238 | n.a. | n.a. | n.a. | n.a. | 950,833 | 80,349 |
| 31. 1990 | n.a. | 315,047 | 442,200 | n.a. | n.a. | 67,097 | 497,482 | n.a. | n.a. | n.a. | n.a. | 663,869 | 73,978 |
| 32. 1991 | n.a. | 302,196 | 419,600 | n.a. | n.a. | 84,212 | 542,813 | n.a. | 422,464 | n.a. | n.a. | 1,003,059 | 98,458 |
| 33. 1992 | n.a. | 483,347 | 427,000 | n.a. | n.a. | 66,535 | 534,676 | n.a. | n.a. | n.a. | n.a. | 848,099 | 79,499 |
| 34. 1993 | n.a. | 328,714 | 410,700 | n.a. | n.a. | 72,423 | 492,624 | 29,610 | n.a. | n.a. | n.a. | 612,005 | 84,952 |
| 35. 1994 | n.a. | 322,073 | 422,300 | n.a. | n.a. | 67,656 | 553,503 | 28,943 | n.a. | n.a. | n.a. | 551,935 | 88,294 |
| 36. 1995 | n.a. | 311,577 | 380,000 | n.a. | n.a. | 74,698 | 484,849 | 25,469 | n.a. | n.a. | n.a. | 541,308 | 83,733 |
| 37. 1996 | 61,868 | 347,996 | 458,100 | 54,991 | 78,966 | 71,393 | 463,938 | 34,925 | n.a. | n.a. | n.a. | 663,429 | 87,273 |
| 38. 1997 | 62,666 | 317,090 | 415,200 | 84,724 | 65,003 | 71,875 | 487,861 | 45,526 | n.a. | n.a. | n.a. | 602,141 | 102,682 |
| 39. 1998 | 85,117 | 340,677 | 431,500 | 92,954 | 86,802 | 66,284 | 467,064 | 48,689 | n.a. | 1,750,000 | n.a. | 554,024 | 85,678 |
| 40. 1999 | 91,369 | 277,589 | 501,661 | 90,432 | 109,000 | 68,081 | 509,377 | 32,331 | n.a. | 1,500,000 | 481,049 | 1,328,765 | 75,398 |
| 41. 2000 | 73,880 | 290,299 | n.a. | 100,156 | 120,000 | 72,134 | 534,162 | 25,545 | 380,425 | 1,400,000 | 138,016 | 597,409 | 110,910 |

*Note:* n.a. = not available.

changes in attendance on annual percentage changes in the Mei and Moses (2002) art index. We also perform each regression separately by city, and finally we stack all cities together and estimate the coefficient on art under the assumption of equality of coefficients. Table 2.11 reports the regression results, showing no evidence of a relationship between attendance and art returns. Assuming our tests have power, we can interpret this negative evidence as favoring the hypothesis that the demand at the high end and the demand at the low end for the nonmonetary dividends supplied by art are essentially disjoint.

Figure 2.2 also suggests little relationship among the museums in the

**Table 2.9**    (continued)

| Metropolitan | Museum of Fine Arts | National | Norton | Philadelphia | Princeton | St. Louis | Dali | Guggenheim | Walker | Walters | Whitney | Yale |
|---|---|---|---|---|---|---|---|---|---|---|---|---|
| n.a. | n.a. | n.a. | n.a. | n.a. | n.a. | n.a. | n.a. | n.a. | n.a. | n.a. | n.a. | 99,196 |
| n.a. | n.a. | n.a. | n.a. | n.a. | n.a. | n.a. | n.a. | n.a. | n.a. | n.a. | n.a. | 92,989 |
| n.a. | n.a. | n.a. | n.a. | n.a. | n.a. | n.a. | n.a. | n.a. | n.a. | n.a. | n.a. | 94,372 |
| n.a. | n.a. | n.a. | n.a. | n.a. | n.a. | n.a. | n.a. | n.a. | n.a. | n.a. | n.a. | 83,440 |
| n.a. | n.a. | n.a. | n.a. | n.a. | n.a. | n.a. | n.a. | n.a. | n.a. | n.a. | n.a. | 79,302 |
| n.a. | n.a. | n.a. | n.a. | n.a. | n.a. | n.a. | n.a. | n.a. | n.a. | n.a. | n.a. | 92,019 |
| n.a. | n.a. | n.a. | n.a. | n.a. | n.a. | n.a. | n.a. | n.a. | n.a. | n.a. | n.a. | 101,424 |
| n.a. | n.a. | n.a. | n.a. | n.a. | n.a. | n.a. | n.a. | n.a. | n.a. | n.a. | n.a. | 114,211 |
| n.a. | n.a. | n.a. | n.a. | n.a. | 41,811 | n.a. | n.a. | n.a. | n.a. | n.a. | n.a. | 131,811 |
| n.a. | n.a. | n.a. | n.a. | n.a. | 43,641 | n.a. | n.a. | n.a. | n.a. | n.a. | n.a. | 126,253 |
| n.a. | n.a. | n.a. | n.a. | n.a. | 43,850 | n.a. | n.a. | n.a. | n.a. | n.a. | n.a. | 119,004 |
| n.a. | n.a. | n.a. | n.a. | n.a. | 47,575 | n.a. | n.a. | n.a. | n.a. | n.a. | n.a. | 101,482 |
| 2,225,530 | n.a. | n.a. | n.a. | n.a. | 59,770 | n.a. | n.a. | n.a. | n.a. | n.a. | n.a. | 120,946 |
| 2,272,212 | n.a. | n.a. | n.a. | n.a. | 99,706 | n.a. | n.a. | n.a. | n.a. | n.a. | n.a. | 118,366 |
| 2,590,851 | n.a. | n.a. | n.a. | n.a. | 123,722 | n.a. | n.a. | n.a. | n.a. | n.a. | 261,342 | 87,496 |
| 3,326,012 | n.a. | n.a. | n.a. | n.a. | 84,338 | n.a. | n.a. | n.a. | n.a. | n.a. | 231,829 | 96,293 |
| 2,871,417 | n.a. | n.a. | n.a. | n.a. | 89,519 | n.a. | n.a. | n.a. | n.a. | n.a. | 278,981 | 144,290 |
| 3,337,040 | n.a. | n.a. | n.a. | n.a. | 86,779 | n.a. | n.a. | n.a. | 417,380 | n.a. | 401,489 | 75,392 |
| 3,235,684 | n.a. | n.a. | n.a. | n.a. | 77,228 | n.a. | n.a. | n.a. | 436,040 | n.a. | 458,547 | 98,546 |
| 4,687,277 | 490,888 | n.a. | n.a. | n.a. | 76,031 | n.a. | n.a. | n.a. | 423,362 | n.a. | 369,791 | 96,423 |
| 3,369,934 | 390,604 | n.a. | n.a. | n.a. | 59,551 | n.a. | n.a. | n.a. | 645,799 | n.a. | 441,405 | 106,677 |
| 3,574,138 | 327,431 | n.a. | n.a. | n.a. | n.a. | n.a. | n.a. | n.a. | 360,793 | n.a. | 637,578 | 110,223 |
| 3,232,876 | 341,901 | n.a. | n.a. | n.a. | n.a. | n.a. | n.a. | n.a. | 415,340 | n.a. | 420,150 | 99,346 |
| 4,333,918 | 335,142 | n.a. | n.a. | n.a. | 61,817 | n.a. | n.a. | n.a. | 401,305 | n.a. | 426,547 | 110,914 |
| 3,945,708 | 437,685 | n.a. | n.a. | n.a. | 61,145 | n.a. | n.a. | n.a. | 396,554 | n.a. | 387,743 | 97,130 |
| 3,889,471 | 491,603 | n.a. | n.a. | n.a. | 68,281 | n.a. | n.a. | n.a. | 352,099 | n.a. | 310,595 | 117,746 |
| 3,290,133 | 507,507 | n.a. | n.a. | n.a. | n.a. | n.a. | n.a. | n.a. | 473,259 | n.a. | 340,781 | 185,951 |
| 4,871,698 | 511,838 | n.a. | n.a. | n.a. | n.a. | n.a. | n.a. | n.a. | 473,074 | n.a. | 457,471 | 118,467 |
| 3,767,018 | 665,887 | n.a. | n.a. | n.a. | n.a. | n.a. | n.a. | n.a. | 334,033 | n.a. | 399,564 | 137,867 |
| 4,585,554 | 560,187 | n.a. | n.a. | n.a. | 48,118 | n.a. | n.a. | n.a. | 350,044 | 220,000 | 313,143 | 135,981 |
| 4,329,474 | 510,992 | n.a. | n.a. | n.a. | 75,713 | n.a. | n.a. | n.a. | 335,996 | 200,000 | 338,090 | 155,085 |
| 4,479,344 | 760,868 | n.a. | n.a. | n.a. | 81,345 | n.a. | n.a. | n.a. | 371,672 | 247,000 | 260,800 | 119,834 |
| 4,453,441 | 544,804 | n.a. | 52,494 | n.a. | 103,589 | n.a. | n.a. | 671,303 | 356,801 | 275,000 | 273,986 | 120,630 |
| 4,399,542 | 579,466 | 5,597,973 | 54,174 | n.a. | 119,211 | 542,656 | n.a. | 919,191 | 406,910 | 306,000 | 273,426 | 121,436 |
| 4,308,881 | 1,247,768 | 4,042,044 | 55,092 | n.a. | 78,836 | 447,436 | n.a. | 745,526 | 456,825 | 255,000 | 231,100 | 103,786 |
| 4,657,430 | 1,259,642 | 4,684,095 | 40,268 | 873,515 | 72,188 | 479,738 | n.a. | 788,717 | 499,693 | 267,000 | 293,040 | 96,873 |
| 4,566,579 | n.a. | 4,731,418 | 87,689 | 841,683 | 85,385 | 645,738 | n.a. | 789,182 | 509,123 | 200,000 | 421,867 | 100,968 |
| 5,309,076 | 1,801,924 | 5,637,841 | 98,309 | 1,148,816 | 84,797 | 553,853 | 209,312 | 875,118 | 516,568 | 275,000 | 291,800 | 98,848 |
| 4,950,136 | 1,323,380 | 6,198,523 | 123,212 | 734,149 | 68,144 | 653,016 | 225,685 | 1,048,302 | 518,398 | 344,000 | 385,836 | 111,547 |
| 4,850,913 | 1,251,094 | 5,969,528 | 150,436 | 748,966 | 76,722 | 494,848 | 216,340 | 1,029,638 | 430,252 | 143,676 | 464,244 | n.a. |
| 5,152,884 | 1,784,332 | 5,126,954 | 69,487 | 645,999 | 69,980 | 499,944 | 212,057 | 1,129,366 | 581,590 | 110,952 | 570,255 | 116,400 |

*Note:* n.a. = not available.

sample. This is even more surprising. While the low correlation between attendance and art prices may not be surprising given that auctions reflect demands by a relatively affluent clientele, (indeed, a group whose wealth may depend upon a different set of factors than does the wealth of those who regularly attend art galleries) it is surprising to us to see low intercity relationships in museum attendance trends. In fact, the average correlation among the cities, reported in table 2.12, is close to zero. One way to interpret this is that all art appreciation, like all politics, is local. In some ways, this result reinforces our earlier finding on the importance of both city- and museum-specific factors in determining attendance patterns. An alternative explana-

| Table 2.10 | Summary Statistics, Annual Percentage Changes in Attendance Index of American Art Museums, 1961–2000 | | |
|---|---|---|---|
| | Geographical Growth | Average Growth | Standard Deviation |
| 1961–1970 | –0.0105 | –0.0100 | 0.0930 |
| 1971–1980 | 0.0422 | 0.0461 | 0.1064 |
| 1981–1990 | 0.0307 | 0.0414 | 0.1046 |
| 1991–2000 | 0.0205 | 0.0414 | 0.0599 |

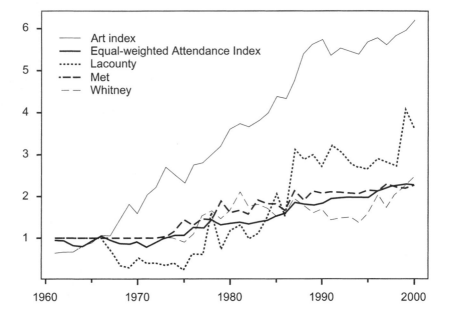

Equal-weighted average of available museums, and three large institutions

**Fig. 2.2   Comparison of the performance of art at auction to measures of growth in attendance**

*Notes:* For an equal-weighted index of museum attendance, and for three museums: Los Angeles County Museum, New York Metropolitan Museum of Art, and the Whitney Museum of American Art. Equal-weighted average of available museums, and three large institutions

tion is that traveling shows are important determinants of attendance with the biggest drawing shows are in different cities in different years.

## 2.5   Conclusions

Art museums in the United States come in a range of ownership forms. In this paper, we have found striking differences in the performance of

Table 2.11    Regressions of Equal-Weighted Percent Changes in Attendance on Art Returns

| | Coefficient | $T$-statistic | $N$ | $R^2$ |
|---|---|---|---|---|
| Asia Society and Museum | −0.033 | −0.037 | 4 | 0.001 |
| Baltimore Museum of Art | 0.381 | 1.006 | 10 | 0.112 |
| Dallas Museum of Art | 0.210 | −0.651 | 10 | 0.050 |
| DeCordova Museum and Sculpture Park | −1.179 | −2.203 | 4 | 0.708 |
| Georgia Museum of Art | 0.962 | 1.629 | 4 | 0.570 |
| Johnson | −0.064 | −0.480 | 16 | 0.016 |
| Huntington Library and Art Gallery | −0.175 | −2.181 | 30 | 0.145 |
| Illinois Art Gallery | −0.747 | −1.298 | 7 | 0.252 |
| Indianapolis Museum of Art | 0.000 | n.a. | 1 | n.a. |
| J. Paul Getty Museum | 0.528 | n.a. | 2 | 1.000 |
| Kimbell Art Museum | 0.000 | n.a. | 1 | n.a. |
| L.A. County Museum of Art | 0.286 | 0.742 | 34 | 0.017 |
| Memorial Art Gallery of Rochester | −0.394 | −1.362 | 12 | 0.156 |
| Metropolitan Museum of Art | −0.131 | −0.851 | 28 | 0.027 |
| Museum of Fine Arts | −0.451 | −1.315 | 19 | 0.092 |
| National Gallery of Art | 0.123 | 0.302 | 7 | 0.018 |
| Norton Museum of Art | −0.749 | −0.665 | 8 | 0.069 |
| Philadelphia Museum of Art | −1.502 | −3.109 | 5 | 0.763 |
| Princeton University Art Museum | 0.178 | 0.863 | 25 | 0.031 |
| Saint Louis Art Museum | 0.506 | 1.035 | 7 | 0.177 |
| Dali | 0.127 | 0.145 | 3 | 0.021 |
| Guggenheim Museum | 0.001 | 0.002 | 8 | 0.000 |
| Walker Art Center | −0.143 | −0.709 | 23 | 0.023 |
| Walters Art Museum | −0.490 | −1.43 | 11 | 0.127 |
| Whitney Museum of American Art | 0.320 | 1.517 | 26 | 0.088 |
| Yale University Art Gallery | 0.152 | 1.087 | 38 | 0.032 |
| Equal-weighted index | −0.008 | −0.122 | 40 | 0.004 |
| Stacked regression | −0.014 | −0.215 | 343 | 0.001 |

Note: City-by-city regression, index regression, and stacked regression.

these museums that are consistent with our expectations about differences in institutional economic incentives. Based on our work comparing art prices and museum attendance, we further find that the levels of demand for art by the various sectors of the market are disjoint. In this light, it is interesting to consider the recent Italian proposal to begin moving some of the major museums into the nongovernmental sector. Our own work suggests that changing governance in this way may well change the operating behavior of those museums, perhaps in ways unanticipated by the government.

Our work also suggests that art collections housed in museums, although often treated as noncommercial assets, have considerable ability to generate revenues. Moreover, the productivity of a collection varies significantly by the characteristics of the city in which it is located. In our his-

**Table 2.12**     Correlations in Attendance (museums with at least ten years of data)

| | V1 | Baltimore | Dallas | Johnson | Huntington | L.A. County | Memorial | Metropolitan | Museum of Fine Arts | Princeton | Walker | Walters | Whitney | Yale |
|---|---|---|---|---|---|---|---|---|---|---|---|---|---|---|
| V1 | 1.00 | 0.05 | 0.06 | 0.06 | -0.11 | -0.10 | -0.07 | 0.09 | -0.11 | 0.12 | -0.03 | 0.09 | -0.03 | 0.01 |
| BaltimcreMOA | 0.05 | 1.00 | 0.09 | -0.67 | -0.06 | -0.26 | -0.32 | -0.05 | -0.43 | 0.20 | -0.09 | 0.13 | 0.19 | 0.09 |
| DallasMOA | 0.06 | 0.09 | 1.00 | -0.51 | 0.37 | 0.03 | -0.28 | -0.22 | -0.31 | 0.73 | -0.24 | -0.52 | 0.35 | 0.38 |
| Johnson | 0.06 | -0.67 | -0.51 | 1.00 | 0.15 | 0.59 | 0.60 | 0.45 | 0.21 | -0.23 | 0.19 | 0.11 | -0.12 | -0.48 |
| Huntington | -0.11 | -0.06 | 0.37 | 0.15 | 1.00 | 0.24 | 0.24 | 0.10 | 0.30 | 0.08 | -0.20 | -0.23 | -0.18 | -0.20 |
| Lacounty | -0.10 | -0.26 | 0.03 | 0.59 | 0.24 | 1.00 | -0.22 | 0.06 | -0.12 | -0.04 | -0.23 | -0.47 | 0.31 | -0.16 |
| MemorialAG | -0.07 | -0.32 | -0.28 | 0.60 | 0.24 | -0.22 | 1.00 | 0.14 | 0.81 | -0.25 | 0.48 | 0.08 | -0.25 | -0.27 |
| Met | 0.09 | -0.05 | -0.22 | 0.45 | 0.10 | 0.06 | 0.14 | 1.00 | -0.06 | -0.07 | -0.22 | 0.13 | -0.04 | -0.05 |
| MFA | -0.11 | -0.43 | -0.31 | 0.21 | 0.30 | -0.12 | 0.81 | -0.06 | 1.00 | -0.54 | 0.14 | -0.25 | -0.39 | -0.31 |
| Princeton | 0.12 | 0.20 | 0.73 | -0.23 | 0.08 | -0.04 | -0.25 | -0.07 | -0.54 | 1.00 | -0.39 | -0.11 | 0.04 | 0.03 |
| Walker | -0.03 | -0.09 | -0.24 | 0.19 | -0.20 | -0.23 | 0.48 | -0.22 | 0.14 | -0.39 | 1.00 | 0.10 | -0.05 | 0.11 |
| Walters | 0.09 | 0.13 | -0.52 | 0.11 | -0.23 | -0.47 | 0.08 | 0.13 | -0.25 | -0.11 | 0.10 | 1.00 | -0.47 | -0.11 |
| Whitney | -0.03 | 0.19 | 0.35 | -0.12 | -0.18 | 0.31 | -0.25 | -0.04 | -0.39 | 0.04 | -0.05 | -0.47 | 1.00 | -0.02 |
| Yale | 0.01 | 0.09 | 0.38 | -0.48 | -0.20 | -0.16 | -0.27 | -0.55 | -0.31 | 0.03 | 0.11 | -0.11 | -0.02 | 1.0 |

torical work on the relationship between social elite and museums, we find remarkable stability: big donors continue to found new museums and support those museums with largesse earned in traditional, old-economy ways.

In this paper, we have focused on the role of governance structure in museum decision making. An interesting example of the dynamics of museum governance can be witnessed in the extraordinary set of western American art collections accessible to the public in Denver, Colorado. In the 1980s and early 1990s, the Denver area had not one, but three, superb collections of art of the American West. The Museum of Western Art (MWA) was founded in the early 1980s as a private, not-for-profit institution by cattleman William Foxley to display his personal collection of paintings and sculpture, which were on loan to the organization for which he served as the chairman of the board. The MWA collection focused on nineteenth- and early-twentieth-century "masterpieces" of western art—from the action paintings of Remington and Russell to the later, much-admired modernist paintings by Taos and Santa Fe artists. The Philip Anschutz collection, similarly, is composed of major works of western American art, and it was somewhat more widely known than the MWA collection. Anschutz amassed a fortune on oil, railroads, and telecommunications, and, like William Foxley, began to collect prize western American paintings and sculpture as a private collector. Over the past two decades, he has exhibited it widely to the public by publishing a catalogue of the collection and underwriting traveling exhibitions of the works to major art museums around the country. The Denver Art Museum (DAM) recently organized a show of the Anschutz collection that traveled to the Jocelyn Museum in Omaha and the Corcoran Gallery in Washington, D.C. The third major collection in Denver was in the Denver Art Museum itself. Dorothy and William Harmsen, founders of the Jolly Rancher Candy Company, assembled a collection of noteworthy western paintings and American Indian art over several decades, which they donated in 2001 to the DAM. The artists whose works are represented in the Harmsen collection are essentially the same as those in the Foxley and Anschutz collections, but they are a part of a public museum, not a private collection or a private, not-for-profit museum.

The constellation of collections is instructive, first because of the apparent rivalry within Denver among some of the leading businessmen at the time to form top western art collections—perhaps as a way of "keeping score" and perhaps as a way of demonstrating refinement, taste, and "western" values. In this respect, it is tempting to draw a parallel to the rivalries among turn-of-the-century Pittsburgh's captains of industry as they vied to buy European masterpieces.

Perhaps more interesting for our purposes is that these founders chose different governance forms for the context of their philanthropy. The collection of the Museum of Western Art, until it was ultimately moved and partly dispersed, was largely in the control of the founder, who was able to sell and to augment the exhibit. The museum relied, to a large extent, upon his financial support. Nevertheless, it was a not-for-profit organization with a mission to serve the public through its exhibitions. The Anschutz collection, on the other hand, was not necessarily formed with the public good in mind: The founder has complete control and no special mandate to use it for philanthropic goals, although lending to a traveling show is certainly a benefit to the public. Although Anschutz and Foxley undoubtedly had the option to give their collections to the Denver Art Museum, they both chose to maintain control of their collections to a greater or lesser degree. In contrast, the Harmsen collection is no longer under the control of the founder, nor does it receive top billing at the museum. The DAM prides itself on displaying an extensive survey collection of world art, as opposed to a regionally focused collection. While Harmsen can probably exert influence on the mission of the museum through his philanthropic activities, the director of the DAM has a larger range of choices about the strategic deployment of the institution's assets. In addition, the DAM serves a broader constituency—a community with an interest in world art, not solely focused on western Americana. Thus, institutional forms facilitate different donor and community goals, even when the art itself is similar.

# References

Ait-Sahalia, Yacine, Jonathan A. Parker, and Motohiro Yogo. 2001. Luxury goods and the equity premium. NBER Working Paper no. W8417. Cambridge, Mass.: National Bureau of Economic Research.

Association of Museum Directors. 1989. *Statistical survey of members.* Washington, D.C.: Association of Museum Directors.

———. 1999. *Statistical survey of members.* Washington, D.C.: Association of Museum Directors.

Anheier, Helmut, and Stefan Toepler. 1998. Commerce and the muse: Are art museums becoming commercial? In *To profit or not to profit,* ed. Burton Weisbrod, 233–48. New York: Cambridge University Press.

Bakshi, Gurdip, and Zhiwu Chen. 1996. The spirit of capitalism and stock market prices. *American Economic Review* 86 (March): 133–57.

Boylan, Patrick. 1999. Universities and museums: Past, present and future. *Museum Management and Curatorship* 18 (1): 43–56.

Campbell, John, and John Cochrane. 2001. By force of habit: A consumption-based explanation of aggregate stock market behavior. *Journal of Political Economy* 107 (April): 205–51.

d'Harnoncourt, Anne, Paul DiMaggio, Marilyn Perry, and James Wood. 1991. The museum and the public. In *The economics of art museums,* ed. Martin Feldstein, 35–60. Chicago: University of Chicago Press.

DiMaggio, Paul. 1986. *Nonprofit enterprise in the arts.* New York: Oxford University Press,

———. 1987. Nonprofit organizations in the production and distribution of culture. In *The nonprofit sector,* ed. Walter W. Powell, 195–220. New Haven, Conn.: Yale University Press.

Goetzmann, William N. 1993. Accounting for taste: An analysis of art returns over three centuries. American Economic Review 83 (5): 1370–76.

Goetzmann, William N., and Matthew Spiegel. 1995. Private value components and the winner's curse in an art index. *European Economic Review* 39 (May): 549–55.

Grana, Cesar. 1971. The private lives of public museums: Can art be democratic? In *Fact and symbol: Essays in the sociology of art and literature,* 95–111. New York: Oxford University Press.

Hansmann, Henry. 1981. The role of nonprofit enterprise. *Yale Law Journal* 89:835–901.

Ingham, John N. 1997. Reaching for respectability: The Pittsburgh industrial elite at the turn of the century. In *Collection in the Gilded Age: Art and patronage in Pittsburgh, 1890–1910,* ed. Gabriel P. Weisberg, DeCourcy E. McIntosh, and Alison McQueen, Pittsburgh: Frick Art and Historical Center.

Kotler, Neil, and Philip Kotler. 2001. Can museums be all things to all people? In *Museum Management and Curatorship* 18 (3): 271–87.

Leo, John. 2001. But where's the art? *US News and World Report,* 14 May, p. 14.

MacDonald, Heather. 2001. The Met's triumphant democratic elitism. *City Journal* 11 (Winter): 76–91.

Mei, J. P., and Michael Moses. 2002. Art as an investment and the underperformance of masterpieces: Evidence from 1875–2000. *American Economics Review,* forthcoming.

Meyer, Ruth Krueger, and Madeleine Fidfell Beaufort. 1997. The rage for collecting: Beyond Pittsburgh in the Gilded Age. In *Collection in the Gilded Age: Art and patronage in Pittsburgh, 1890–1910,* ed. Gabriel P. Weisberg, DeCourcy E. McIntosh, and Alison McQueen, Pittsburgh: Frick Art and Historical Center.

Rosett, Richard. 1991. Art museums in the U.S.: A financial portrait. In *The economics of art museums,* ed. Martin Feldstein, 129–76. Chicago: University of Chicago Press.

Silver, Stuart. 1982. Almost everyone loves a winner. *Museum News* (November–December): 25–35.

Temin, Peter. 1991. An economic history of American art museums. In *The economics of art museums,* ed. Martin Feldstein, 179–93. Chicago: University of Chicago Press.

# HMO Penetration, Ownership Status, and the Rise of Hospital Advertising

Jason R. Barro and Michael Chu

## 3.1 Introduction

Advertising is a pervasive component of many product markets in the United States, from soda to real estate to clothing. Until recently, the providers of health care in America had been conspicuously absent in this activity. In fact, for a great deal of the last century, advertising by physicians and hospitals was explicitly banned by their respective professional organizations. In the American Medical Association's (AMA's) first code of ethics, it was written that "[advertising is] highly reprehensible in a regular physician" (AMA 1848).

Although still relatively small compared with other industries,[1] advertising among hospitals has increased dramatically in recent years. Figure 3.1 shows average advertising expenditures among hospitals in the United States from 1995 to 1998. Of the roughly 5,000 acute care hospitals in the United States, 1,800 advertised in 1995. Among those hospitals, the average advertising budget was $79,000. By 1998, 2,500 hospitals advertised, and the average spending among those hospitals had increased by 56 percent in real dollars to $123,000 per hospital (Video Monitoring Services

Jason R. Barro is assistant professor of business administration at Harvard Business School and a faculty research fellow of the National Bureau of Economic Research. Michael Chu is an analyst at Credit Suisse First Boston.

We want to thank Martin Feldstein, Edward Glaeser, Fiona Scott Morton, and all other conference participants for their helpful comments. The opinions expressed in this paper are the authors' and do not necessarily reflect those of our respective institutions. Any errors remaining in the paper are our own.

1. Hospital advertising is, on average, 0.1–2.0 percent of hospital revenues. Other industries that are better known for their advertising have much larger advertising budgets. Soda companies, for instance, spend 7–8 percent of revenues on advertising. Car companies spend a little over 2 percent (CompuStat).

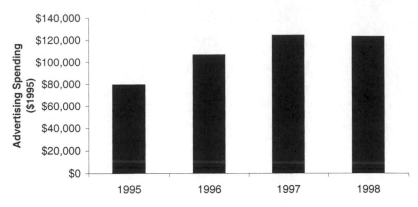

Fig. 3.1    Average hospital advertising spending, 1995–1998

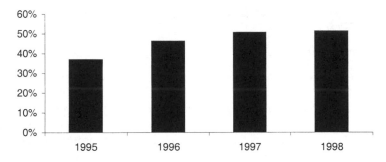

Fig. 3.2    Percentage of hospitals that advertise, 1995–1998

[VMS]). Over this same period, average hospital expenditures increased by only 10 percent in real terms (American Hospital Association [AHA] 1995–98). Figure 3.2 illustrates the increase in participation in advertising for hospitals over this time period. Less than 40 percent of hospitals advertised in 1995, compared with a little more than half by 1998.

Average advertising spending across all hospitals masks the most dramatic increase. Figure 3.3 breaks out the hospitals into five categories: not-for-profit teaching hospitals, other not-for-profit hospitals, for-profit hospitals, religious hospitals, and public hospitals. Figure 3.3 illustrates that the true source of the overall advertising increase among U.S. hospitals has been the not-for-profit teaching hospitals. The spending levels in figure 3.3 are adjusted for bed size so that any differences in ad spending due to differences in hospital size are removed. The average not-for-profit teaching hospital has increased its bed-adjusted ad expenditures by 140 percent. For-profit hospitals, however, have actually decreased their spending in real terms over this time.

In this paper, we examine the underlying cause of this rapid increase in

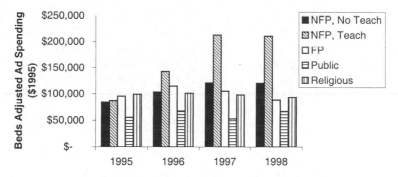

**Fig. 3.3    Average advertising spending by hospital type, 1995–1998**

advertising among hospitals. We utilize a panel data set of hospital and market characteristics along with a unique data set of hospital advertising expenditures. In the end, a critical component of the explanation is the rise of managed care across the country. Those hospitals—particularly the large teaching hospitals—in markets that have experienced the greatest rise in managed care influence had the most rapid increase in advertising.

The paper continues as follows. The next section discusses the history of hospital advertising along with a discussion of the economics behind advertising for hospitals. The third section presents various hypotheses as to why hospitals would have changed their advertising behavior at this time. In the fourth section, we discuss the data. The fifth section presents the empirical results, and the final section concludes.

## 3.2    The History and Economics of Hospital Advertising

One basic model of health care consumption in the United States involves patients' depending on their physicians as well-informed, benevolent agents. When a patient needs to receive treatment in a hospital, the physician suggests the course of treatment and the hospital in which it will be done. Within this view of medical care, advertising directly to patients can play very little positive role and may, in fact, be detrimental to patient outcomes.

If the advertising signals lead the patient to disagree with the well-informed, benevolent physician, then the patient may seek alternative treatments. This may be positive if the physician was not fully informed or if the physician was not truly acting in the patient's best interest. But if the physician was truly acting in the patient's best interest, then the patient will only disagree with the physician's choices when the advertising is false and the patient is unable to determine its veracity. This appears to have been the argument behind the restriction of advertising by hospitals and physicians for the bulk of the twentieth century.

In 1847, when the AMA discussed advertising in its Code of Ethics, the concerns focused on exaggerated or outright fictitious claims perpetrated by some supposed healers. Until the late 1970s, the AMA, as well as the AHA, explicitly banned advertising for its members. A successful Federal Trade Commission suit in 1980 made advertising a legal, if not accepted, part of medical care. Prior to the final decision, the AHA had already decided to allow some regulated advertising for its member hospitals, as long as the "truthful" advertising was not done at the "expense of the competitor" (Rosenstein 1985, 34). Even now the AMA is careful to remind its members that although there are no restrictions on advertising, there is a concern that the public will be easily "deceived" and that information transmitted to the public should be done in a "readily comprehensible manner" (AMA 1848).

### 3.2.1   Not-for-Profit Hospitals and Advertising

Prior to the recent upsurge in advertising, not-for-profit hospitals historically engaged in less advertising than their for-profit counterparts. Figure 3.3 shows that, at the beginning of our sample in 1995, not-for-profits advertised less than for-profits, adjusting for the size of the hospital. The anecdotal evidence, and the fact that the AMA and the AHA had so long banned the practice, suggests that not-for-profits had never relied on advertising in the hospital industry. The nonreliance on advertising among not-for-profit hospitals has several possible explanations.

A situation in which not-for-profits all choose to do little advertising requires some degree of collusion among the market participants. Two facts about not-for-profit hospitals may help the hospitals collude not to advertise: First, not-for-profits are typically thought to have more complicated objective functions than the typical profit-maximizing for-profit hospital, and second, once a not-for-profit generates profits, it is restricted in how those profits are distributed. Both of these facts may make it easier to reach a collusive agreement in which the hospitals are essentially agreeing not to attempt to increase profits.

There are many theories suggesting that the managers at not-for-profits may care less about profits and are instead concerned with the provision of public goods, such as charity care and research (Weisbrod 1988), or are concerned with providing high-quality care (Hansmann 1980). According to those theories, hospital managers may not advertise because the increased profits that the advertising brings are not the core concern of those operating the organization. The nondistribution constraint also may create less of an incentive for management to increase profits, since there are no official owners to distribute the money.

Additionally, the managers at not-for-profits may simply feel that advertising, in its own right, is not an honorable activity. This is consistent with the historical view of the AMA and the AHA. Hospital managers may like profits because they help the hospital provide all of the services they want to provide, but some methods of achieving that profitability are simply not worth the moral cost.

Finally, not-for-profit managers may enjoy spending their time on activities other than marketing and advertising. Without the pressure to do all that is necessary to maximize profits, perhaps the managers would simply prefer to use their time to do other things—focus on medical services, research, and so on. Regardless of which reason was the principle reason behind the historically low level of advertising among hospitals prior to the 1990s, something has occurred to change the reality in the health care marketplace.

### 3.3     Theories of Advertising Changes

There are several possible explanations for the current rise in hospital advertising. The first possibility is the unraveling from one equilibrium, in which few hospitals advertise, to another in which many hospitals advertise. Perhaps all hospitals, particularly the large teaching hospitals, would do little advertising as long as all of the other hospitals followed suit. Once that equilibrium begins to unravel, it will unravel quickly; hence the rapid increase in advertising.

Another hypothesis may be that the not-for-profit hospitals have undergone a fundamental change in their objectives. One explanation as to why hospitals have historically done so little advertising, as we indicated above, is that marketing is unbecoming for a not-for-profit institution—hence the statement in the code of ethics. The corollary to that idea is that marketing is a perfectly acceptable activity for an organization concerned with profits. Perhaps advertising is increasing because for-profit hospitals and their ethics are becoming more dominant in today's hospital market. This hypothesis leads to two predictions. First, for-profit hospitals should advertise more than not-for-profits, and second, advertising should increase more rapidly for not-for-profit hospitals that have more contact with for-profit competitors.

Another explanation is that hospitals and their executives are more willing to engage in activities, such as advertising, that were once shunned because the new financial realities in health care have made them necessary. If the financial strains become large enough, the choice for the hospital can be to stay open and advertise, or not to advertise and either close or curtail valued activities. The financial situation for hospitals has gradually deteriorated through the 1980s and 1990s as reimbursements from government and private payers have decreased. In addition to price reductions, hospitals have experienced a steady decline in admissions and inpatient days. This decline has been caused by technological improvements that have rendered some inpatient procedures obsolete (e.g., cataract surgery) or have greatly reduced the length of stay for other procedures. In addition, hospitals have faced pressures from managed care organizations to reduce lengths of stay. The result has been that inpatient days in U.S. hospitals have fallen by roughly 35 percent over the last twenty years (AHA 1995–98).

A final hypothesis is that changes in the market structure and the manner in which hospital reimbursements are determined have resulted in an increased return to advertising. Perhaps the return to hospital advertising had historically been very low, and the hospital executives chose not to advertise because they had little to gain. If the marketplace changes such that there are significant gains to be had by advertising, then hospital managers will begin to advertise.

One major change in the health care market structure over the last twenty years has been the rise of managed care. In 1998, health maintenance organizations (HMOs) provided health insurance to roughly 30 percent of the U.S. marketplace (InterStudy 1998). Only four years earlier, that percentage was less than 20 percent, and twenty years ago, that percentage was essentially zero. Health maintenance organizations reduce health care costs, at least in part, by negotiating lower reimbursement rates with providers. They achieve leverage in those negotiations by only offering a subset of a market's providers in their ultimate network. It is the threat to leave a provider out of the network that provides HMOs with their power.

In a market with managed care organizations, advertising can potentially provide leverage to the providers. The threat for managed care companies to leave providers out of the networks is much more empty to the extent that providers can render themselves indispensable in the eyes of the patients. In the extreme, if an insurer has very little chance of being able to sell a product that lacks one key hospital, then that hospital has all of the power in setting the reimbursement fees. Advertising directly to patients may be a tool for the hospitals in creating this sense of necessity. The rise of managed care has increased the returns to advertising to the extent that advertising plays this new role in the negotiation process between hospitals and managed care.

In the sections that follow, we test several of the hypotheses outlined above. Given the large variation across hospitals and hospital markets, it is possible to test each of the hypotheses empirically. The *change in objective function* hypothesis can be tested using variation across markets in the influence of for-profit hospitals. In particular, those markets that have experienced the greatest increase in for-profit influence should have the greatest impact on the objectives of the other hospitals in the market.

CHANGE IN OBJECTIVE FUNCTION HYPOTHESIS. *Not-for-profit hospitals with more and increasing contact with for-profit hospitals will advertise more.*

The *financial distress* hypothesis can be tested using variation in financial performance across hospitals and using differences in market structure changes across markets. Theoretically, if the financial distress story is driving the change in hospital advertising, then hospitals that experience more financial distress should advertise more. The alternative story is that hospitals with less money will do less of everything, including advertising.

FINANCIAL DISTRESS HYPOTHESIS. *Hospitals in financial distress will respond by increasing advertising expenditures.*

The penetration of HMOs into markets is a form of financial distress for hospitals. This means that the relationship between HMO penetration and hospital advertising will combine two effects: the effect of financial distress and the effect of HMO presence on the returns to advertising. Empirically, it is possible to disentangle these two effects if the returns to advertising do not change universally for all hospitals.

In the *increasing returns to advertising* hypothesis, advertising by hospitals would focus on hospital quality in order to create the sense of necessity among the patients. Some hospitals, particularly those that are large or are teaching hospitals, may be more credible in their advertising than others. Those hospitals for which their high-quality claims are more believable should increase their ad spending more than those hospitals for which their claims are less credible. The empirical test is then whether hospitals that are more likely to be credible (i.e., teaching and large hospitals) increase their advertising more in response to HMO penetration than do other hospitals.

INCREASED RETURNS TO ADVERTISING HYPOTHESIS. *More credible hospitals in markets with higher HMO penetration should respond with more advertising than other hospitals.*

We will not focus directly on the initial hypothesis that the increase in advertising is due to an equilibrium shift from no advertising to everyone advertising. If none of the other hypotheses were to be supported in the data, then the cascading equilibrium theory could be the explanation. Even if the other hypotheses prove to have some validity, it is impossible to prove that some form of equilibrium cascade did not occur. For instance, in the data, it appears that large teaching hospitals responded to increased HMO penetration by increasing ad spending. That provides support to the increasing returns hypothesis, and it may also be true that once some teaching hospitals decided to advertise, many others decided to follow. More generally, it may be that any of the other hypotheses can act as triggers in creating a cascade from one equilibrium to another. Additionally, if not-for-profit hospitals were not advertising before because their lack of concern for profits made collusion easier, then any change (in objective function, financial distress, or increased pressure from insurers) that would increase their concern for profits could lead to an equilibrium cascade.

### 3.4     Data

The data we employ in this paper come from four sources: the AHA, the Medicare Cost Reports, Interstudy, and VoiceTrak. Each source provides a panel of data across U.S. hospitals from 1995 to 1998. The AHA data contain information on hospital ownership, size, and location. The AHA data are also used to generate data characterizing a hospital's market, including information on the number of competitors. The Medicare data contain financial information for the hospitals, including revenues, expenses, and income numbers. The Interstudy data provide the information on HMO penetration over time at the metropolitan statistical area (MSA) level.

VoiceTrak is the source for the hospital advertising data (VMA): Voice-Trak surveys roughly 11,000 media outlets each year, achieving a response rate of over 85 percent by offering the respondents some of the survey results. VoiceTrak surveys radio, print, and television outlets and compiles an annual advertising spending number for each firm, including hospitals. The VoiceTrak data were merged with the other data sources to create a panel of roughly 5,000 hospitals over four years. Any advertising expenditures attributed to hospital holding companies or hospital networks were distributed among the member hospitals in the market, according to size and to the amount possible. The network and affiliation data in the AHA are far from complete. That should dampen the advertising numbers for hospitals more likely to be in networks, to the extent that some expenditures are not distributed.

### 3.5     Empirical Results

The first hypothesis as to why hospital advertising has increased in recent years is that the objectives of the hospitals have changed. In order to test this, we first examine whether hospitals of different ownership types in fact exhibit different behavior with respect to marketing. If the difference in advertising expenditures is caused by differences in objectives, then that is presumably driven by not-for-profits' having an objective function that differs from profit maximization. Most of the differences that would be proposed, such as ethical concerns, should lead to not-for-profits' advertising less than for-profits. If the objectives of the hospitals are changing, then not-for-profits should behave more like for-profits through time.

Table 3.1 presents results of a simple least-squares regression to illustrate the average advertising behavior by hospital types. The following regression is estimated:

$$(1) \quad \text{AdSpending}_{h,t} = \alpha + \gamma_t + \beta_1 \cdot \text{Beds} + \text{ForProfit}_{h,t} + \text{Pub}_{h,t}$$
$$+ \text{TeachingHosp}_{h,t} + \varepsilon_{h,t}$$

| | (1) | (2) |
|---|---|---|
| **Table 3.1** | **Relationships of Hospital Types To Hospital Advertising** | |

| | (1) | (2) |
|---|---|---|
| Hospital beds | **443.9** | **442.0** |
| | **(13.25)** | **(13.20)** |
| For-profit | 7,093.6 | 10,091.3 |
| | (1.68) | (1.96) |
| Year interactions | | |
| 1996 | | 9,124.9 |
| | | (1.88) |
| 1997 | | 4,346.1 |
| | | (0.74) |
| 1998 | | **−19,785.9** |
| | | **−(3.35)** |
| Public | **−20,653.3** | **−8,610.0** |
| | **−(5.14)** | **−(2.26)** |
| Year interactions | | |
| 1996 | | **−9,837.8** |
| | | **−(3.24)** |
| 1997 | | **−19,751.6** |
| | | **−(4.90)** |
| 1998 | | **−20,281.1** |
| | | **−(4.40)** |
| Teaching hospital | **48,183.4** | −11,692.0 |
| | **(5.63)** | −(1.29) |
| Year interactions | | |
| 1996 | | **45,116.2** |
| | | **(5.85)** |
| 1997 | | **98,315.0** |
| | | **(8.19)** |
| 1998 | | **103,087.4** |
| | | **(8.36)** |
| Year Effects | | |
| 1996 | **20,116.7** | **13,078.6** |
| | **(11.66)** | **(6.14)** |
| 1997 | **35,103.3** | **22,408.0** |
| | **(13.07)** | **(7.89)** |
| 1998 | **35,024.6** | **23,777.5** |
| | **(12.51)** | **(8.08)** |
| Constant | **−33,782.7** | **−25,689.7** |
| | **−(6.71)** | **(5.34)** |
| $N$ | 19,539 | 19,539 |
| $R^2$ | 0.21 | 0.22 |

*Note:* Dependent variable-real hospital advertising expenditures. *T*-statistics in parentheses; boldface indicates significance at the 5 percent confidence level.

where $h$ is "hospital" and $t$ is "time." The regression includes the VoiceTrak advertising expenditures as the dependent variable. The number of hospital beds as well as dummy variables indicating hospital ownership type are included on the right-hand side.

The results help illustrate that the general pattern is not entirely consistent with the change in objectives hypothesis. If the hypothesis is correct, for-profits should advertise more than not-for-profits, but the relationship should narrow over this period of time while advertising spending is increasing so rapidly. In the regressions, the omitted hospital category is nonteaching, not-for-profit hospitals. The regression in column (1) shows that, over the whole time period, for-profits do advertise more than nonteaching, not-for-profit hospitals and public hospitals, but less than teaching hospitals. The difference between for-profits and nonteaching not-for-profits is not significant at standard levels of significance.

The regression in column (2) presents results with each hospital type interacted with the year effects. These results highlight the regime shift in hospital advertising that was evident in figure 3.3. By the end of the period, for-profit hospitals advertise significantly *less* than all not-for-profit hospitals, and the teaching hospitals have increased their advertising expenditures significantly.

Again, this result is a little too strong for the change in objectives hypothesis, since the not-for-profits not only begin to advertise as much as the for-profits, but even surpass them. It is possible that a change in objectives could still be a driver behind the rise in advertising if it were true that the returns to advertising are higher for the not-for-profits and the teaching hospitals, in particular. Then, once all hospitals are comfortable advertising, the not-for-profits would actually do more, not just the same amount.

Another test of the change in objectives hypothesis is to see whether hospitals that interact more with for-profit hospitals advertise more. The assumption behind this theory is that not-for-profit hospitals have historically had an ethic of not advertising, while for-profit hospitals have not felt restricted with respect to marketing. As not-for-profit hospitals increasingly interact with for-profits, they may begin to absorb some of their behaviors. In table 3.2, the following fixed-effects regression is estimated:

(2)   $\text{AdSpending}_{h,t} = \alpha_h + \gamma_t + \beta_1 \cdot \text{ForProfitMktShare}_{h,t} + \beta_2 X_{h,t} + \varepsilon_{h,t}$

Again, the advertising expenditures are the dependent variable. Year and hospital fixed effects are included on the right-hand side along with other hospital and market characteristics including; ownership status (for-profit, public, or religious), teaching status, hospital occupancy rate, net income, and whether the hospital is a local monopoly (i.e., no other hospital within ten miles). The key variable of interest is the percentage of hospital beds in the hospital's ten-mile market that are in for-profit hospitals— the for-profit market share. This variable, as well as interactions of this

**Table 3.2**              **Advertising and For-Profit Market Share**

|  | (1) | (2) |
|---|---|---|
| For-profit | 24,153.35 | 21,895.91 |
|  | (0.60) | (0.55) |
| Public | 10,138.95 | 9,911.42 |
|  | (0.88) | (0.86) |
| Religious | 27,237.89 | 27,305.66 |
|  | (1.61) | (1.61) |
| Teach |  | −489.59 |
|  |  | −(0.04) |
| Hospital beds | 77.72 | 78.11 |
|  | (0.75) | (0.75) |
| For-profit market share in ten-mile market | **86,845.62** | **78,777.74** |
|  | **(1.88)** | **(1.75)** |
| Interactions |  |  |
|   For-profit market share • For-Profit | −101,889.95 | −94,168.86 |
|  | −(1.58) | −(1.50) |
|   For-profit market share • Public | −62,834.33 | −62,119.12 |
|  | −(1.11) | −(1.10) |
|   For-profit market share • Religious | −72,150.87 | 28,076.80 |
|  | −(0.69) | (0.85) |
|   For-profit market share • Teach |  | −70,884.33 |
|  |  | −(0.67) |
| Monopoly in ten-mile market | 5,988.82 | 6,699.86 |
|  | (0.41) | (0.46) |
| Occupancy rate | −7,985.25 | −7,995.76 |
|  | −(0.65) | −0.65 |
| Net income | 0.00 | 0.00 |
|  | −(1.02) | −(1.02) |
| Year effects |  |  |
|   1996 | **19,526.48** | **19,441.07** |
|  | **(9.29)** | **(9.26)** |
|   1997 | **33,367.15** | **33,309.83** |
|  | **(10.46)** | **(10.41)** |
|   1998 | **33,870.10** | **33,824.83** |
|  | **(8.75)** | **(8.73)** |
| Constant | 23,509.50 | 23,438.83 |
|  | (1.23) | (1.23) |
| Hospital fixed effects | Yes | Yes |
| $N$ | 15,791 | 15,791 |
| $R^2$ | 0.78 | 0.78 |

*Notes:* Dependent variable-real hospital advertising expenditures. *T*-statistics in parentheses. Boldface indicates significance at the 5 percent confidence level. Standard errors are heteroscedasticity robust and clustered by hospital.

variable with the various ownership types, are included in the regression. The hypothesis is that as a hospital is increasingly interacting with for-profit hospitals, the more likely that hospital is to begin behaving as a for-profit.

The results are presented in table 3.2. The only difference between columns (1) and (2) is that teaching status is not included in the first regression. The coefficient on for-profit market share (86,845) represents the impact of increased for-profit market share on the omitted category—nonteaching, not-for-profit hospitals. This coefficient is marginally significant and positive, but the magnitude is small relative to the overall change in advertising. The result suggests that an increase in for-profit market share of 10 percent leads to an increase in advertising of $8,600. The average change across hospitals in for-profit market share from 1994 to 1998 is less than 1 percent. The standard deviation is 15 percent, so there were some hospitals that experienced a significant increase in for-profit influence. The effect for teaching hospitals is essentially zero. Since the largest increase in hospital advertising over this time period has been from large teaching hospitals, the impact of for-profit hospitals does little to explain the general trend.

The coefficients on net income and occupancy rate are not significantly different from zero. This is the first test of the financial distress hypothesis. The regressions in table 3.2 provide no evidence that tougher financial conditions lead to an increase in advertising.

Table 3.3 presents results on the relationship between HMO penetration and hospital advertising. These results provide insight into both the financial distress hypothesis and the change in returns to advertising hypothesis. At one level, an increase in HMO penetration is a negative financial shock to hospitals. This may affect advertising in either direction. The financial distress hypothesis suggests that the rise in advertising may be due to increasing financial strain on hospitals. Alternatively, a strain on hospital budgets may require a decrease in all types of spending, including advertising. At another level, the presence of HMOs in the market may increase the returns to advertising. This affect may differ across hospitals, as some hospitals may have more credibility in their claims of high quality. The regressions in table 3.3 estimate the following regression:

$$(3) \quad \text{AdSpend}_{h,t} = \alpha_h + \gamma_t + \beta_1 \cdot \text{ForProfit}_{h,t} + \beta_2 \cdot \text{TeachingHosp}_{h,t}$$
$$+ \beta_3 L_{h,t} + \beta_4 \cdot \text{TeachingHosp}_{h,t} \cdot L_{h,t} + \beta_5 \cdot \text{HMO}_{\text{MSA},t}$$
$$+ \varepsilon_{h,t}$$

where $L$ equals more than 200 beds. As with equation (2), the regression includes hospital and year fixed effects, as well as controls for hospital type and the HMO penetration at the MSA level. The regression in column (2) contains interaction terms between HMO penetration and the for-profit, teaching, large, and large-teaching variables.

The coefficient on the HMO penetration variable is the result of interest.

Table 3.3          **Advertising and HMO Penetration**

|  | (1) | (2) |
|---|---|---|
| Hospital beds | 129.97 | 145.43 |
|  | (1.21) | (1.38) |
| HMO penetration at MSA level | 52,735.47 | **−88,180.58** |
|  | (1.66) | **−(2.94)** |
| HMO penetration interactions |  |  |
| For-profit |  | −92,630.49 |
|  |  | −(1.69) |
| Teach |  | **249,337.49** |
|  |  | **(3.72)** |
| Hospital beds > 200 |  | 104,938.15 |
|  |  | (1.75) |
| Teach and hospital beds > 200 |  | **165,839.40** |
|  |  | **(2.21)** |
| For-profit | −3,206.56 | 16,463.46 |
|  | −(0.16) | (0.76) |
| Teach | −3,597.88 | **−88,083.94** |
|  | −(0.24) | **−(3.83)** |
| Hospital beds > 200 | 8,537.69 | −40,640.50 |
|  | (0.53) | −(1.85) |
| Year Effects |  |  |
| 1995 | **−54,556.12** | **−55,111.42** |
|  | **−(8.77)** | **−(8.69)** |
| 1996 | **−20,026.40** | **−20,373.52** |
|  | **−(3.60)** | **−(3.63)** |
| 1997 | 2,801.80 | 3,640.46 |
|  | (0.63) | 0.81 |
| Constant | **92,948.34** | **129,955.48** |
|  | **(3.61)** | **(5.17)** |
| Hospital fixed effects | Yes | Yes |
| $N$ | 10,387 | 10,387 |
| $R^2$ | 0.76 | 0.77 |

*Notes:* Dependent variable-real hospital advertising expenditures. *T*-statistics in parentheses. Boldface indicates significance at the 5 percent confidence level. Standard errors are heteroscedasticity robust and clustered by hospital.

Without the interaction terms (column [1]), there is no significant relationship between HMO penetration and hospital advertising. The coefficient is positive, but not significant at normal levels. Once the interactions are included, an interesting pattern is revealed. The omitted group—nonteaching, not-for-profit hospitals—responds to increased HMO penetration by advertising less. Every 10 percent increase in HMO penetration leads to $8,800 less in advertising. For-profit hospitals also respond to increased HMO penetration by advertising less, not more (as either the financial distress or the increased returns hypotheses would suggest). Increased financial distress appears to lead to less spending on advertising for small and for-profit hospitals.

The final groups—teaching and large hospitals—provide evidence consistent with the increased returns to advertising theory. Both teaching hospitals and large hospitals respond to increased HMO penetration with additional advertising. The effect for a large, nonteaching hospital is not significantly different from zero, although the effect is no longer negative as with the previous groups. For large teaching hospitals, the effect of HMO penetration on advertising is significant and large. Each 10 percent increase in HMO penetration leads to a $43,000 increase in hospital advertising. Among large teaching hospitals, the average change in HMO penetration from 1995 to 1998 was 8 percent, with a standard deviation of 14 percent. On average, this category of hospitals increased its advertising spending by $150,000. The increased influence of managed care appears to explain a significant percentage of that change.

### 3.6   Conclusions

The rise of hospital advertising in the late 1990s is best characterized by the significant increase in marketing activity by large, not-for-profit teaching hospitals. There is little evidence to suggest that any increased influence of for-profit hospitals explains the recent pattern in marketing behavior. Over this time period, for-profit hospitals have actually decreased their marketing expenditures. Nonteaching, not-for-profit hospitals that were exposed to more for-profit competition increased their ad expenditures in a marginally significant manner, but the magnitude of the effect is small.

Changes in managed care penetration are positively correlated with increased advertising, but only for the teaching hospitals (particularly for large teaching hospitals). For all other hospitals, increased managed care reduces ad spending, suggesting that HMOs represent a financial shock to hospitals. For the large teaching hospitals, the results, with respect to HMOs, suggest support for the increased return to advertising hypothesis. The presence of HMOs in the marketplace introduces a new negotiating dynamic, in which hospitals can attain higher reimbursement fees if they can dampen the HMOs' ability to threaten to leave them out of insurance contracts. Advertising directly to patients, if effective, can perhaps help to create a sense of necessity for a hospital. Only hospitals with credible high-quality claims (i.e., large teaching hospitals) will gain through this type of advertising. For all the other hospitals, HMOs are simply a financial shock, and, consequently, advertising expenditures should fall.

## References

American Hospital Association (AHA). 1995–98. *Annual survey of hospitals, 1995–98.* Chicago: AHA.

American Medical Association (AMA). 1848. *Code of ethics.* Philadelphia: Collins.

———. Ethical opinions, E-5.02, advertising and publicity. http://www.ama-assn. org/apps/pf_online/pf_online?f_n=browse&doc=policyfiles/CEJA/E-5.02.HTM.

Hansmann, H. 1980. The role of nonprofit enterprise. *Yale Law Journal* 89:835–901.

InterStudy. 1998. The InterStudy HMO trend report, 1987–97. Bloomington, Minn.: InterStudy.

Rosenstein, A. 1985. The changing trends of medical care and its impact on traditional providers: Adaptation and survival via a marketing approach. In *Marketing ambulatory care services,* ed. W. J. Winston, 11–34. New York: Haworth Press.

Video Monitoring Services (VMS). VoiceTrak local multimedia expenditure reports. http://www.VoiceTrak.com.

# 4

## Objective Functions and Compensation Structures in Nonprofit and For-Profit Organizations
### Evidence from the "Mixed" Hospital Industry

Burcay Erus and Burton A. Weisbrod

### 4.1 Introduction

We examine the behavior of two forms of nonprofit organizations, religious nonprofit (RNP) and secular nonprofit (SNP), as well as that of private for-profit (FP) firms, when they coexist in a mixed industry—hospitals.[1] In an attempt to determine whether each type of nonprofit organization can be characterized by the same objective function as a for-profit

Burcay Erus is a Ph.D. candidate in economics at Northwestern University. Burton A. Weisbrod is the John Evans Professor of Economics, and a faculty fellow at the Institute for Policy Research, Northwestern University.

This research was supported by grants to Weisbrod from the Andrew W. Mellon Foundation and the Searle Fund, and by an Investigator Award in Health Policy Research from The Robert Wood Johnson Foundation. We also thank the Hay Group, and particularly Richard Sperling and Janet Snow, for making their survey data available, and Nancy Kirby for her patience in answering our questions about the data. The views expressed are those of the authors and do not imply endorsement by any of these organizations. We appreciate the helpful comments of Jeffrey Ballou, Edward Glaeser, Sendhil Mullainathan, Maxim Sinitsyn, William Vogt, and an anonymous reviewer; National Bureau of Economic Research conference participants; and participants in the Northwestern University Public Economics Seminar and the January 2002 Health Economics Research Organization session at the Allied Social Science Association meetings. We also thank Richard Lindrooth for his comments and for providing data on health maintenance organization penetration.

1. There are many mixed industries, including higher education, day care, the arts, and museums, as well as hospitals and nursing homes. Behavior of organizations in such industries has been studied in a wide variety of dimensions. In nursing homes, for example, consumer complaints and regulatory violations have been found to differ not only at FP and governmental facilities, but also at RNPs and SNPs (Weisbrod and Schlesinger 1986); in the mentally handicapped facilities and nursing home industries, the use of waiting lists, rather than price to ration access, and the use of volunteer labor have been found to vary among institutional forms (Weisbrod 1988, 1998a; Kapur and Weisbrod 2000); and in day care centers, levels of staffing and consumer information have been found to vary across institutional forms (Mauser 1998). In general hospitals, charity care has been a particular focus of attention (Sloan 1998).

firm, but recognizing the difficulty of observing objective functions, we study the reflections of objective functions in employee compensation structures.

Specifically, we determine whether each form of nonprofit (NP) hospital provides incentives that differ from each other and from those of FP hospitals (a) in terms of "total" monetary compensation and its composition between base salary and performance-based bonus; (b) for each of fifteen types of jobs ranging from chief executive officer (CEO) to middle managers and technical workers; and (c) both cross-sectionally and over time in response to exogenous revenue constraints.

Our focus on relationships between employee reward structures and organization form has two justifications. One involves the difficulty of identifying the arguments in an organization's objective function. Measuring a private firm's "performance"—profit—relative to its presumed objective of profit maximization is not devoid of problems, as the recent Enron Corporation accounting practices made clear (Eichenwald 2002). Nevertheless, the problems of measurement and valuation of performance by FP firms pose considerably fewer challenges than is the case with the types of public-good outputs that are often identified with NP organizations—e.g., charity care (in hospitals), basic research (at universities), cultural preservation (at museums and zoos), and environmental protection. Thus, insofar as NPs pursue these hard-to-monitor, public-good goals rather than behaving as "for-profits-in-disguise" (Weisbrod 1988), they would utilize weaker reward structures (Holmstrom and Milgrom 1991), relying less on "performance"-based bonus compensation and more on base-salary compensation.

The second reason for focusing on employee compensation structures across institutional forms relates to understanding labor markets in which NPs operate. The question is whether NP and FP organizations compete in unified labor markets for particular types of labor, or whether they operate in distinct markets. On the labor supply side, employees could have preferences for working in one or another institutional form of organization for any given type of job.[2] On the demand side of the market, employers from various institutional forms could have preferences for distinct kinds of workers—i.e., in terms of worker-utility functions, which could influence the cost to employers of monitoring particular forms of performance.

The hypotheses we test relate particularly to the use of relatively strong, high-powered incentives in the form of performance-based bonuses, compared with weaker incentives in the form of base salary. The easier it is for

---

2. There is some evidence that such preference differentials do exist. In a survey of hospital volunteers (Wolf, Weisbrod, and Bird 1993), it was found that, while half of the respondents reported no preference as to volunteering to a FP or a NP hospital, the other half reported a preference for volunteering to a nonprofit.

the organization to monitor its agents' contribution to the organization mission, the stronger would be the incentives employed by any organization, regardless of ownership form or objectives. Thus, we test hypotheses that (a) NP organizations use weaker incentives than FPs when compensating their CEOs; (b) there are no differences—or, at most, smaller differences—in the incentive structures at FP and NP organizations for workers down the job ladder (middle managers and technical workers); and (c) exogenous tightening of fiscal constraints cause nonprofits to alter incentive structures to become more like for-profit firms. The hypotheses also distinguish between religious and secular nonprofits, for prior research has found systematic differences between them (see references cited in note 1, above).

The next section describes the theoretical setting and hypotheses. Empirical methodology is in section 4.3, followed by results in section 4.4. Section 4.5 interprets the full set of our findings and concludes.

## 4.2   Theoretic Setting and Hypotheses

Measurement and valuation of outputs are the fundamental challenges to all attempts to specify a NP organization objective function and then derive testable predictions. If an objective function includes outputs that are hard to measure and to value—as is the case with basic research (at universities), health care to the poor (at hospitals), or cultural preservation (at museums)—it will necessarily be difficult for the organization's trustees and directors to reward "performance" and for outside researchers to test for differential performance among FP, RNP, and SNP organizations.[3]

Thus, rather than attempting to observe differential outputs directly, we take an alternative tack. Making use of the theoretical relationship between any organization's objective function and the reward structures it utilizes to provide incentives for its employee-agents, we study the reflection of unobserved objectives in observable employee reward structures.[4]

3. For an interesting attempt to measure such output by FP and NP providers, though not to value it, see Schlesinger and Dorwart (1984), who examined psychiatric hospitals' provision of unpaid emergency psychiatric services by telephone. For a recent study of the "value" of hospital "charity care" at FP and NP hospitals see Nicholson et al. (2000). At the theoretic level, Hirth (1999), focusing on informational asymmetries, has shown that competition between FP and NP suppliers will lead FPs to emulate NPs if the latter are believed by consumers to be less opportunistic. However, that model does not deal with provision of public goods, such as charity care and medical research.

4. In recent years there has been increasing attention to managerial incentives in NP and FP hospitals. Roomkin and Weisbrod (1999), for example, examined data on CEO compensation and its decomposition into base salary and bonus and found significantly stronger incentives for CEOs at FP hospitals. Brickley and Van Horn (2002) found significant relationships between "financial performance" at nonprofit hospitals and both CEO turnover and compensation, but they did not have compensation information for FP hospitals and so could not compare the strength of incentives at the two institutional forms. Arnould, Bertrand, and Hallock (2000) focused on the effect on CEO incentives of market competition, finding that

If NPs were essentially disguised FP firms (Weisbrod 1988), they would want to offer the same strong rewards as private firms. Even if NPs pursued goals other than profit, they would use strong rewards if the desired outputs were easily monitored. The managerial rewards, while strong and in that sense like rewards by FP firms, would reward different variables.

We turn now to the theoretic structure underlying our empirical work. Consider an NP organization as a producer of two goods: a mission good (M) that is socially desirable but privately unprofitable and a revenue good (R) that finances the provision of M (James 1983; Schiff and Weisbrod 1991; Weisbrod 1998b, chap. 3).[5] If provision of M is difficult to measure and value, the firm would provide low-powered incentives, so as to discourage managers from focusing on profitable activities at the expense of mission outputs (Holmstrom and Milgrom 1991; Weisbrod 1988).

Profit from a revenue good, while necessary to maximize output of the mission good, is not sufficient. The organization must also be efficient in using the resources to maximize output of M subject to the available revenue. That efficiency, however, is more difficult to reward than is the generation of revenue. The optimal strength of managerial incentives thus requires a balancing of the incentive to generate revenue from R, which is relatively easily measured and rewarded, and the incentive to expend managerial effort on maximization of M, for given revenue, which can be difficult to measure. Under these conditions an NP would not fully exploit profit opportunities.

This two-good model of NP organization behavior, together with the assumptions that NPs are efficient in the pursuit of their mission good[6] but confront measurement problems with respect to the mission good, leads to some testable predictions. Assume that (a) for any organization, its CEO is the key agent through whom its mission is pursued; (b) the mission may differ among institutional forms; and (c) the mission may involve outputs that are difficult to monitor and reward ("type 2" attributes, contrasted with "type 1," easily-observed attributes; Weisbrod 1988). Assume further that (d) employees down the job ladder are expected to perform specific

---

increased competition leads to closer ties between executive compensation and performance at nonprofit hospitals. Again, however, comparisons with FP hospitals were not made.

5. Under existing U.S. tax law, a NP organization's mission is not limited to unprofitable activities. The charging of patient fees by hospitals, tuition by universities, and admission fees by museums is generally treated as "substantially related" to the organization's tax-exempt mission. From a theoretic perspective, however, it is useful to think of such "user fees" as income from revenue goods, because the social rationale for granting tax-exempt status to NPs is, presumably, their provision of socially desirable outputs that private enterprise markets would not engage in.

6. The assumption that NP organizations are efficient in optimizing their objective functions subject to the constraints they face can be questioned. It has been argued that NP as well as governmental organizations are less efficient than private firms because their executives are not legally permitted to share in the profits that greater efficiency would bring (Alchian and Demsetz 1972).

duties that involve easily observable, type 1 dimensions of performance that differ little, if at all, across institutional forms. A janitor, for example, might well be expected to perform the same duties by a profit-maximizing firm or the most public-goods-oriented NP. Under these assumptions a model in which objective functions differ across institutional forms would imply that CEO reward structures would vary substantially across institutional forms. Going down the job ladder we expect to find that the differences across institutional forms disappear. Whether that occurs at the middle-management or technical-worker levels, or at lower levels, is not clear, but we expect relatively smaller differences among institutional forms than is found for CEOs. Accordingly, our first two hypotheses are:

HYPOTHESIS 1. *Nonprofit organizations offer their CEOs weaker incentives that are less tied to observable performance. Weak incentives are made operational in the form of payment of a base salary, while strong incentives are measured in two ways: by the CEO's contractual eligibility for a performance-based bonus and by the actual amount of bonus received, conditional on eligibility.*

HYPOTHESIS 2. *Lower-level workers—middle managers and technical workers—confront incentive structures that are more similar across institutional forms. That is, there are smaller differences, compared with CEOs, in base salaries, eligibility for a bonus, amount of bonus, conditional on eligibility for it, and total compensation (base salary plus bonus).*

In this model, managerial effort in an NP organization would be directed toward the mission in two ways: directly, in the production of M, the mission good, and indirectly, through the budget obtained from R, the revenue good. Thus, in response to a tightening of the revenue constraint, whether an NP would alter its CEO incentives would depend on the relative productivity of managerial effort in each activity. It would also depend on any aversion to commercial activity that would reduce the marginal attractiveness of the R good to the NP (on the effects of such aversion, see Schiff and Weisbrod 1991 and Segal and Weisbrod 1998). For example, charging impecunious clients for medical care and generating some revenue may be feasible, but may be regarded by the organization as inconsistent with its mission of both providing medical care and not impoverishing patients in the process (Steinberg and Weisbrod 2002).

For NP organizations the tightening of an exogenous revenue constraint thus poses a choice[7]: The NP can retain its weaker CEO incentives com-

---

7. This assumes that, in the case in which there are multiple R goods, a decrease in the profitability of one does not alter the profitability of the others. That is, for example, an exogenous reduction in revenue from patient fees, for example, may or may not alter an organization's optimal behavior in other revenue markets, such as donations or ancillary commercial activity.

pared with FP firms and, confronted by reduced revenue, contract its output of M. Alternatively, it can strengthen the CEO incentives in order to generate additional profit, assuming that there was some revenue source that had not been fully exploited.

No strong prediction can be made regarding how that choice will be made at an NP (relative to an FP) organization in response to an exogenous cut in revenue, even if, as we predicted above, the NP was operating at a less-than-profit-maximizing level in the R market. However, we suspect that the net effect of the forces luring the NP to seek increased revenue from the R good, and any aversion to such commercial activity, is to seek more revenue and, hence, to strengthen managerial rewards.[8] In the empirical section we test the proposition that both types of NP hospitals alter their pay structures so as to more closely approximate FPs. Thus:

HYPOTHESIS 3. *When all forms of hospitals are confronted by a tightened revenue constraint—as might result from increased competition or HMO penetration—NP and FP organizations alter their CEO compensation structures differently, so that differences across institutional forms narrow.*[9]

Turning to lower-level employees, we predicted smaller systematic differences in reward structures across institutional forms (hypothesis 2), and now we hypothesize the following:

HYPOTHESIS 4. *When all forms of hospitals are confronted by a tightened revenue constraint, compensation structures for middle management and technical workers at NP and FP organizations will become even more alike.*

With respect to all four hypotheses, we explore the differences not only between FPs and NPs, but also between FPs and each of the two types of NPs—religious and secular. There has been little research about the modeling or empirical behavior of RNP and SNP organizations (see, however, references cited in note 1, above, and also Ballou and Weisbrod 2003). Both forms are subject to the same legal constraints—e.g., the nondistribution constraint, eligibility for tax subsidies for charitable donations, and exemption from property and sales taxation. However, they may face other constraints that differ—e.g., donor preferences—or have different goals. By examining the labor reward structures in these two forms of NPs and their responses to a change in budget constraint, we can learn whether they should be modeled differently.

Before turning to empirical work, we should note that our expectation

8. The logic is symmetric. Thus, in respect to a loosening of fiscal constraints, we expect managerial reward structures at NPs to increasingly deviate from FPs. Our data do not cover such conditions. However, during the 1960s, for example, expansive governmental and private health care insurance programs were making it easier for NPs to pursue their missions.

9. Relatedly, Sloan (2000, 1142) argued that "As competition among hospitals increases, differences in behavior among hospitals with different ownership forms should narrow. . . . Private not-for-profit hospitals will have less latitude than previously to produce outputs they deem to be socially worthy."

that NPs use weaker rewards than FPs is consistent with a number of models. The one on which we have focused is that NPs' objective functions, by contrast with those of FP firms, encompass hard-to-monitor outputs, such as public goods. A second, also focusing on objective functions, is that NPs are pursuing profit maximization, despite the nondistribution constraint, but are inefficient at doing so, failing to provide optimal managerial incentives. A third model emphasizes the importance of the nondistribution constraint (NDC; Hansmann 1980) as a restriction on the use of strong incentives to reward profitability.[10] Thus, if an NP seeks to act like a profit maximizer, it would use weaker incentives than an FP, assuming the NDC is at least partially enforced.[11]

Some evidence to help in model identification can come from other findings. If our empirical evidence showed that compensation down the job ladder differs little across institutional forms, even though CEO compensation differs markedly, this would weaken the appeal of the inefficiency model, because inefficiency might be expected to appear at all levels, not just at the CEO level.

### 4.3   Data and Econometric Model

We utilize data from annual surveys administered by a proprietary compensation-consulting firm, the Hay Group, for the years 1992 and 1997.[12] The survey asks questions about compensation policies of hospitals for dozens of job titles. We utilize data on general nongovernmental hospitals, excluding specialty hospitals.

Although Hay Group contacted each hospital listed by the American Hospital Association (AHA), 3,732 and 3,593 general nongovernmental hospitals in 1992 and 1997, respectively, the number of respondents (908 and 857 in 1992 and 1997) constituted a rate of less than 25 percent. With respect to possible selection bias, it is clear that respondent hospitals are disproportionately for-profit, large, and in urban areas (that is, in metropolitan statistical areas [MSAs]). Not all respondent hospitals report compensation data for all jobs: We cannot distinguish, however, between cases in which a hospital does not have an employee with a specific job title and in which the hospital chooses not to provide the information.

10. It should be noted that NDC does not constrain the use of performance-based bonuses per se—only the rewarding of profit. NPs may legally utilize strong managerial reward structures to reward behavior other than profit.

11. Adjustment to NDC might be in form of offering job perquisites (see Glaeser and Shleifer 2001; Migue and Belanger 1974) or hiding incentives in the salary (see Brickley and Van Horn 2001; Arnould, Bertrand, and Hallock 2000).

12. The earliest year we could obtain is 1992. We also have data for years 1998 through 2000. We choose not to use these later years because of an extraneous exogenous shock to bonus policies of FP hospitals. After a fraud lawsuit against a major FP hospital chain, Columbia/HCA Health Corporation (now the Health Care Company), the chain ceased using bonuses to reward managers, in order to reduce the incentives to expand profit by using questionable business practices.

It is also the case that hospitals that responded in one of the years 1992 and 1997 did not necessarily respond in the other. With respect to data on CEOs, 731 hospitals reported in 1992 and 696 in 1997, but only 249 reported CEO information in both years (table 4.1 lists summary statistics for those hospitals). For CEOs we used a balanced sample, but for middle-management- and technician-level jobs the balanced samples were too small at for-profit hospitals to be useful, and so we use the full, unbalanced samples for each year. We analyze all middle-management and technician-level jobs (table 4.2) for which we had at least fifteen observations for each ownership type.

Hay data provide the following details about compensation structures for each job title: (a) base salary paid in the prior year; (b) whether the job is bonus eligible; and (c) the amount of bonus paid in the prior year. Regarding bonus eligibility, we treat a hospital as offering a bonus as part of its compensation package if the survey respondent either checked the bonus-eligible box or reported a positive amount of bonus paid.

For controls we utilize a number of variables characterizing each hospital and job title: (a) the complexity of each job with a given title—"Hay Points." Developed by Hay Consultants, job complexity at each hospital reflects specialized know how, problem solving, and accountability requirements of the job. This measure helps us account for possible differences in job definition and scope of responsibilities across hospitals. For jobs other than CEO, missing values led us to drop the Hay Points variable in order to obtain a useful sample size.

Control variables for other, arguably exogenous, characteristics of each hospital were obtained by matching the Hay Group survey data with data from the American Hospital Association (AHA) hospital surveys for the years 1992 and 1997. These include (b) the ownership type, (c) number of licensed beds, and (d) location, a dummy for whether the hospital is in an urban area (MSA), and other dummies for geographic region:[13] Northeast, South, and Midwest, with West being the omitted class. Summary statistics are in table 4.3 for CEOs; data for other job titles are available from the authors.

The effects of revenue constraints are analyzed using two measures: (a) Competition and (b) the HMO penetration rate. Greater competition and greater HMO penetration are hypothesized to bring intensified budgetary pressure on all hospitals in the county. Competition is measured by $1 - $ Herfindahl index (HHI). To construct the HHI from the AHA Hospi-

---

13. It could be argued that state dummies would be preferable to regional dummies insofar as states differ in their Medicaid policies and other hospital regulatory policies. Use of state dummies, however, is impractical because, in our sample of 248 hospitals, most states have only a few hospitals. Moreover, even with a larger sample, the usefulness of state dummies is somewhat questionable insofar as hospitals are near state borders (e.g., in New York, Chicago, and St. Louis), and have significant numbers of patients crossing the borders.

**Table 4.1**   Summary Statistics (CEO)

|  | 1992 | | | | 1997 | | | |
|---|---|---|---|---|---|---|---|---|
|  | For-Profit | Secular | Religious | All | For-Profit | Secular | Religious | All |
| Base salary | 97.6 | 152.3 | 137.3 | 124.5 | 122.5 | 179.5 | 152.2 | 148.7 |
|  | (33.8) | (46.0) | (45.5) | (47.8) | (35.0) | (51.3) | (48.9) | (51.0) |
| Bonus (conditional on offering) | 46.9 | 18.5 | 15.3 | 34.9 | 56.6 | 37.1 | 24.9 | 47.4 |
|  | (51.8) | (18.7) | (22.9) | (44.3) | (41.6) | (31.0) | (19.6) | (38.4) |
| Total compensation | 143.7 | 162.4 | 146.9 | 151.0 | 176.0 | 203.6 | 161.7 | 183.7 |
|  | (72.0) | (51.5) | (57.3) | (630) | (66.3) | (68.4) | (57.0) | (67.3) |
| HMO penetration | 0.09 | 0.14 | 0.15 | 0.12 | 0.21 | 0.26 | 0.21 | 0.23 |
|  | (0.11) | (0.12) | (0.12) | (0.12) | (0.16) | (0.17) | (0.13) | (0.16) |
| Competition | 0.57 | 0.52 | 0.60 | 0.56 | 0.57 | 0.50 | 0.60 | 0.55 |
|  | (0.32) | (0.33) | (0.27) | (0.32) | (0.32) | (0.34) | (0.25) | (0.32) |
| Number of beds | 164.4 | 295.2 | 250.1 | 226.9 | 164.7 | 290.4 | 223.6 | 221.4 |
|  | (100.6) | (181.3) | (154.1) | (155.5) | (96.1) | (169.8) | (127.7) | (144.2) |
| Job points | 1253.5 | 1781.6 | 1508.7 | 1489.9 | 1310.4 | 1916.4 | 1590.5 | 1583.0 |
|  | (226.0) | (491.0) | (397.8) | (440.9) | (239.2) | (594.0) | (385.7) | (506.0) |
| MSA | 0.7 | 0.7 | 0.7 | 0.7 | 0.7 | 0.7 | 0.7 | 0.7 |
|  | (0.5) | (0.4) | (0.5) | (0.5) | (0.5) | (0.4) | (0.5) | (0.5) |
| South | 0.8 | 0.3 | 0.2 | 0.5 | 0.8 | 0.3 | 0.2 | 0.5 |
|  | (0.4) | (0.4) | (0.4) | (0.5) | (0.4) | (0.5) | (0.4) | (0.5) |
| West | 0.2 | 0.2 | 0.2 | 0.2 | 0.2 | 0.2 | 0.2 | 0.2 |
|  | (0.4) | (0.4) | (0.4) | (0.4) | (0.4) | (0.4) | (0.4) | (0.4) |
| Northeast | 0.0 | 0.2 | 0.1 | 0.1 | 0.0 | 0.2 | 0.1 | 0.1 |
|  | (0.0) | (0.4) | (0.3) | (0.3) | (0.0) | (0.4) | (0.3) | (0.3) |
| N | 110 | 88 | 43 | 242 | 110 | 88 | 43 | 242 |
| N (offering bonus) | 109 | 48 | 27 | 184 | 104 | 58 | 15 | 177 |

*Notes*: Standard errors are in parentheses. Total compensation, base salary, and bonus are in thousands of dollars. Competition = 1 − Herfindahl index (HHI). HMO penetration = HMO enrollment/population. Both competition and HMO enrollment are county based.

Table 4.2          Job Titles

|  | Title |
| --- | --- |
| CEO | |
| Middle-management level | Head of dietary and food services |
| | Head of housekeeping |
| | Head of imaging/radiology (nonmedical) |
| | Head of medical records |
| | Head of patient accounting/business office |
| | Head of purchasing/materials management |
| Technician level | Nurse supervisor |
| | EKG technician |
| | Nuclear medicine technologist |
| | Radiology technologist |
| | Respiratory therapist |
| | Staff dietitian |
| | Staff medical technologist |
| | Ultrasound technologist |

tal Surveys we used the county as the market area and calculated market shares using number of beds.[14] The use of 1 – HHI, rather than HHI, is intended to simplify the interpretation. HMO penetration is calculated for each hospital as the percentage of the total population in the county that is enrolled in an HMO (see Wholey, Christianson, Engberg, and Bryce 1997 on how the data was constructed).

HMO penetration as an influence on hospital behavior is relevant under the realistic assumption that the price negotiated by a HMO with a hospital, which we do not observe, is lower than the price for non–HMO patients. It is likely, however, that non–HMO patients are not a homogeneous class. Preferred provider organization (PPO) members, Medicare patients, Medicaid patients, and private-pay patients (insured or uninsured) may all present a hospital with distinct prices. Thus, it would be ideal to have data not only on market penetration by HMOs, but also by each of these other market groups. By omitting them, we implicitly assume that their relative importance across hospital types is a constant.[15]

14. In the literature, a number of measures of market area have been used, including county (Lynk 1995), MSA (Dranove, Simon, and White 1998), and measures based on geographic flow of patients (Keeler, Melnick, and Zwanziger 1999). While we use county, we have also considered MSA for those hospitals located in MSAs (and county for others), and results did not change markedly. Significance levels and signs were unchanged, but magnitude of some coefficients was different. For example, the coefficient for religious hospitals in total compensation decreased from –58 to –34, and the coefficient for secular hospitals decreased from –34 to –24.

15. It should be noted that the importance of each of these market groups depends on their size in each "market area," not their importance in the actual patient structure of each specific hospital. Even if, for example, a hospital were found to have no HMO patients, the HMO penetration rate in the market might well affect the hospital's behavior.

**Table 4.3** CEO: Coefficients of Ownership Dummies and of Their Interactions with MSA, Competition, and HMO Penetration Measures, 1992 and 1997

| | Total Compensation | | Base Salary | | Bonus Amount[a] | | Bonus Eligibility[b] | |
|---|---|---|---|---|---|---|---|---|
| | 1992 | 1997 | 1992 | 1997 | 1992 | 1997 | 1992[c] | 1997[c] |
| Religious (vs. for-profit) | -58.3*** | -57.2*** | 5.4 | -2.8 | -85.7*** | -57.8* | -11.0* | -4.48*** |
| | (17.8) | (16.1) | (10.4) | (11.5) | (27.6) | (31.2) | (6.2) | (1.56) |
| Secular (vs. for-profit) | -34.7** | -21.8 | 21.1** | 14.8 | -68.3*** | -45.9*** | -10.7* | -1.2 |
| | (17.4) | (16.7) | (10.1) | (10.2) | (19.6) | (16.4) | (6.2) | (1.2) |
| MSA | 10.3 | 4.4 | -2.2 | 6.0 | 13.4 | 1.9 | -1.4** | -0.099 |
| | (20.6) | (14.1) | (7.6) | (6.3) | (13.0) | (10.5) | (0.6) | (0.53) |
| MSA · Religious | 0.7 | -9.1 | 13.2 | -5.5 | -3.1 | -21.7 | | |
| | (22.1) | (21.2) | (11.3) | (11.4) | (25.1) | (17.4) | | |
| MSA · Secular | -5.1 | -9.2 | 8.7 | -4.0 | 0.9 | -7.9 | | |
| | (22.1) | (18.6) | (10.9) | (11.5) | (27.0) | (27.1) | | |
| HMO penetration | -1.26 | -0.59 | -0.32 | 0.03 | -1.12* | -0.83** | 0.02 | 0.074* |
| | (0.79) | (0.51) | (0.35) | (0.23) | (0.61) | (0.33) | (0.08) | (0.05) |
| HMO · Religious | 2.22** | 1.87*** | 0.72 | 1.00* | 2.06* | 0.75 | 0.04 | -0.058 |
| | (1.11) | (0.69) | (0.61) | (0.54) | (1.09) | (0.95) | (0.09) | (0.06) |
| HMO · Secular | 1.01 | 1.01 | 0.04 | 0.38 | 1.35 | 1.43** | 0.01 | -0.112** |
| | (0.77) | (0.64) | (0.43) | (0.34) | (0.90) | (0.55) | (0.09) | (0.05) |
| Competition | 0.05 | 0.26 | 0.21* | 0.09 | -0.17 | 0.18 | -0.08 | -0.025 |
| | (0.28) | (0.22) | (0.11) | (0.10) | (0.19) | (0.15) | (0.07) | (0.02) |
| Competition · Religious | 0.32 | -0.03 | 0.15 | 0.03 | 0.11 | 0.07 | 0.09 | 0.043 |
| | (0.32) | (0.29) | (0.17) | (0.22) | (0.46) | (0.50) | (0.07) | (0.03) |
| Competition · Secular | 0.15 | -0.13 | 0.01 | 0.02 | 0.15 | -0.22 | 0.08 | 0.029 |
| | (0.32) | (0.27) | (0.16) | (0.16) | (0.31) | (0.24) | (0.07) | (0.02) |
| Beds | 6.57 | 5.89 | 6.40* | 4.36 | -0.87 | -0.61 | 0.24 | 0.251 |
| | (5.45) | (4.93) | (3.66) | (3.89) | (5.64) | (4.06) | (0.25) | (0.27) |

*(continued)*

**Table 4.3** (continued)

| | Total Compensation | | Base Salary | | Bonus Amount[a] | | Bonus Eligibility[b] | |
|---|---|---|---|---|---|---|---|---|
| | 1992 | 1997 | 1992 | 1997 | 1992 | 1997 | 1992[c] | 1997[c] |
| Jobpoint | 4.79** | 7.15*** | 3.64*** | 5.55*** | 1.64 | 3.32** | -0.03 | -0.04 |
| | (1.87) | (1.69) | (1.19) | (1.13) | (2.12) | (1.36) | (0.09) | (0.08) |
| South | 0.39 | 19.79* | 12.02* | 10.39 | -12.83 | -4.93 | 0.08 | 1.385*** |
| | (12.62) | (11.53) | (6.83) | (6.67) | (11.37) | (10.01) | (0.50) | (0.52) |
| West | 16.15 | -1.29 | 9.85 | 0.28 | 10.64 | -19.96* | 0.38 | 2.286*** |
| | (15.38) | (11.08) | (7.59) | (7.19) | (13.02) | (11.58) | (0.58) | (0.67) |
| Northeast | 9.12 | -3.26 | 16.17** | 4.05 | -13.41 | -14.25 | -0.27 | -0.576 |
| | (10.38) | (13.29) | (7.95) | (9.43) | (18.52) | (13.82) | (0.57) | (0.58) |
| Constant | 72.19*** | 52.35*** | 23.13* | 25.05** | 45.48* | 26.90 | 11.06* | 1.861 |
| | (17.9) | (19.3) | (12.8) | (11.7) | (23.3) | (16.3) | (6.3) | (1.31) |
| N | 242 | 242 | 242 | 242 | 184 | 177 | 242 | 242 |
| $R^2$ | 0.3 | 0.45 | 0.6 | 0.67 | -839 | -811 | -90.8 | -91 |
| Expected salary for for-profit hospital[d] | 153.0*** | 191.3*** | 110.6*** | 129*** | 41.134*** | 70.1*** | 6.697*** | 3.4*** |
| | (16.5) | (13.0) | (6.9) | (6.2) | (11.0) | (8.6) | (2.1) | (1.2) |

*Notes:* Standard errors in parentheses. Results are obtained by OLS for Total Compensation and Base Salary, tobit for Bonus Amount, and logit for Bonus Eligibility. Total Compensation, Base Salary, and Bonus Amount are in thousands. Italics indicate that religious and secular hospitals are significantly different from each other.

[a] For the amount of bonus there were twenty-eight and nineteen hospitals offering $0 bonus in 1992 and 1997, respectively.

[b] All results that are presented are logit coefficients rather than derivatives.

[c] We were unable to estimate a model with full interaction variables. Results are from one with no MSA interaction variables.

[d] At mean values of independent variables, except for MSA set equal to zero.

***Significant at the 1 percent level.

**Significant at the 5 percent level.

*Significant at the 10 percent level.

Cost containment pressures[16] also operate through other mechanisms, such as Medicare and Medicaid pricing, which we do not measure. To investigate whether hospitals of different ownership type reacted differently in terms of compensation structures to changes in financial constraints, we also compare the compensation structures over a time interval in which constraints were tightening, specifically from 1992 to 1997. We interpret changes in compensation structures as reflections of the effect of cost containment policies other than the HMO penetration and competition variables. Thus, we assume that there were no systematic changes across institutional forms that affect compensation structure other than those captured by the control variables.[17]

Specifically, we analyze determinants of four measures of compensation structure referred to above: (a) base salary, (b) bonus eligibility (whether a hospital offers a bonus or not), (c) amount of bonus (for those hospitals that offer a bonus), and (d) total compensation (base salary plus bonus). We have no data on other forms of compensation, such as stock options, expense accounts, and fringe benefits, which may also vary in systematic ways across institutional forms and over time. All monetary values are in 1992 dollars corrected with the Consumer Price Index–Health. We analyze institutional form differences in reward structures as a function of financial constraints at a given time, 1992, between 1992 and 1997, down the job ladder, and in response to changes in financial constraints, controlling for hospital size, job complexity, and location.

That is, for each of the years 1992 and 1997, we regress each of the four dependent variables—base salary, bonus eligibility, bonus payment, and total compensation—on ownership dummies (FP is the omitted class), competition, and HMO penetration measures, both independently and interactively with institutional form and other control variables. For the total compensation and base salary estimates we use ordinary least squares (OLS).[18] For the bonus eligibility equations, in which the dependent vari-

16. In the latter half of the 1980s and in the 1990s, "managed care," especially HMOs, expanded, as private and public insurers shifted emphasis from quality enhancement to cost containment. Lengths of hospital stays were cut by insurers. Patients were increasingly directed by insurers to hospitals with which discounted prices had been negotiated. Price competition intensified (Dranove, Shanley, and White 1993; Keeler, Melnick, and Zwanziger 1999). An important change affecting hospitals' revenues was the system of Medicare payments to hospitals. Beginning in late 1985 Medicare no longer reimbursed hospitals based on "actual costs" of treating a given patient. The Prospective Payment System, based on a set of 368 Diagnosis Related Groups of illnesses and therapies, each with a price attached, was increasingly adopted by other insurers in subsequent years. Hospitals were paid fixed prices for treating specific diseases, regardless of the actual cost incurred for a given patient, and downward pressure on those prices ensued.

17. William Vogt pointed out, however, that improvements in information technology might have helped NPs to better measure their mission-good performance, in which case they would use stronger incentives over time.

18. A Cook-Weisberg test (Stata command hettest) signals heteroscedasticity, which, while not causing OLS regression coefficients to be biased, does increase the estimated variances.

able is a dichotomous dummy indicating whether the hospital offers a bonus, we utilize a logit model. For the amount of bonus, conditional on the job being bonus-eligible at a specific hospital, we estimate a tobit model to account for the occurrence of bonuses of size zero (28 out of 184 and 19 out of 177 in 1992 and 1997, respectively).[19] That is, some CEOs whose jobs are bonus eligible do not receive a bonus. Since FP status is the omitted category, coefficients for SNP and RNP hospitals give the estimated differences between these types of hospitals and FP hospitals. Coefficients for the interaction of competition and HMO penetration with ownership dummies show how different types of ownership react to these financial constraints.

## 4.4    Results

In this section we first report findings for CEOs and then down the job ladder. For each job category we show the cross-sectional effects of institutional form on each of the four compensation structure variables. Estimates are then presented for the interactive effects of institutional forms with HMO penetration and competition. Finally, changes over time are estimated, by examining coefficients in both years and estimating the cross-institutional differences at low, high, and medium levels of HMO penetration and competition variables.

### 4.4.1   CEO

*Institutional Differences—Base Case, 1992*

Table 4.3 shows the estimated coefficients in 1992, our base year, for total compensation, base salary, amount of bonus, and bonus eligibility. The differential institutional effects of the HMO and competition variables are of particular interest. Table 4.3 also shows estimates for 1997, to capture the effects of changes over time. Table 4.4 shows predicted differences from FPs at each of several combinations of values of HMO penetration, competition, and MSA. With respect to bonus eligibility, we note that sample size limitations prevented estimation of equations with the interaction of MSA with each institutional form. Thus, we estimated equations without those interactions—that is, we did not estimate the differential effects of

---

Thus we use a Huber/White/Sandwich estimator for robust variances. In the tobit analyses, by contrast, coefficients are biased when heteroscedasticity exists. To deal with this we assume that the error term variance can be expressed as a function of hospital size, which we suspect to be the reason for heteroscedasticity, and then estimate the model accordingly.

19. Our estimation assumes that the data are reported accurately, i.e., those hospitals reporting no bonus payment did, indeed, pay no bonus to their CEOs. If that were not the case and a hospital reported zero dollars as bonus payment, even though it paid a positive amount of bonus, a two-part model that distinguishes between positive amounts and zeros would be more accurate.

**Table 4.4    Differences between Institutional Forms under Different Specifications of Competition, HMO Presence and MSA for CEOs**

| | Total Compensation | | Base Salary | | Bonus Amount | | Bonus Eligibility[a] | | | |
| | | | | | | | Logit Coefficient | | Probability[b] | |
| HMO/Competition | 1992 | 1997 | 1992 | 1997 | 1992 | 1997 | 1992 | 1997 | 1992 | 1997 |
|---|---|---|---|---|---|---|---|---|---|---|
| | *Religious versus for-profit, MSA = 0* | | | | | | | | | |
| Low | -34.3** | -49.1*** | 14.9* | 3.4 | -71.1*** | -51.3** | -7.3** | -3.0*** | -0.5*** | -0.6*** |
| | (17.2) | (15.6) | (8.3) | (10.2) | (20.1) | (20.0) | (3.4) | (0.95) | (0.1) | (0.2) |
| Middle | -5.7 | -31.0* | 25.1*** | 14.0 | -48.4** | -42.4** | -5.2** | -2.7*** | -0.4*** | -0.5*** |
| | (18.9) | (16.0) | (8.8) | (10.0) | (20.9) | (18.3) | (2.2) | (0.70) | (0.1) | (0.1) |
| High | 23.0 | -12.9 | 35.3*** | 24.6 | -25.6* | -33.5* | -3.0*** | -2.5*** | -0.2** | -0.4*** |
| | (45.0) | (7.9) | (12.8) | (20.6) | (13.7) | (18.5) | (1.0) | (0.86) | (0.1) | (0.1) |
| | *Religious versus for-profit, MSA = 1* | | | | | | | | | |
| Low | -39.4** | -58.3*** | 23.7** | -0.6 | -70.2*** | -59.2** | | | | |
| | (19.0) | (19.2) | (10.2) | (1.0) | (22.4) | (28.6) | | | | |
| Middle | -10.7 | -40.2** | 33.8*** | 10.0 | -47.4*** | -50.3** | | | | |
| | (14.6) | (16.5) | (8.3) | (9.7) | (15.9) | (19.5) | | | | |
| High | 18.0 | -22.2** | 44.0*** | 20.6 | -24.7*** | -41.3** | | | | |
| | (63.5) | (10.7) | (11.5) | (24.1) | (9.0) | (16.9) | | | | |

*(continued)*

Table 4.4    (continued)

| HMO/Competition | Total Compensation | | Base Salary | | Bonus Amount | | Bonus Eligibility[a] | | | |
| | | | | | | | Logit Coefficient | | Probability[b] | |
| | 1992 | 1997 | 1992 | 1997 | 1992 | 1997 | 1992 | 1997 | 1992 | 1997 |
|---|---|---|---|---|---|---|---|---|---|---|
| *Secular versus for-profit, MSA = 0* | | | | | | | | | | |
| Low | -23.7 | -22.1 | 21.8** | 17.6 | -55.5*** | -47.5*** | -7.3** | -0.6 | -0.5*** | -0.1 |
| | (18.2) | (18.0) | (9.7) | (10.8) | (17.7) | (16.3) | (3.4) | (0.83) | (0.1) | (0.1) |
| Middle | -10.6 | -14.6 | 22.4** | 21.8* | -39.1* | -37.6** | -5.5** | -1.1 | -0.4*** | -0.1 |
| | (19.9) | (18.7) | (10.8) | (11.2) | (20.4) | (16.6) | (2.2) | (0.70) | (0.1) | (0.1) |
| High | 2.5 | -7.1 | 23.1* | 26.1* | -22.6 | -27.6** | -3.7*** | -1.7** | -0.3*** | -0.2** |
| | (8.0) | (9.1) | (12.9) | (15.7) | (14.8) | (12.9) | (1.0) | (0.84) | (0.1) | (0.1) |
| *Secular versus for-profit, MSA = 1* | | | | | | | | | | |
| Low | -23.0 | -31.1 | 35.0*** | 12.1 | -58.6*** | -69.2*** | | | | |
| | (18.9) | (22.3) | (9.2) | (11.6) | (21.2) | (17.3) | | | | |
| Middle | -9.9 | -23.7 | 35.7*** | 16.3* | -42.1*** | -59.3*** | | | | |
| | (14.6) | (18.8) | (7.4) | (9.8) | (15.2) | (13.7) | | | | |
| High | 3.2 | -16.2 | 36.3*** | 20.5 | -25.6** | -49.4*** | | | | |
| | (7.4) | (13.0) | (8.3) | (13.5) | (10.0) | (11.7) | | | | |

*Notes:* Low: HMO penetration = .05, competition = .4. Middle: HMO penetration = .15, competition = .6. High: HMO penetration = .25, competition = .8. Standard errors are in parentheses. Results are obtained from coefficients presented in table 4.3. Total Compensation, Base Salary, and Bonus Amount are in $ thousands.

[a]As we are unable to estimate the interaction of MSA and ownership forms, we present the estimates from equations without those interaction terms; thus, the bonus eligibility coefficients do not distinguish between MSA = 0 and MSA = 1.

[b]Differences in probabilities are calculated at the mean values of independent variables other than ownership dummies, HMO Penetration, and Competition.

***Significant at the 1 percent level. **Significant at the 5 percent level. *Significant at the 10 percent level.

MSA location for RNPs and SNPs. In table 4.4, "middle" refers to the mean values (over both years) of competition (0.6) and HMO penetration (0.15), while "low" and "high" refer, respectively, to first and third quartile values of competition and HMO penetration (0.4 and 0.8 for competition and 0.05 and 0.25 for HMO penetration). For example, –34.3 on the top left cell of table 4.4 means that total compensation at a RNP in 1992 is estimated to be $34,300 less than at a FP when competition is 0.4, HMO penetration is 0.05, and the hospital is not in a MSA (This number is derived from table 4.3 as –58.3 + 0 · 0.7 + 5 · 2.22 + 40 · 0.32 = –34.3). Also, note that for bonus eligibility we report differences both in logit coefficients and average probabilities.

In terms of institutional differences our overall results support hypothesis 1 that FP hospitals use higher-powered incentive mechanisms to reward CEOs compared with NP hospitals. As seen in table 4.4, regardless of which assumptions are used for HMO penetration and competition, the findings are robust: Bonus eligibility and bonus amount are significantly smaller and base salary is significantly higher at NPs than at FPs. For example, under the middle-level assumptions, RNP and SNP hospitals located in a non–MSA pay $22,000–$25,000 greater base salaries than FP hospitals, far smaller bonuses—$39,000–$48,000—conditional on offering a bonus, and total compensation that is lower, though not significantly, by $6,000–$10,000, while being significantly less likely to offer a bonus.

Do the two types of NPs behave alike? Table 4.3 shows coefficients for the RNP and SNP variables—independently and interactively—in *italics* when they differ significantly at the 10 percent level or better. In 1992, CEO total compensation is significantly lower at SNPs than at RNPs, by $23,000, and base salaries are also significantly lower, by about $16,000. However, with respect to interactive effects of each institutional form with the HMO penetration and competition variables, there are no significant differences between RNPs and SNPs.

### Institutional Differences—Effects of Tightened Revenue Constraints

We move now to the effects of varied financial constraints crosssectionally and over time. While we report findings on base salary and total compensation, we focus on strength of incentives as captured by bonus eligibility and amount of bonus. We find some evidence in 1992 that tighter fiscal constraints, proxied by competition and HMO penetration, led NPs to use stronger reward structures, more closely emulating FPs in terms of use of bonus compensation, and consistent with hypothesis 3 (hypotheses 2 and 4 will be considered below). Results are weaker for 1997 and mixed for changes across years, as cost containment pressures mounted.

From table 4.4 we see that in 1992 a shift from low levels of HMO penetration and competition to high levels is estimated to reduce the differences in bonus eligibility probabilities compared with FPs, by about half (from –.5 to –.2 for RNPs and to –.3 for SNPs). Similarly, the differences in bonus amount, compared with FPs, fall by almost two thirds (from –$71,000 to –$26,000 for RNPs and from –$56,000 to –$23,000 for SNPs not in MSAs). In 1997, while table 4.4 again shows that the differences in the amount of bonus narrow as conditions change from the low to high assumptions, this narrowing is smaller absolutely and proportionately, than in 1992 (from –$51,000 to –$34,000 for RNPs and from –$48,000 to –$28,000 for SNPs not in MSAs). In terms of bonus eligibility, both types of NPs remain less likely than FPs to offer a bonus, but a SNP hospital differs more from a FP under the assumption of high (–.2) than low (–.1).

We turn now to comparison of compensation structures across years, in order to estimate the effects of cost containment policies that operate other than through HMO penetration and competition. Table 4.4 shows that between 1992 and 1997 differences between SNP and FP hospitals (lower two panels) in bonus amount increased in absolute value in some HMO/ Competition cases (e.g., hospitals in MSAs), and decreased in others (e.g., low HMO/Competition in non–MSA hospitals). In terms of bonus eligibility, SNP hospitals consistently became more like their FP counterparts over the period. Differences in bonus eligibility became insignificant in 1997 under both low and middle conditions. RNPs, however, displayed a contrasting pattern (upper panel), becoming less like FPs in terms of bonus eligibility.

Finally, in order to capture the combined effects of changing coefficients over time and changing levels of HMO penetration, we consider the change from middle in 1992 to high in 1997. Between those years, HMO penetration nearly doubled, from 12 percent to 23 percent (table 4.1), which is close to the values of 15 percent and 25 percent that we use to define middle and high groups.[20] Table 4.4 shows that, under those assumptions, differences in the amount of bonus paid, conditional on bonus eligibility, between FPs and both types of NPs narrowed substantially for hospitals not in MSAs, from about $48,000 to $34,000 for RNPs and from about $39,000 to $28,000 for SNPs. For hospitals in MSAs, the narrowing also occurred for RNPs, from –$47,000 to –$41,000, but for SNPs the differential increased, from –$42,000 to –$49,000. For bonus eligibility, we find that as conditions change from middle to high—reflecting greater HMO penetration and competition—SNPs became more like FPs (the difference in bonus eligibility probability decreasing from –.4 to –.2), while for RNPs the differential probability remained the same.

### 4.4.2   Middle Management

Predicted differences between institutional forms at middle-level jobs are presented in table 4.5, analogous to table 4.4 (coefficients behind this

20. The growth was particularly great in the markets where FP hospitals were concentrated, where it increased from 9 percent to 21 percent (table 4.1). In 1992, FPs tended to be located in markets in which HMO penetration was substantially lower than was the case for NPs. By 1997, the gap narrowed, disappearing for the RNPs.

**Table 4.5**    Differences between Institutional forms under Different Specifications of Competition, HMO Presence and MSA in Middle-Level Jobs

| | Total Compensation | | | | Base Salary | | | | Bonus Eligibility | | | |
|---|---|---|---|---|---|---|---|---|---|---|---|---|
| | 1992 | | 1997 | | 1992 | | 1997 | | 1992 | | 1997 | |
| | Low | High | Low | High | Low | High | Low | High | Low | High | Low | High |
| | | | | | *Secular versus for-profit* | | | | | | | |
| Head of dietary services | 9.1 | -1.4 | 1.8 | 1.1 | 9.2 | -0.9 | 2.5 | 1.6 | | | -1.1 | -0.6 |
| | (6.6) | (2.2) | (2.0) | (2.4) | (8.6) | (2.2) | (2.3) | (2.3) | | | (3.4) | (0.6) |
| Head of housekeeping | 1.5**| 2.0 | 6.5 | 3.7 | 1.3*** | 1.7 | 7.1 | 3.5 | | | -2.3 | 0.5 |
| | (0.3) | (2.0) | (9.4) | (4.0) | (0.2) | (2.0) | (11.7) | (4.0) | | | (2.5) | (0.9) |
| Head of imaging | 3.0** | -1.3 | 1.0** | 2.2 | 3.2** | -0.9 | 2.6** | 2.4 | | | -1.8 | -0.5 |
| | (1.4) | (3.0) | (0.4) | (2.3) | (1.2) | (2.5) | (1.0) | (2.2) | | | (2.3) | (0.5) |
| Head of medical records | -0.6** | 2.3 | 2.6*** | 5.0** | -0.4* | 2.9 | 3.5*** | 5.0** | | | -1.5 | -0.3 |
| | (0.3) | (3.5) | (0.9) | (2.3) | (0.2) | (3.0) | (1.1) | (2.3) | | | (6.8) | (0.5) |
| Head of patient accounting | -1.5 | -0.5 | 3.3 | 0.4 | -1.8 | -1.0 | 4.0 | 0.1 | | | -0.8 | -0.4 |
| | (4.9) | (2.5) | (33.1) | (3.0) | (8.8) | (2.5) | (39.9) | (0.5) | | | (2.1) | (0.6) |
| Head of purchasing | 5.9** | 3.5 | 7.5*** | 6.4*** | 5.9* | 3.9* | 8.0*** | 6.2*** | | | -1.0 | -0.6 |
| | (2.9) | (2.2) | (2.9) | (2.4) | (3.6) | (2.1) | (2.9) | (2.4) | | | (0.9) | (0.5) |

*(continued)*

Table 4.5 (continued)

|  | Total Compensation | | | | Base Salary | | | | Bonus Eligibility | | | |
|---|---|---|---|---|---|---|---|---|---|---|---|---|
|  | 1992 | | 1997 | | 1992 | | 1997 | | 1992 | | 1997 | |
|  | Low | High | Low | High | Low | High | Low | High | Low | High | Low | High |
| *Religious versus for-profit* | | | | | | | | | | | | |
| Head of dietary services | 13.4 | -2.0 | 3.8 | 0.6 | 13.9 | -1.3 | 4.6 | 1.0 | | | -2.1* | -1.1 |
|  | (10.0) | (2.6) | (5.6) | (2.7) | (16.1) | (2.6) | (4.6) | (2.5) | | | (1.2) | (0.7) |
| Head of housekeeping | 1.5*** | 0.8 | 6.5 | 2.9 | 1.6*** | 0.4 | 7.3 | 2.6 | | | -1.8 | 0.3 |
|  | (0.4) | (2.2) | (5.3) | (4.1) | (0.4) | (2.1) | (6.0) | (4.0) | | | (5.0) | (0.9) |
| Head of imaging | 4.2** | -3.1 | 3.0* | 3.0 | 4.6*** | -2.3 | 4.5** | 3.3 | | | -2.3* | -1.0* |
|  | (1.9) | (3.0) | (1.7) | (2.6) | (1.7) | (2.6) | (2.3) | (2.5) | | | (1.2) | (0.6) |
| Head of medical records | 1.8* | 1.3 | 4.0* | 3.9 | 2.2 | 1.9 | 5.0* | 3.7 | | | -1.7 | -0.4 |
|  | (1.0) | (3.7) | (2.4) | (2.6) | (1.5) | (3.1) | (2.8) | (2.5) | | | (1.4) | (0.6) |
| Head of patient accounting | 0.4 | -3.8 | -0.6 | -3.7 | 0.5 | -3.8 | -0.1 | -3.2 | | | -0.9* | -0.7 |
|  | (1.0) | (2.7) | (0.6) | (3.5) | (1.1) | (2.7) | (0.1) | (3.5) | | | (0.5) | (0.6) |
| Head of purchasing | 5.6 | 2.2 | 4.8 | 6.7** | 5.9 | 2.9 | 6.1 | 6.4** | | | -3.0** | -0.7 |
|  | (4.0) | (2.2) | (4.7) | (2.8) | (6.1) | (2.0) | (5.0) | (2.6) | | | (1.3) | (0.6) |

*Notes:* Low: Competition = .4, HMO Penetration = .05, MSA = 0; High: Competition = .8, HMO Penetration = .25, MSA = 1. Results are obtained by OLS for Total Compensation and Base Salary, and by logit for Bonus Eligibility. Values are in $ thousands for Total Compensation and Base Salary; for Bonus Eligibility, logit coefficients are presented.

***Significant at the 1 percent level.

**Significant at the 5 percent level.

*Significant at the 10 percent level.

table—analogous to table 4.3    are available from the authors). We present the differences under two sets of assumptions. The first evaluates the differences across institutional forms at the 25th percentiles of the distributions of competition and HMO penetration over the two years for the full samples (0.4 and 0.05 for competition and HMO penetration, respectively—corresponding to low in table 4.4) and considers a non–MSA hospital. The second specification evaluates the differences across institutional forms at the 75th percentile (0.8 for competition and 0.25 for HMO penetration—corresponding to high in table 4.4) and considers a MSA hospital.

With respect to hypothesis 2—that there are relatively smaller differences in compensation between NP and FP hospitals for lower-level jobs compared with CEOs—we find a mixed pattern. We are unable to estimate a full interaction model for bonus eligibility in 1992 and for amount of bonus in both years. Estimation without interactions indicated no significant difference between FPs and either type of NP (available from the authors). The estimates for bonus eligibility in 1997 (table 4.5) show a regular pattern, in that FPs are estimated to be more likely than NPs to offer a bonus in almost all job titles, even though most of the differences are insignificant. For total compensation and base salary, whether in 1992 or 1997 and whether the focus is SNPs or RNPs relative to FPs, there is evidence that significant differentials exist for some jobs but not for others.

### 4.4.3   Technician-Level Jobs

With respect to hypothesis 2, we expect to find results that are less mixed as we go further down the job ladder. Results for technician-level jobs are presented in table 4.6, which is similar to table 4.5. As very few hospitals offer bonuses for such jobs, we were unable to estimate either the bonus eligibility or bonus amount equations with interactions. A regression of bonus eligibility without interaction variables, however, showed no significant differences between FP and either type of NP hospital for any of the eight jobs regarding their tendency to offer bonuses. The fact that few hospitals of any form offer bonuses for technician jobs is consistent with hypothesis 2—that the use of strong rewards, as measured by the use of bonus compensation, does not differ across institutional forms as one moves down the job ladder.

Hypothesis 2, if correct, holds that the levels of total compensation will also not differ among institutional forms at technical-level jobs, nor will it differ for base salaries. Here the evidence is not clear. In 1992, with the low assumptions, table 4.6 shows that NPs and FPs do not differ in total compensation, as hypothesized, for four of eight at RNPs and for two of the eight jobs at SNPs. In terms of base salary, there are no significant differences for five of the eight jobs between either type of NP and the FPs.

Over time, from 1992 to 1997, table 4.6 shows that under the low assumptions many of the cross-form differences that were significant in 1992

**Table 4.6    Differences between Institutional Forms under Different Specifications of Competition, HMO Presence and MSA in Technician Level Jobs**

| | Total Compensation | | | | Base Salary | | | |
|---|---|---|---|---|---|---|---|---|
| | 1992 | | 1997 | | 1992 | | 1997 | |
| | Low | High | Low | High | Low | High | Low | High |
| | *Secular versus for-profit* | | | | | | | |
| Nurse supervisor | -3.3*** | 2.1 | 3.2** | 0.6 | -3.3*** | 2.2 | 3.0** | 0.7 |
| | (0.8) | (1.7) | (1.3) | (1.4) | (0.8) | (1.6) | (1.2) | (1.3) |
| EKG technician | 9.6 | -1.4 | 5.1 | 0.3 | 9.7 | -1.3 | 4.9 | 0.3 |
| | (14.4) | (1.9) | (20.6) | (1.2) | (14.1) | (1.9) | (18.5) | (1.2) |
| Nuclear medical technician | -2.4* | -4.0*** | 0.3 | -1.1 | -2.1 | -3.7 | 0.2 | -1.1 |
| | (1.4) | (1.0) | (0.2) | (0.9) | (1.3) | (0.9) | (0.1) | (0.9) |
| Radiology technologist | -9.0** | -0.9 | -0.1*** | -0.2 | -8.8* | -0.8 | -0.2*** | -0.2 |
| | (4.6) | (1.1) | (0.0) | (0.7) | (4.5) | (1.0) | (0.1) | (0.7) |
| Respiratory therapist | 7.17* | -0.66 | 1.5* | -0.8 | 7.4 | -0.5 | 1.4 | -0.9 |
| | (4.0) | (1.6) | (0.8) | (0.8) | (4.4) | (1.6) | (0.7) | (0.8) |
| Staff dietician | -0.1 | -1.4 | 1.0 | -0.7 | 0.2 | -1.3 | 1.0 | -0.7 |
| | (0.3) | (1.1) | (2.5) | (0.9) | (0.5) | (1.1) | (2.6) | (0.9) |
| Staff medical technician | -2.7*** | -1.7 | 1.4** | -0.8 | -2.3 | -1.5 | 1.4 | -0.9 |
| | (0.9) | (1.5) | (0.7) | (0.7) | (0.8) | (1.3) | (0.6) | (0.7) |
| Ultrasound technician | -11.9*** | 0.1 | 0.7 | -0.1 | -11.6** | 0.3 | 0.6 | -0.2 |
| | (4.5) | (1.5) | (2.8) | (0.9) | (4.7) | (1.4) | (2.2) | (0.9) |

| | Religious versus for-profit | | | | | | | |
|---|---|---|---|---|---|---|---|---|
| Nurse supervisor | -4.1*** | 1.8 | 0.6* | 0.4 | -3.9*** | 1.8 | 0.6* | 0.4 |
| | (1.4) | (1.8) | (0.3) | (1.4) | (1.4) | (1.8) | (0.3) | (1.4) |
| EKG technician | 5.7 | -1.6 | 1.6 | 0.5 | 5.8 | -1.4 | 1.6 | 0.5 |
| | (7.7) | (2.0) | (2.0) | (1.3) | (7.7) | (2.0) | (2.2) | (1.3) |
| Nuclear medical technician | 0.0 | -3.9*** | -1.5 | -1.3 | 0.4 | -3.6 | -1.6 | -1.3 |
| | (0.0) | (1.2) | (3.5) | (1.0) | (0.3) | (1.1) | (4.2) | (1.0) |
| Radiology technologist | -9.7* | -1.8 | -0.7 | 0.2 | -9.5* | -1.6 | -0.8 | 0.2 |
| | (5.1) | (1.1) | (0.5) | (0.8) | (5.1) | (1.1) | (0.6) | (0.8) |
| Respiratory therapist | 6.08 | -0.76 | -0.4 | -1.5* | 6.2 | -0.6 | -0.4 | -1.5 |
| | (4.7) | (1.6) | (2.7) | (0.8) | (5.1) | (1.6) | (2.5) | (0.8) |
| Staff dietician | 0.5 | -1.3 | -2.1 | -0.4 | 0.9 | -1.2 | -2.2 | -0.4 |
| | (3.8) | (1.2) | (4.5) | (1.0) | (2.5) | (1.2) | (4.1) | (1.0) |
| Staff medical technician | -2.7** | -2.2 | 0.1 | -0.8 | -2.3 | -2.0 | 0.1 | -0.9 |
| | (1.1) | (1.5) | (0.1) | (0.8) | (0.9) | (1.4) | (0.1) | (0.8) |
| Ultrasound technician | -12.7** | -0.4 | 0.1 | -0.4 | -12.5** | -0.2 | 0.0 | -0.4 |
| | (5.5) | (1.5) | (0.2) | (1.0) | (5.8) | (1.4) | (0.1) | (1.1) |

*Notes:* Low: Competition = 4, HMO Penetration = .05, MSA = 0; High: Competition = 4, HMO Penetration = 8, HMO Penetration = 25, MSA = 1. Standard errors are in parentheses. Results are obtained by OLS for Total Compensation and Base Salary. Values are in $ thousands for Total Compensation and Base Salary.

***Significant at the 1 percent level.

**Significant at the 5 percent level

*Significant at the 10 percent level

become insignificant—three of four at RNPs and two of six at SNPs. When we consider the high assumptions, with hospitals facing more competition and HMO penetration, there are almost no significant differences between different types of hospitals in either year, consistent with hypothesis 4.

### 4.5    Conclusion

We analyzed compensation structures for CEOs, as well as middle managers and technical workers, and changes in those structures in response to financial constraints at nonprofit—both religious and secular—and for-profit hospitals. While there are many reasons for wanting to understand patterns of compensation and their reaction to financial constraints, our principal motivation was to increase understanding of the objective functions of NP organizations that may or may not pursue goals other than profit maximization.

We hypothesized that compensation schemes and responses to exogenous fiscal stringency would differ across institutional forms, reflecting differential objective functions but only for top management, not for middle management or technical workers.

Overall, our findings are broadly consistent with the four hypotheses, but it is clear that there are forces other than we have considered that influence compensation structures and incentives. We find that NP and FP organizations act very differently in the labor markets for top management, CEOs. This is consistent with a model in which organizations of different institutional forms have different objective functions, with particular reference to outputs that are difficult to monitor and, hence, to reward. It is also consistent, however, with other models, including models in which NPs are less efficient or are legally constrained from adopting profit-sharing reward structures. Importantly, however, we noted that NPs are not constrained from linking compensation to performance in dimensions other than profit, such as the organization's provision of certain public goods or delivery of selected services to "deserving" consumers. The reason for using weaker rewards may well be the difficulty of measuring such outputs.

In lower-level jobs, differences in bonus and other compensation measures between NPs and FPs are far more limited. During the period, 1992 to 1997, a period of increasingly intense downward pressure on revenues at both FP and NP hospitals, we find that both types of NPs came to look somewhat more like FPs in terms of the use of performance-based bonus compensation.

Considering jointly our findings for top managers, middle managers, and technical workers, we judge that institutional form does convey information about organization objective functions. There is considerable evidence that is not consistent with the hypothesis that NP and FP hospitals are essentially "carbon copies."

Public policy does not distinguish between NP organizations that are religiously affiliated and those that are secular. Tax subsidies are offered to both without distinction. Antitrust law makes no distinction between the forms of NPs, applying equally to both. We find some but rather limited evidence that RNPs and SNPs behave differently.

Behavior of any organization reflects both its objective function and the constraints faced. More effective modeling of behavior of various forms of organizations in mixed industries requires better understanding of how to characterize both objective functions and constraints. This paper, utilizing employee compensation structures as indicators of organization goals, permits some limited inferences about the interplay of objective functions and constraints. Attention to other institutionally mixed industries, such as higher education, day care, the arts, and museums, as well as hospitals and nursing homes, is needed to facilitate generalizations about differential institutional behavior.

# References

Alchian, Armen A., and Harold Demsetz. 1972. Production, information costs, and economic organization. *American Economic Review* 62 (5): 777–95.

Arnould, Richard, Marianne Bertrand, and Kevin F. Hallock. 2000. Does managed care change the mission of nonprofit hospitals? Evidence from the managerial labor market. NBER Working Paper no. 7924. Cambridge, Mass.: National Bureau of Economic Research.

Ballou, Jeffrey P., and Burton A. Weisbrod. 2003. Inferring behavior of nonprofit and governmental organizations from managerial rewards: An application to the hospital industry. *Journal of Public Economics,* forthcoming.

Brickley, James R., and Lawrence Van Horn. 2002. Managerial incentives in nonprofit organizations: Evidence from hospitals. *Journal of Law and Economics* 45 (1): 227–49.

Dranove, David, Mark Shanley, and William D. White. 1993. Price and concentration in hospital markets. *Journal of Law and Economics* 36:179–204.

Dranove, David, Carol J. Simon, and William D. White. 1998. Determinants of managed care penetration. *Journal of Health Economics* 17 (6): 729–45.

Eichenwald, Kurt. 2002. Enron paid huge bonuses in '01: Experts see a motive for cheating. *New York Times,* 1 March 2002, pp. A1, C8.

Glaeser, Edward, and Andrei Shleifer. 2001. Not-for-profit entrepreneurs. *Journal of Public Economics* 81 (1): 99–115.

Hansmann, Henry B. 1980. The role of nonprofit enterprise. *Yale Law Journal* 89 (5): 835–901.

Hirth, Richard. 1999. Consumer information and competition between nonprofit and for-profit nursing homes. *Journal of Health Economics* 18 (2): 219–40.

Holstrom, Bengt, and Paul Milgrom. 1991. Multitask principal agent analyses: Incentive contracts, asset ownership, and job design. *Journal of Law, Economics, and Organization* 7:24–52.

James, Estelle. 1983. How nonprofits grow: A model. *Journal of Policy Analysis and Management* 2 (3): 350–65.

Kapur, Kanika, and Burton A. Weisbrod. 2000. The roles of government and nonprofit suppliers in mixed industries. *Public Finance Review* 28 (4): 275–308.

Keeler, Emmett B., Glenn Melnick, and Jack Zwanziger. 1999. The changing effects of competition on nonprofit and for-profit hospital pricing behavior. *Journal of Health Economics* 18:69–86.

Lynk, William J. 1995. Nonprofit hospital mergers and the exercise of market power. *Journal of Law and Economics* 38:437–61.

Mauser, Elizabeth. 1998. "The importance of organizational form: Parent perceptions versus reality in the day care industry." In *Private action and the public good,* ed. Walter W. Powell, 124–33. New Haven: Yale University Press.

Migue, Jean Luc, and Gerard Belanger. 1974. Toward a general theory of managerial discretion. *Public Choice* 17:27–47.

Nicholson, Sean, Mark V. Pauly, Lawton R. Burns, Agnieshka Baumritter, and David A. Asch. 2000. Measuring community benefits provided by for-profit and nonprofit hospitals. *Health Affairs* 19 (6): 168–77.

Roomkin, Myron J., and Burton A. Weisbrod. 1999. Managerial compensation and incentives in for-profit and nonprofit hospitals. *Journal of Law, Economics and Organization* 15:750–81.

Schiff, Jerald, and Burton A. Weisbrod. 1991. Competition between for-profit and nonprofit organizations in commercial markets. *Annals of Public and Cooperative Economics* 62 (4): 619–39.

Schlesinger, Mark, and Robert Dorwart. 1984. Ownership and mental health services: A reappraisal of the shift toward privately owned facilities. *New England Journal of Medicine* 311:959–65.

Segal, Lewis, and Burton A. Weisbrod. 1998. Interdependence of commercial and donative revenues. In *To profit or not to profit: The commercial transformation of the nonprofit sector,* ed. Burton A. Weisbrod, 105–27. Cambridge: Cambridge University Press.

Sloan, Frank A. 1998. Commercialism in nonprofit hospitals. In *To Profit or not to Profit: The commercial transformation of the nonprofit sector,* ed. Burton A. Weisbrod, 151–68. Cambridge: Cambridge University Press.

———. 2000. Not-for-profit ownership and hospital behavior. In *Handbook of health economics,* ed. A. J. Culyer and J. P. Newhouse, 1142–74. New York: Elsevier Science.

Steinberg, Richard, and Burton A. Weisbrod. 2002. To give or to sell? That is the question: Or, price discrimination by nonprofit organizations with distributional objectives. Northwestern University, Department of Economics. Unpublished manuscript.

Weisbrod, Burton A. 1988. *The nonprofit economy.* Cambridge: Harvard University Press.

———. 1998a. Institutional form and organizational behavior. In *Private action and the public good,* ed. Walter W. Powell and Elisabeth S. Clemens, 124–33. New Haven, Conn.: Yale University Press.

———, ed. 1998b. *To profit or not to profit: The commercial transformation of nonprofit sector.* Cambridge: Cambridge University Press.

Weisbrod, Burton A., and Mark Schlesinger. 1986. Public, private, and nonprofit ownership and the response to asymmetric information: The case of nursing homes. In *The economics of nonprofit institutions: Studies in structure and policy,* ed. Susan Rose-Ackerman, 133–51. New York: Oxford University Press.

Wholey, Douglas R., Jon B. Christianson, John Engberg, and Cindy Bryce. 1997. HMO market structure and performance, 1985 to 1995. *Health Affairs* 16 (6): 75–84.

Wolf, Nancy, Burton A. Weisbrod, and Edward Bird. 1993. Supply of volunteer labor: The case of hospitals. *Nonprofit Management and Leadership* 4:23–45.

# A Renaissance Instrument to Support Nonprofits
## The Sale of Private Chapels in Florentine Churches

Jonathan Katz Nelson and Richard J. Zeckhauser

## 5.1 Introduction

The United States has long been "the land of nonprofits." When Alexis de Tocqueville visited in 1831–32, he noted America's distinctively widespread and successful use of voluntary associations (1976, 191–98). In recent decades, secular nonprofits in the United States have grown dramatically in size and importance. But the nonprofit as a crucial player in society is neither an exclusively modern nor a predominantly American phenomenon, and many nonprofits have a religious base. Our paper considers the operation of a historic, non-American, religious-based nonprofit: the Roman Catholic Church. The most important nonprofit in Renaissance Florence, the Church had two clear objectives: to address the needs of the parishioners, and to build churches in order to propagate the faith. To meet these objectives and to grow as an institution, the Church needed substantial private support from donors. It sold private chapels within churches to get such support, and these sales brought in significant tie-in revenues from burials, funerals, and commissioned masses. The monies supported the construction, expansion, and renovation of churches, and the religious services celebrated in the chapels provided employment for many priests and

Jonathan Katz Nelson teaches renaissance art history at Syracuse University in Florence and is a research associate at Harvard University's John F. Kennedy School of Government. Richard J. Zeckhauser is the Frank Plumpton Ramsey Professor of Political Economy at Harvard University's John F. Kennedy School of Government.

The authors thank conference participants, participants in the February 2002 College Art Association Annual Conference session on Conspicuous Commissions: Status Signaling Through Art in the Italian Renaissance, and Edward Glaeser and Bruce Weinberg, in particular, for helpful comments. We also thank Marta Alvarez Gonzalez for excellent research assistance.

members of religious orders. Those who provided financial support enjoyed the satisfaction of contributing to noble and spiritual endeavors—but they also reaped considerable private benefits, notably status, permanent recognition, and expectations of salvation. The Church thus sold benefits to donors to raise private funds, and transformed the private funds into public goods.

This "transformation" of contributions from wealthy merchants and bankers involved the production of art. In Renaissance Florence, the Church played a major role in stimulating the visual arts, architecture, and music, although this was not the mission of this institution. (Support of the arts is often a role of modern nonprofits, but the history of the Church demonstrates how faith-based organizations can deliver public services in this area.) Most visitors to Florence today assume that the extraordinary examples of religious art and architecture were commissioned by the local church, and that each church was largely controlled by the Vatican. In fact, most church art was privately commissioned and privately owned, and the local churches had a large degree of local autonomy. Even the chapels themselves, which contained most of the art, remained private property until modern times. The sale, decoration, and staffing of private chapels played a fundamental role in the fund-raising and financing of local churches in Renaissance Florence. The art produced benefited not only the donors, but also the general public and the Church. Most Florentines believed that works of art contributed to the glorification of God, the dignity of the Church, and the status of the city.

This paper focuses on Florentine churches over the course of about 250 years. This period begins in about 1280, when construction began on the first two churches to contain significant numbers of private chapels: the late medieval basilicas of Santa Croce and Santa Maria Novella. It ends in the early 1530s, when Renaissance Florence became a duchy, and the Medici family began to exercise much greater control over local churches, and specifically on the sale and decoration of private chapels. Sections 5.2–5.5 address the historical context of our analysis. Section 5.2 looks at the similarities between the functions and needs of modern nonprofits and the Renaissance Church, and how the selling of chapels provided a useful way to raise money. Section 5.3 discusses the currency and prices of Renaissance Florence, and the reasons for our chronological and geographic focus. Section 5.4 discusses the layout of Renaissance churches, including a description of private chapels, and the construction of these spaces. Section 5.5 explores funding, especially for construction costs, with special attention to the sale of private chapels.

Sections 5.6 and 5.7 consider why churches offered such spaces for sale, and why donors bought them. Section 5.6 addresses the supply side of chapels, reviewing the experience of three major churches. It argues that local churches supplied private chapels because the benefits they received—the direct payments for the chapels, tie-in revenues, and enhancements to the church—substantially outweighed the costs. Section 5.7 looks at the demand for chapels. Why were donors willing to pay significant amounts to obtain and decorate private chapels, and to pay for masses in these spaces? It argues that the demand arose because the donors could buy benefits not available elsewhere, primarily status and the hope for salvation. (Similarly, the donation of a building to a university both establishes a form of immortality for one's name and enhances one's status.) Section 5.8 consists of some short concluding remarks.

## 5.2 Renaissance and Modern Nonprofits

### 5.2.1 The Renaissance Church as a nonprofit

Lester Salamon noted that all nonprofits share six characteristics: They are organized, private, self-governing, voluntary, public benefit in nature, and they do not distribute any surplus or profits (Salamon 1999, 10–11). Clearly, the Renaissance Church in Italy was a highly organized and self-governing institution. It can, on the whole, be considered voluntary: Although virtually all Italians were Roman Catholics, and Church regulations demanded participation in certain activities, most people rarely attended mass. The Church also fits the "functional definition" of nonprofits, that they work in the public interest or for public purposes.[1] In Renaissance Italy, it offered several essential services that the local government could not or would not provide: education for children, charity for the poor, medical assistance for the sick, and of course the meeting of spiritual needs.

In theory, there were severe nondistribution constraints within the Renaissance Church:[2] the abbot of a monastery, for example, could not simply pocket surplus revenue. Nevertheless, the power of the Church and the high degree of local authority led to widespread abuses. Perhaps the most infamous example is one that stirred protests by Martin Luther in the early 1500s. After the Archbishop of Magdeburg, Germany, raised considerable funds through the sale of indulgences, he sent half to Rome for the construction of the church of St. Peter's, and kept half to pay off his debt with the local banking family. Among local churches in Florence, however, the profit derived from the sale of chapels and masses was used primarily to construct, maintain, and staff the building.

1. Weisbrod (1978) shows how nonprofit organizations overcome market failures in the provision of public goods to particular groups.
2. For the "nondistribution constraint" as a criterion for a nonprofits, see Hansmann (1990).

### 5.2.2   Free-Riders and Private Beneficiaries

The most critical challenge to many nonprofits, regardless of era or locale, is to secure financial support. Nonprofits that provide subsidized benefits to the community, but receive insufficient government funding to provide them, need support from private parties. Rarely will altruistic concerns be sufficiently powerful to ensure the needed funding. As Olson (1965) demonstrated in *The Logic of Collective Action,* voluntary organizations (those that lack coercive powers to tax) confront serious free-rider problems. Few individuals will provide substantial support to a truly collective undertaking; all will seek to capitalize on the contributions of others.

Olson (1965) perused the American landscape and found that successful nonprofit organizations had found a clever solution: They provided private benefits that are not readily available elsewhere in exchange for contributions. For example, the American Medical Association, once very powerful, could charge stiff dues because it provided its members with a valuable referral network. Similarly, as we shall see, the churches of Renaissance Florence provided individuals with aid to salvation—private masses, indulgences, and intramural burial spaces—in exchange for contributions.

Olson also briefly observed that individuals donate to charity "because of a desire for respectability or praise" (1965, 160 n. 91). We provide strong evidence that such status-seeking motivated church contributions in late medieval and early modern Italy. In particular, it motivated major donations to purchase chapels and significant expenditures to decorate them. Whether in Renaissance Florence or modern America, nonprofits capitalize on their distinctive capability to convey status. They publicly associate the donor with other distinguished individuals and families, and provide a socially acceptable way to signal one's wealth.[3]

### 5.2.3   Profits from the Provision of Private Benefits

To sell at a high markup, nonprofits must focus on goods and services where they have market power. Modern churches that own regular businesses can at best charge a modest "feel-good" premium beyond market price. Big premiums require major advantages in the market. Many wealthy churches today are able to accumulate wealth by providing the hope for a better afterlife in exchange for contributions. The most successful in this domain, such as the Mormon church (which requires tithing to stay in good stead), are often very explicit about possible states for one's eternal life.

---

3. For an action to be an effective signal, the prestigious group must find that action less costly to take than would others. For example, a college degree is less costly for smarter people to secure, and a costly chapel is more likely to be purchased by someone who is rich. See Spence (1974, especially chap. 8, "Status, Income, and Consumption," pp. 62–68); and Zeckhauser and Marks (1996).

What net profit does a nonprofit receive when it provides a private benefit in exchange for a contribution? Its net is the whole contribution less fund-raising costs and the costs of providing benefits to donors. Most Renaissance churches offered private masses, which could reduce the time that donors would spend in purgatory. These services required private masses, which led to the need for priests to conduct them.

Physical structures offer a different story. Contemporary universities tend to sell buildings at or sometimes below cost. However, they often sell rooms and spaces within them as well. Such double sales afford the potential for profit. The amount of profit depends significantly upon how essential the building is for the nonprofit. A needed dorm essentially reaps a 100 percent surplus from any donations; the university would have built the structure even if it had not received outside funds. But if the new building will house some little-used museum, say, even a contribution of the full construction cost may entail a loss, since the land will likely be given for free and maintenance will be required.

We demonstrate that chapels provided a wonderful way to finance the Renaissance church. First, the monopoly on afterlife benefits allowed churches to sell their goods and services—chapels and masses—at prices well above cost. Second, although chapels were sold to private parties, donors were rarely physically present in their chapels. These individuals selected and paid for the expensive decorations within chapels, and both the art and architecture added significantly to the magnificence of churches. Third, the church, like the modern university selling buildings, could boost prices due to the status benefits donors received.

The benefits to a church from the sale of a private chapel can be summarized as follows:

$$\text{Benefits} = (\text{price of chapel} - \text{cost of chapel})$$

$$+ \text{ value of benefits from tie-in sales}$$

$$+ \text{ value to church of decorated chapel}$$

The last term is what the church itself would have paid to secure the decorated chapel if no one would donate it. Our analysis shows that chapels generally sold at prices far above cost; the term in parentheses was solidly positive. The two additional terms made the proposition of selling private chapels even more attractive.

### 5.2.4  Residual Claimants

One characteristic feature of for-profit organizations is a clear residual claimant, namely the shareholders. This implies that all parts of the organization are working toward a common purpose. In many contemporary nonprofits, it is unclear who is the residual claimant. Theoretically, it would be the board, but the board members are not allowed to take any surplus. It might be posited that the board's preferences will guide the allocation of the surplus, but directors of the same nonprofit may have vastly different ideas of what the organization should do. Interestingly, the intended residual claimants in monastic churches were the religious orders, whose members had taken vows of poverty. They could not accept sums of money beyond living expenses, but they could accept prestigious buildings and beautiful decorations. These made their lives more pleasant, raised the respect of their profession, and, by adding to the glorification of God, contributed to one of the stated goals of the nonprofit to which they had dedicated their lives.

Lay people usually dominated the building committees of medieval and Renaissance churches, and thus they often made key decisions on chapel sales. As we shall see, this was the situation in the church of Santo Spirito, where the building committee did not maximize revenues from the sale of chapels. Rather, it set low prices for some of the most prestigious chapels, which were purchased by members of the building committee. It is not clear to what extent this was self-dealing, as opposed to representing rewards for past and contemplated future contributions.

### 5.2.5   Focus on Posterity and Mission Drift

Nonprofit organizations can last much longer than the human life span. Harvard University has passed the 350-year mark, and the Catholic Church is into its third millennium. Conspicuous association with such an institution—say, by paying for a named and long-lived physical structure that it uses—provides a form of immortality. Such immortality is not achievable through either family or personal possessions, which change their names and ownership. How can a nonprofit assure current donors that the assets promised in return for their contributions will not be taken back in the future? Part of the answer is that since the nonprofit must continue to raise new funds, current management has to show fidelity to past donors; drawing down an endowment or allowing physical structures to languish can sound a death knell for a nonprofit.

Nevertheless, nonprofits can compromise their missions if they have a strong fund-raising orientation, especially one that relies heavily on the sale of private benefits. An organization may shift its goals in order to attract donors and funds. Fund-raising performance often becomes a prime marker of the success of the organization's leader, which further shifts his or her activities. In addition, donors may gain some control over the organization, and influence its direction. The original objectives of the organization then receive relatively less emphasis, and new goals emerge. With time, the mission of the organization tends to drift.

The history of the Catholic Church helps illustrate these dangers. In the late medieval period, it began to sell private benefits in order to support itself, and then to grow in numbers of physical structures and personnel. The activities surrounding these sales noticeably influenced the behavior of the individual churches involved. To support their staffs, many churches became virtual mass-and-funeral factories for a small number of wealthy benefactors. Partially as a reaction against these abuses, the Vatican in the late sixteenth century took an increasingly active role in regulating the sale of privately owned chapels (Swanson 1995). By the nineteenth century, private ownership of chapels had virtually disappeared, although private burial areas in churches can still be purchased today.[4] The Church, like other nonprofits, must balance its focus on posterity—and thus its fundraising activities—with efforts to limit the drift of its original mission.

### 5.3    Measures for and Focus of the Analysis

#### 5.3.1    Prices and Currency

Most studies of Renaissance art and architecture provide prices in florins only, but these figures are difficult to compare, given the ever increasing value of the florin in the Renaissance, and they are even harder to relate to our own times.[5] Following the example of Goldthwaite (1980), we compare prices to the rate of pay for unskilled construction workers, which remained extremely stable at roughly one-half lira per day from 1350 to 1527. A full-time laborer could hope to work at most about 270 days a year, given the large number of religious holidays. Goldthwaite estimated that during the entire period under consideration one man-year of unskilled labor was worth about 150 lire; the total yearly cost to provide one adult with essentials was 55 to 75 lire.[6]

#### 5.3.2    Chronological and Geographic Limits

We focus on Florence from about 1280 through the 1530s, for three reasons. First is the extraordinary reputation enjoyed then and now by the art and architecture produced in late medieval and Renaissance Florence. The Church not only employed and encouraged the patronage of major artists,

4. The new Catholic cathedral in Los Angeles is offering prestigious final resting spots for sale (1,300 crypts and 5,000 niches for ashes), with crypts starting at $50,000. See, "Cathedral in Los Angeles Sets Premium on Its Crypts," *New York Times,* 10 February 2002, p. 20.
5. The price of buildings, chapels, and their artistic decorations were usually calculated in florins, an internationally recognized gold-based coin, but wages and living expenses were usually given in lire. Between 1350 and 1500, the value of the lire to the florin fell in half from 3.5:1.0 to 7:1 (Goldthwaite and Mandich 1994; Cipolla 1990). Different currencies were used for different types of items. Similarly, some countries today employ dollars for major transactions, but the local currency for day-to-day purchases.
6. Man-year figures are always approximate, and we round off those above 20. Goldthwaite's (1980) data allow one to determine the lire/florin exchange rate and the rate of pay for any given year, and therefore enable us to hone the calculation of the cost of a man-year.

but also played a crucial role in the preservation of their work. Most surviving Renaissance works were made for private chapels in churches, and many of these objects and structures are now owned or protected by modern nonprofits.

A second reason to focus on Florence is the unusually rich quantity, quality, and variety of surviving documentation. The best known original source are the records of the *Catasto;* these and related financial records were made on several occasions in the 1400s and beyond (Herlihy and Klapish-Zuber 1988). Other significant documents include the private account books kept by merchants, a type of financial record particularly popular in Florence, and the account books and memorials kept by churches. Although this treasure trove of documentary material is exceptional for a major Renaissance city in Europe, it is highly fragmentary in comparison with the material available for modern economic studies.

As a result of the abundant source material, there are far more studies on the history and society of medieval and Renaissance Florence than on any other Italian city. The research of five scholars has been particularly important for this paper: Richard Goldthwaite (1968, 1980, 1993) on the construction industry, banks, and private wealth; Sharon Strocchia (1992) on Tuscan funerary rituals; and Samuel Cohn (1988, 1992) on wills in Tuscany.[7] In addition, the doctoral dissertations by Annegret Höger (1976) and Ena Giurescu (1997) offer crucial information on the origins of private chapels in Florence. Remarkably, given the plethora of research and publications on Renaissance architecture, no study has established a complete financial record of the total expenses and funding sources for the construction of a church. Very few sustained studies address the phenomenon of private chapels over the course of our period.[8]

A third motivation for our geographic focus is that private citizens played a particularly large role in the economy and government of late medieval and Renaissance Florence. Bankers and merchants paid for the vast majority of the church decorations and made substantial contributions toward the construction of churches. Perhaps in no other city were so many churches remodeled or rebuilt in order to accommodate private chapels. The economic sophistication of the Florentines, their abundance of liquid wealth, and their business leaders' need to display their status all contributed to the success and refinement of this fund-raising instrument for the leading Renaissance nonprofit (Goldthwaite 1993). The direct funding of the Renaissance Church in Florence by private individual and family donors provides a useful parallel to modern American nonprofits.

---

7. Unless otherwise stated, Strocchia provided the source for all references to funerals in the paper. On burials and strategies for preserving the memory of Florentines, see also Ciappelli and Rubin (2000).

8. For general essays, see Colvin (1991, chap. 10, "The Family Chapel in Renaissance Italy," pp. 190–217); and Nelson (forthcoming).

## 5.4   The Organization and Construction of Churches

### 5.4.1   Definitions

Since the Middle Ages, every major city in Europe has had a cathedral, the principal church of the diocese (which contained the cathedra or throne of the bishop) and several parish churches under the bishop's direct supervision.[9] In addition, vast numbers of monastic churches were built in this period; these constitute most of the examples in our study. Monastic churches were open to the general public but designed to meet the needs of the religious community that lived in the adjacent monastery or convent. Nearly all were basilicas; that is, they had an oblong plan and longitudinal axis, usually consisting of a central nave and side aisles. Transept arms extended from both sides of the main chapel or high altar, both located at the end of the nave (figs. 5.1, 5.3). Two significant architectural features in monastic churches were the choir, an enclosed structure usually located in front of the high altar, where the members of the order prayed and sang, and the rood screen, which bisected the nave, keeping women in the area further from the high altar (Hall 1979). The "religious" were the members of the orders—the friars, nuns, monks, and canons. Most male religious were not priests, so they could participate in but not officiate at mass. The most prominent orders throughout Europe, including Tuscany, were the Franciscans and Dominicans. Both were mendicant orders; their rule embraced collective poverty. The friars had no personal property, and thus they had to seek donations to support themselves, their churches, and their mission goals.

### 5.4.2   Private Chapels

During our period, the term "chapel" referred to any area where mass was conducted, and was virtually synonymous with the term "altar." Altar tables were attached to the side and entrance walls of churches, to columns, and even to rood screens. In this paper, however, we usually use "chapel" in the modern sense to refer to a discrete architectural area, with the altar table opposite the entrance. A chapel could be a spatial box defined by three walls, with the fourth side originally closed off by a metal gate, as in the churches of Santa Maria Novella and Santa Croce (figs. 5.1–5.5), or a shallow niche, as in the church of Santo Spirito (figs. 5.6–5.7). In most churches such spatial boxes were built in both arms of the transept; in many churches, such as San Lorenzo, chapels of this type also lined the side aisles.

9. For Renaissance Tuscany, see Bizzocchi (1987). Sources for the following general comments about the nature and organization of the church can be found in the volumes already mentioned (Goldthwaite 1993; Strocchia 1992; Cohn 1992; Colvin 1991) as well as Swanson (1995) and Vauchez (1998–1999).

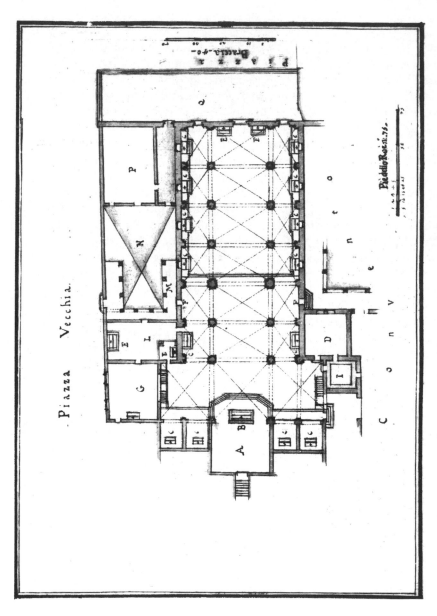

**Fig. 5.1**  **Florence, Church of Santa Maria Novella, plan of interior, drawing, eighteenth century**

*Source:* Florence, Kunsthistorisches Institut.

*Notes:* Entrance at right; main chapel at left (A); high altar (B); private chapels (C) in aisles along the nave and in transept arms on either side of main chapel; "exceptional" chapels (I, G); sacristy (D).

**Fig. 5.2   Florence, Church of Santa Maria Novella, nave and side aisles**

*Source:* See figure 5.1.

*Notes:* View is toward high altar and main (Tornabuoni) chapel, with frescoes by Domenico Ghirlandaio, late fifteenth century. Chapels visible in side aisles, including the Lenzi Chapel on the left, with Masaccio's *Trinity,* early fifteenth century.

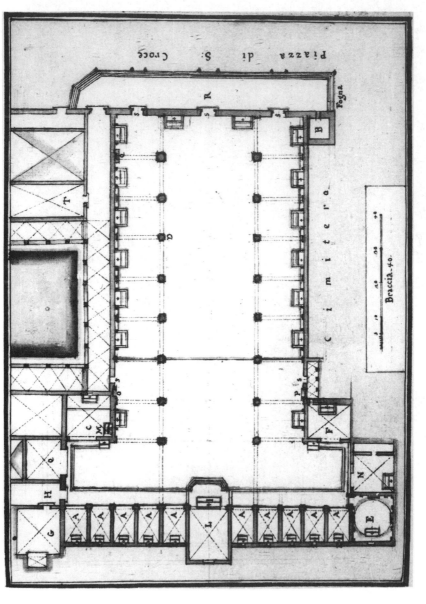

**Fig. 5.3   Florence, Church of Santa Croce, plan of interior, drawing, eighteenth century**

*Source:* See figure 5.1.

*Notes:* Entrance at right (L); high altar (I); private chapels in aisles along the nave, and in transept arms on either side of main chapel (A); "exceptional" chapels (N, E); sacristy (G).

*Interno del Tempio di S. Croce di Firenze*

**Fig. 5.4    Florence, Church of Santa Croce, view of interior, engraving, nineteenth century**

*Source:* See figure 5.1.

*Notes:* View is toward high altar and main (Alberti) chapel; chapels visible in side aisles.

**Fig. 5.5    Florence, Church of Santa Croce, view of two chapels to right of high altar**

*Source:* See figure 5.1.

*Notes:* Bardi Chapel (left), Peruzzi Chapel (right), both with frescoes by Giotto, early fourteenth century.

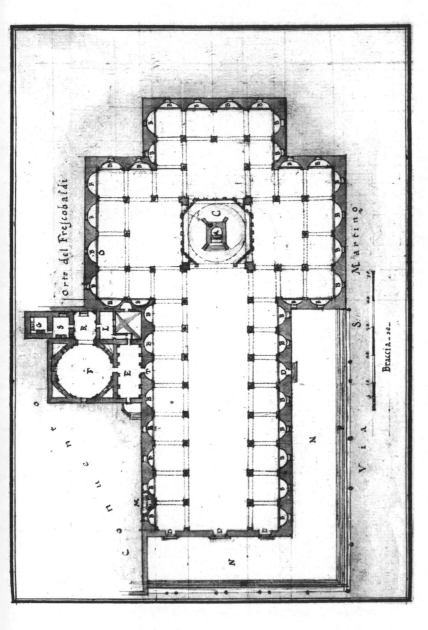

**Fig. 5.6  Florence, Church of Santo Spirito, plan of interior, drawing, eighteenth century**

*Source:* See figure 5.1.

*Notes:* Entrance at left (D); main chapel at right (C); high altar (A); private chapels in aisles along the nave and transept (B); sacristy (F).

**Fig. 5.7    Florence, Church of Santo Spirito, view of three chapels in transept**
*Source:* See figure 5.1.

*Notes:* The chapel on the far right is indicated with an "O" in figure 5.6, on the "Orto del Frescobaldi" side. All chapels have original architectural elements designed by Brunelleschi, early fifteenth century, and original altar tables, altarpieces, frames, and altar frontals from the late fifteenth to the early sixteenth centuries.

Most chapels and wall altars were private property. The main exceptions in Florence were the cathedral, which did not have private chapels, and the high chapels in some monastic churches, which remained the property of the religious orders. The rights to private chapels were sold most often to individuals or families, including brothers and extended clans, but at times to groups such as lay brotherhoods or trade associations.[10] The main function of a chapel was as a setting for memorial masses, not as a place for individuals to attend mass. In addition, many private chapels provided burial places for donors and their families.

In Florence, the first churches with significant numbers of private chapels are in two basilicas built for the leading mendicant orders, which were both rebuilt in the late 1200s and early 1300s. The Dominican church of Santa Maria Novella has four spatial box chapels in the transept (figs. 5.1–5.2), and the slightly later Franciscan church of Santa Croce has ten

10. By way of contrast, most private chapels in Venice were owned by confraternities or *scuole.* Although the purchasers of chapels received private property in return, they were regularly described in Renaissance Italy as benefactors, and we refer to them as donors.

(figs. 5.3–5.5). In the later Middle Ages, the new class of extremely wealthy and status-conscious merchants created a strong demand for private chapels. By the late 1300s, these chapels had became popular across Europe, especially in affluent commercial cities such as Florence, and they line the walls of most late medieval and Renaissance churches.

The sale of private chapels strongly affected church architecture. In fifteenth-century Florence, architects created plans that allowed for more of these privately owned spaces (Goldthwaite 1993, 122–23). In San Lorenzo and Santo Spirito, for example, Brunelleschi abandoned the tradition of wall altars along the aisles and made plans for a series of spatial chapels (Saalman 1993; and figs. 5.6–5.7 of this chapter). The advantages of this arrangement were sufficiently great that other churches, including Cestello, were remodeled, and the designs for new churches provided for spatial chapels along the side walls (Luchs 1977; and fig. 5.8).

For most practical purposes, these chapels were private property, and identified as such by conspicuous inscriptions, coats of arms, and banners. Chapels were purchased, left to heirs, and in many cases resold. Other than priests, few people ever entered these spaces. Since the spatial box chapels were located in the transept, beyond the rood screen, they were off limits to women, and men would have found them locked with gates (Hall 1979). From a distance, visitors could appreciate the architecture and decorations in private chapels. However, the main images of many altarpieces were covered by curtains or shutters (Nova 1994). The paintings would be visible on special occasions, such as feast days or when masses were held at these altars.

Prestigious chapels were expensive. In the late 1400s, Piero del Tovaglia reasoned, "If I spend 2,000 florins on my townhouse [*palazzo*], my dwelling on earth, then 500 devoted to my residence in the next life seem to me money well spent" (Kent 1995, 183). This wealthy Florentine evidently planned on spending 500 florins for his private chapel and tomb. The purchase price of a private chapel constituted only part of the total cost, often less than half. The related tie-in expenses were furnishing the chapel with an altar and required liturgical instruments, decorating the space, and providing funds for priests to say masses. In the late 1400s, Filippo Strozzi spent 300 florins (sixteen man-years)—the standard price for a private chapel in a main church—on a chapel in Santa Maria Novella and over 900 (forty-eight man-years) on the decorations and the tomb within (Sale 1976; the Strozzi chapel is in the right transept, adjacent to the main chapel, in fig. 5.1). The magnificence of the church benefited from such furnishings and decorations, and the coffers of the church benefited directly from the payment for masses.[11] These additional responsibilities constitute one

11. Some modern nonprofits that have constructed named buildings upon merely receiving their construction costs—or worse, only a fraction of them—have encountered financial difficulties. Many nonprofits now push hard to get some assurance of support for maintenance, recognizing that they may have to settle for fewer and less grand buildings.

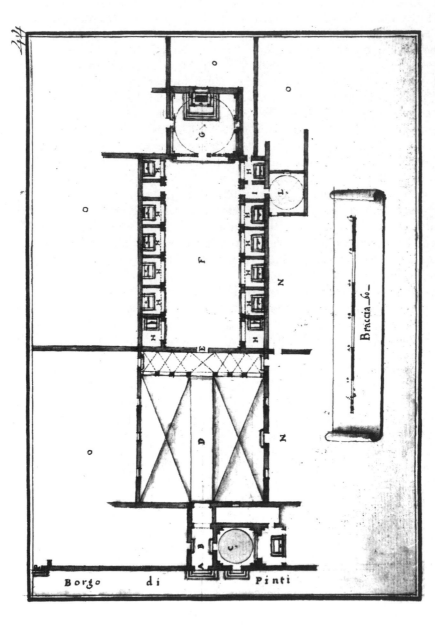

**Fig. 5.8** Florence, Church of Cestello (now Santa Maria Maddalena de' Pazzi), plan of interior, drawing, eighteenth century

*Source:* See figure 5.1.

*Notes:* Street entrance at left (A); courtyard (D); church entrance (E); nave (F); main chapel at right (G); private chapels along nave (H); sacristy (L).

significant difference between chapels and traditional private property: If owners failed in these obligations, they could lose the right to the chapels, as happened repeatedly in various churches during our period. A second unusual characteristic of chapels as private property is that their owners rarely visited them. Most donors probably went only a few times a year.

As context for these figures, in 1427, tax (*Catasto*) officials established the expected maintenance cost of a single adult at 14 florins, just under half of one man-year.[12] The yearly income of higher government officials in the fifteenth century was 100–150 florins, and that of a manager in a merchant-banking house was 100–200 florins (Goldthwaite 1993). Many of the patrons discussed in this paper were extremely affluent, with a personal wealth declared in *Catasto* records at 5,000 to 10,000 florins (Molho 1994). In 1427, Cosimo de' Medici was worth 100,000 florins (3,137 man-years; Kent 2000). Other financial records reveal that the personal assets of some prominent donors were considerably higher: In 1377 Niccolò di Jacopo Alberti was worth 340,000 florins (10,741 man-years; Strocchia 1992, 77), and in 1491 Filippo Strozzi was worth 116,000 florins (6,138 man-years; Goldthwaite 1968, 60, 63).

### 5.4.3    Church Construction Boom

Florence witnessed an explosion in the number and size of its churches in our period. This development was not a response to demographic expansion. Even by the mid-1500s, the population had not regained its level of 1348 when the Black Death wiped out one-half to two-thirds of the residents (Cohn 1992). Nevertheless, the number of churches had dramatically increased, and many of the older buildings had been extensively restored. The quantity of these monuments, the modern style of their architecture, and the quality of the art they contained were not necessary for the traditional functions of the Church: masses, confession, charity, and education. However, the construction boom brought several advantages to the priests and the religious in local churches. The new or renovated buildings enhanced the prestige of the Church and religious orders, and they attracted considerable additional funds that permitted an increase in the number of the priests and religious and an improvement in the quality of their lives.

### 5.4.4    Public Goods from Church Construction

Most Florentines believed that the construction or major renovation of a church brought two major public goods. First, churches glorified God, the Virgin, and the saints—a larger, more beautiful building was inter-

---

12. The *Catasto* was a financial statement that included assessments of real estate and liquid wealth; this provided the basis for the government to levy forced loans. For practical purposes, such loans can be compared with taxes (see Goldthwaite 1968).

preted as expressing greater praise to these holy figures, a benefit to all residents in the city. Within the religious orders, this view had to be balanced against the ideals of austerity and simplicity, especially those championed by St. Francis (Trexler 1989). For his followers, indeed for all Christians, the primary justification for such buildings and their decoration was the glorification of God. New and renovated churches added to a city's beauty and reputation, another public good for its residents. This view was often expressed both explicitly and implicitly by medieval and Renaissance sources. This was a period of extraordinary competition between neighboring Italian city-states, such as Florence, Siena, and Pisa. This atmosphere encouraged governments and citizens to praise their cities in public and private. A wide range of surviving documents, from formal decrees and academic discourses to travel books and private journals, describe the beauty and justify the reputations of cities by celebrating their major architectural monuments, especially each city's cathedral and most prominent churches.

Some of the public goods attributed to local churches benefited a defined population, and might be thought of as "bounded" public goods. In a modern society, this term could apply to a public park in the suburbs, which overwhelmingly helps local residents, although outsiders may also use it occasionally. In our period, the residents of Florence and most other large European cities had an extremely developed sense of belonging to particular neighborhoods (Eckstein 1995). Florence was divided into four quarters, each of which was partitioned into districts. The construction or renovation of a local church would add to the beauty of the entire city, but would especially improve the status of a particular neighborhood. In addition, medieval and Renaissance accounts often refer to churches and the art within as fulfilling an obligation to holy figures, and expressed the hope that such commissions would bring more benefits. These obligations and hopes were felt most strongly by those who worshiped in the new or renovated church.

### 5.4.5   Construction Costs

The single largest expense for local churches was construction costs for the church and related buildings. Other major expenses fall into three main categories: church decoration, including stained glass windows, frescoes, statues, and altarpieces; staff living expenses for the religious, including room, board, and clothing; and religious functions, including liturgical objects, special vestments, and candle wax. Local churches employed architects and workers to construct buildings or chapels. Private individuals rarely paid for these expenses directly but they did hire artists to decorate private chapels, and they purchased the many objects needed for masses at private altars.

Partial construction costs for several fifteen-century churches in Florence have been collected and analyzed by Goldthwaite. The most complete data are for Santo Spirito, largely rebuilt between 1477 and 1491 (figs. 5.6–5.7). For these years, the detailed account books itemize construction costs of 83,172 lire (554 man-years) for the main church. In 1449–1450, the much smaller church of San Pancrazio was said to cost 5,500 florins (176 man-years).[13] For the medium-sized church of San Salvatore, the merchant Castello Quaratesi bequeathed 14,000 florins (523 man-years) in 1465, but when the building was completed at the end of the century, the private chapels were then sold to raise additional funds.[14]

### 5.4.6   Chapel Costs

Original documents and modern authors often indicate the price of chapels, or the amount of money left in wills for these spaces, but the cost of actually building chapels is rarely discussed and is extremely difficult to determine. Since some churches had considerable market power in chapel sales, the gap between price and cost might be great.

One extremely valuable source is the account book for the church of Cestello (Luchs 1977; fig. 5.8). In the early 1480s, this church was built with uninterrupted nave walls that led to the only chapel, the high altar. In 1488, plans were made to add eight new chapels in the nave, four on each side. To build them, the side walls had to be pierced and new spatial box chapels added, a process much more costly than building chapels in a new church. The Cestello patrons paid 50 to 70 florins (2.2–3.1 man-years) for their chapels, about a quarter of the price of chapels at Santo Spirito at the time. Only the Cestello sums correspond to actual building costs. Most of its chapels cost between 50 and 60 florins to build for the walls only, excluding the window, altar table, and decorations.[15] Documents for San Lorenzo also provide some information on chapel costs. Here, the nave was built to include side chapels; between 1463 and 1465, patrons paid 125 florins (5.5 man-years) each to the masons responsible for building the church. This figure probably includes at least some of the cost of the side aisles, and perhaps of the central nave as well.

### 5.4.7   Construction Decisions

Only the Vatican could grant approval for construction of all chapels, and thus for the creation or transformation of local churches. This meant that all major proposals needed powerful political and religious backers,

---

13. Construction of the cloister, or living quarter for the friars, was included in the figure for San Pancrazio but not for Santo Spirito.

14. This approach is much in the spirit of the contemporary university, which sells a building to one person, then sells rooms within it to others. Often such rooms are not sold until years after the building is completed.

15. No explanation is given for the considerable differences in construction costs, which ranged from 50 to 70 florins.

and generous payments to numerous members of the ecclesiastical hierarchy were common. Approval, however, did not translate into financial support or a tax. In a typical arrangement, a religious order was offered a piece of publicly owned or private land, together with some funds for construction. Over a long period, the religious raised additional monies to build. The difficulty of this enterprise helps explain why the construction of major churches often took a century or longer.[16]

The role of the Vatican should not be overstated; the Roman Catholic Church was less centralized in the medieval and Renaissance periods than after the Council of Trent in the 1560s. Even after that date, the Vatican had a more modest role than today in directing local churches. In the period under study, local churches were run by priors or abbots, named (or at least approved) by the local bishops. Priors made most decisions regarding day-to-day operations of the church, but major decisions were subject to approval by Rome.[17] The decision to construct, expand, or renovate a church could be made in many ways, and for a wide variety of reasons. Surviving evidence indicates a very fluid situation that was not regulated by any single procedure or governing body. Proposals could be advanced from a city government, ruling family, wealthy merchant, or religious order.

In late medieval and Renaissance Italy, the management of construction projects, including new churches, was usually directed by the *opera,* the "board of works" or "building committee" (Haines and Riccetti 1996; Goldthwaite 1980, 90–94). The *operai,* or committee members, were responsible for all major decisions concerning the new structure: They raised and distributed funds, selected the architect, approved plans and subsequent alterations, authorized contracts, hired laborers, and purchased materials. They could determine costs and prices of chapels, although sales had to be approved by ecclesiastical officials. Although members of religious orders might serve on a building committee, this institution was dominated by laymen, usually wealthy, respected figures from the local community. Within the city of Florence, most of the powerful church officials, influential building committee members, and principal donors to churches belonged to only a few clans. This was particularly true of monastic churches, since each prominent family would often support and send a family member to a particular religious order. When negotiations were conducted by churchmen and committee members who belonged to the same or allied families, interests often coincided nicely.

16. Many modern nonprofits also have construction activities lasting more than a century, although rarely for a single building.

17. A modern analogy might be a state university system or a large private university; most appointments and financial decisions are made by the local colleges and universities, and are generally approved by the chancellor.

## 5.5    Funding Church Construction

In the 1400s, the construction of most Florentine churches was supported by private donations (usually in exchange for chapels) and not by contributions from the government, Vatican, or religious orders. We now consider what each group contributed for what and when.

### 5.5.1    Government Funding

Government funding does not play a significant role in our model of how the Renaissance Church transformed private funds into public goods. As we shall see, however, government grants served as seed money for the construction of several medieval churches, which then turned to the private sector for additional support. Before 1400, substantial government funds had been given to the three most prominent new churches in Florence—the cathedral, Santa Maria Novella, and Santa Croce—and the commune had plans to finance the church of Santo Spirito.[18] Santa Maria Novella and Santa Croce, both built in the late 1200s for new mendicant orders, were the first churches in Florence to contain significant numbers of private chapels.[19] According to Giurescu (1997), the contributions given by the commune of Florence, together with some unrestricted private donations, covered the basic construction costs of both churches. Despite such support, both churches relied heavily on funds raised through the sale of chapels and their accompaniments.

### 5.5.2    Vatican and Religious Orders

The main financial support from the popes and cardinals for church construction and renovation provided for the basilicas under the direct control of the Vatican and the titular churches of individual cardinals. In the 1200s and early 1300s, the Vatican played a major role in encouraging the new mendicant orders, and contributed to the building and decoration of their churches. In later periods, however, the Vatican and the religious orders usually viewed local churches as sources of income, not as recipients for their largesse. Tithes, for example, were collected at the local level, but they were not given to local churches. Most of these funds remained with the local ecclesiastical officials, who would give a percentage to the Vatican, and to the individuals or organizations that actually collected the tithes, such as the Medici bank.

18. As discussed below, the construction funds for Santo Spirito were raised from the sale of private chapels; but starting in 1445, the friars there and at Santa Maria del Carmine did receive proceeds from a salt tax to help offset expenses.
19. All information relating to the early history of these churches derives from Giurescu (1997).

### 5.5.3   Private Donations and Indulgences

Beginning in the mid-1200s, a series of Vatican regulations provided crucial support for local churches. These bulls allowed for the burial of laymen within the walls of the churches and for the sale of indulgences. With the invention of purgatory in the late medieval period, Christians learned that the souls of most people would reach heaven only after spending an extended period in this transitional area (Le Goff 1981). Priests could absolve the guilt of sinners, but they still had to repay their debt to God by suffering punishment. According to the theory of indulgences, the period of punishment could be reduced by various types of good deeds, including donations. In the late 1400s, for example, Cardinal Albert of Brandenburg calculated that the indulgences he had obtained for himself could reduce his stay in purgatory by 39,245,120 years.

The fund-raising opportunities offered by the sale of indulgences attracted many church officials. One possibility was to sell written indulgences to those who visited the church. In Florence, it was more popular to offer indulgences at no cost to visitors on certain days, guaranteeing high attendance. For example, a papal bull of 1344 informed the faithful that they could reduce their stay in purgatory by 515 days by attending mass on Thomas' feast day at Santa Maria Novella (Giurescu 1997, 207). The indulgences given for attending masses in specific chapels naturally raised the prestige of those spaces; this encouraged contributions by private individuals to purchase and decorate such chapels.

The most direct way to gain indulgences was to donate cash or property. In 1476, Pope Sixtus IV sold indulgences that benefited the souls of the dead to raise funds for the reconstruction of St. Peter's in Rome. The mendicant friars, who took vows of personal poverty, were well suited to warn moneylenders and traders about the punishments awaiting those with ill-gotten riches, and to encourage them to make substantial donations. A series of bulls from the 1200s gave the Dominican and Franciscan friars in Florence the authority to accept funds in exchange for reducing the punishment for usury (Giurescu 1997, 2–3). This practice, however, was not always accepted. Saint Antoninus, the Archbishop of Florence in the mid-1400s, objected to this type of barter-for-salvation (Gaston 1987). (Even today, the question of what constitutes an acceptable quid pro quo for donations is often an issue with nonprofits, and Antoninus' concerns fall in this category.[20])

The desire to reduce one's time in purgatory surely encouraged some of the generous unrestricted grants left to Santa Maria Novella and Santa Croce. Giurescu (1997) states that these funds, combined with the sub-

---

20. For example, what edge, if any, should the children of large donors have in getting into prestigious colleges?

stantial contributions from the commune of Florence, paid for the construction of the main body of both Santa Maria Novella and Santa Croce (figs. 5.1–5.5). This includes the nave and transept, the latter with rows of chapels. Regulations about indulgences and burial encouraged private donations to churches across Europe. In his study of nearly 3,400 wills drawn up between 1276 to 1425 in six central Italian cities, Cohn (1992) documented a major change in the years following the plague of 1362–1363 (and not immediately after Black Death in 1348, as generally expected). In the earlier period, he found a large number of small, unrestricted grants to churches or other institutions, such as hospitals. Testators rarely asked the institutions for anything in return. In the later period, Cohn found a smaller number of far larger gifts, and these grants were usually restricted. As part of the growing "cult of remembrance," testators arranged their bequests to obtain burial rights, private chapels, and commemorative masses.

## 5.6 The Supply Side: Benefits to Churches from the Sale of Chapels and from Tie-in Sales

### 5.6.1 Sale of Chapels

Our principal argument is that churches were eager to sell private chapels as part of their fund-raising strategy. Such sales produced significant additional benefits because donors also had to pay for other goods and services, such as chapel decoration and masses. The churches also received the benefit of more magnificent structures, both in scale and in decoration. Basically, what the churches received far exceeded any costs of provision. Although magnificent churches provided benefits to the neighborhoods and the worshippers, the biggest beneficiaries from the chapel sales were the priests and members of religious orders associated with the individual churches. They were able to work in beautiful surroundings, participate in vibrant and growing institutions, and secure employment.[21] We begin our discussion of supply by considering chapel sales at three major churches.

### Santa Maria Novella and Santa Croce

By the 1330s, the friars at both Santa Maria Novella and Santa Croce had sold the patronage rights to most of the original transept chapels. In exchange for the purchase of a chapel, and the commitment to outfit and

21. Thus, support of a church might be thought of as a "directed good." Although providing benefits to a general public, a directed good provides dramatically disproportionate benefits to a small segment of the population. In the contemporary context, the provision of education is often identified as a public good, since it produces a better citizenry. But citizen X is the overwhelming beneficiary from his or her education, so that education is a directed good.

decorate it, a donor received the chapel together with a stipulated number of perpetual masses in the chapel and the right to burial there. This exchange established a pattern for raising funds that was imitated in virtually all Florentine churches for the rest of our period and beyond. The history and reasons behind the friars' dramatic and influential decision to sell chapels are rarely discussed, and few documents clarify these crucial points. According to Giurescu (1997), the mendicant orders sought funds from the wealthy merchants of Florence only after the completion of the transept and nave of Santa Maria Novella and Santa Croce. One previous document, however, suggests a very different scenario.

In his testament of 1292, the banker Donato Peruzzi left 200 lire (9.3 man-years) for a chapel to be built in the nearby church of Santa Croce, if plans for enlarging the church were completed within ten years of his death (Borsook and Tintori 1965, p. 95, appendix IA).[22] Donato was still alive in 1299, so he witnessed the beginning of the construction of new transept at Santa Croce in 1294. The friars gave the Peruzzi family a chapel in the south transept at an unknown date, but presumably before Giotto painted his celebrated frescoes there (fig. 5.5; about 1311–1316). Donato Peruzzi surely discussed his plans with the Franciscan friars before he drew up his will, and he clearly believed that it was possible to purchase a chapel in the church soon to be built. The friars probably intended to assign him one of the chapels on either side of the high altar, given that the chapels at the end of the transept were a later addition. Nevertheless, Peruzzi's plans to leave funds do not mean that he financed construction—laborers had to be paid in cash daily. The transept was built primarily with public funds; only after the friars received the bequest did they cede one of the chapels to the Peruzzi.

The Franciscan friars may have always intended for one or more chapels in the transept to be sold to donors. This could even help explain why they built ten chapels in the transept, whereas the earlier church of Santa Maria Novella has only four (figures 5.1, 5.3). This hypothesis suggests that the government grants served as seed money that allowed the Franciscans to build their church and thus obtain further funds from the private sector. Donato Peruzzi's will leaves open the possibility that at least some of the Santa Croce chapels were built on speculation. There is no doubt that the patronage rights for most of the transept chapels were sold after their construction. In 1334, Riccardo de' Bardi paid 200 florins (11 man-years) for his chapel in Santa Maria Novella. The price to obtain the rights to the high chapel was considerably higher. In his will of 1348, Albertaccio di Lapo degli Alberti left 2000 florins (67 man-years) for the endowment and

---

22. The original Latin document refers to "libras," which most authors render as *libber* (pounds), but in this context presumably indicates the lire coin.

decoration of the main chapel in Santa Croce, plus another 500 florins (17 man-years) for the materials and construction of his tomb.

Individual donations played an even more important role in the construction of the end chapels in the transepts of both churches. This type of chapel was defined by Trachtenberg as exceptional for its size, often double that of "standard" transept chapels; by its location at the end of the transepts; and by its elevation, atop a flight of stairs (Trachtenberg 1996; figures 5.1, 5.3). The construction history and unusual shape of these chapels indicate that they were built as additions to the transept, and were not part of the original plans for the churches. According to a new and convincing hypothesis by Giurescu (1997), wealthy private individuals left substantial funds to build these new spaces only after the standard chapels were completed. Donors thus commissioned the exceptional chapels, supplied construction costs, and altered the shape of the churches. The chapel at the end of the north transept in Santa Croce, for example, was built only after Michele Castellani, in his will of 1383, left 1,000 florins (24.4 man-years) for the construction costs.

*Santo Spirito*

The sale of private chapels also played a principal role in supplying the construction costs for Santo Spirito (Acidini Luchinat and Capretti 1996; and figs. 5.6–5.7 in this chapter). In 1433, the Augustian friars decided to rebuild their church. The new church, designed by Brunelleschi, was built between 1477 and 1491. According to the analyses of Goldthwaite, the construction was "largely financed by the sale of its many chapels" (1980, 100). If the donations given for the thirty-nine chapels contributed three-quarters of the total cost (83,172 lire), the average price would be about 1,600 lire (10.7 man-years), or about 262.3 florins. Here we can be relatively certain that the chapel price far exceeded the cost of building it. Each chapel consists of two steps and a shallow niche framed in local limestone; the flanking columns outside the chapels can be considered part of the side aisle. The additional cost of each chapel, in comparison to building a straight wall, would hardly add up to even 50 florins, the cost of piercing the wall and adding a chapel to the church of Cestello, implying at least an 80 percent profit on selling cost.[23]

The prices of the chapels at Santo Spirito, and at most other churches, were set by members of the *opera*. In theory, the Church would want the *opera* to maximize income derived from the sale of chapels. Since all chapels are the exact same size and shape, it should charge the highest prices for those in the best spots, close to the high altar. In fact, the very op-

---

23. This comparison understates Santo Spirito's profits, because it was planned to include side chapels, but these were added to Cestello.

posite took place on several occasions (Burke 1999). Each member of the *opera* obtained a chapel, creating the potential for self-dealing. At least some paid highly discounted rates (e.g., only 50 to 100 florins, or 2.2–4.4 man-years) for chapels in the transept; other donors, who were not members of the *opera*, had to pay higher fees (e.g., 150 florins) for less prestigious chapels in the nave. In the 1480s and 1490s, the price for at least six transept chapels was 300 florins (17.3 man-years).[24] But one of the most desirable chapels, behind the high altar, was given at no cost to Luca Pitti, a member of the *opera*. The friars intervened directly in the decision-making process in order to reward the local banker, of whom they said, "with his wisdom he has increased the income of the said *opera*" (Burke 1999). Pitti evidently received a chapel after he had made a large donation to the building committee. As with many nonprofits today, major donors were given valuable gifts in recognition of previous donations, and in hope of future ones. This important example shows that even with extensive documentation, recorded evidence about what churches received for chapels is likely to understate their long-term receipts.

### 5.6.2   Tie-in Arrangements with the Sale of Chapels

Donors were expected to outfit and adorn their chapels at their own expense. Although the church did not profit directly from these activities, it received honorably decorated spaces at no cost. Donors also purchased additional services from the church, sometimes at a later date. The most important such services were paid private masses, and funerals and burials.

*Outfitting Chapels*

Each chapel needed an altar table and crucifix, as well as the objects used during the mass, including missals, candlesticks, chalices, bells, ewers, cloths, censers, and priestly vestments (Gardner 1994). In prestigious chapels these objects were made of precious metals, and were often more expensive than the paintings and sculptures. For his chapel in Santa Maria Novella, for example, Filippo Strozzi spent 135 florins (6.1 man-years) between 1488 and 1490 on priestly vestments alone. For the altar table, tomb, and marble relief sculpture of the Madonna and Child, Filippo and his heirs paid 437 florins (25 man-years) to the sculptor Benedetto da Maiano (Sale 1976).

*Decorations*

Many chapels had altarpieces (usually painted), elaborate frames, frescoes, or stained glass windows, and more prominent chapels often had sev-

24. Blume (1995, 172 n. 33) records the price of 300 florins for the Biliotti, Ridolfi, Lanfredini, and Dei chapels. In 1493 the Nerli chapel cost 300 florins, and in 1495 the Segni chapel cost the unusually high price of 500 florins (31 man-years; see Luchs 1977, 159 n. 5). The Luti chapel cost 300 florins (see Burke 1999).

eral of these decorations (figs. 5.2, 5.5, 5.7). These objects, together with the tombs in chapels, comprise the vast majority of the Renaissance Church art that we admire today. These decorations were not required for the celebration of the mass, although altarpieces did fulfill the obligation that an image or inscription must identify the person, object, or mystery to which the altar was dedicated. During our period, the average cost for an altarpiece by a respected artist was about 100 florins, but some works naturally cost much more. For the fresco decorations in the Strozzi chapel, Filippino was paid 350 florins (19.3 man-years; Sale 1976). Cohn's analysis of wills made by Tuscans of widely different social classes, from humble shopkeepers to wealthy bankers, showed that the average sum left for sacred art was about 27 florins, about 10 percent of the average sum left for obtaining a chapel (Cohn 1992, 245).

*Paid Private Masses*

Like many nonprofits in the modern era, the Renaissance Church offered services for a fee: paid private masses. Donors invariably left funds for masses to be held in their chapels; for the churches, these represented a form of tie-in sale. These masses usually consisted of post mortem commemorations, and masses in honor of the patron saint or saints of the chapel and of the donor. These commemorations often included a meal, which could range from a simple repast for the celebrant to banquets for a large number of priests, friars, and other invited guests. The study of one community of friars shows that during eight months of 1528, the friars ate commemorative meals on more than one day in three (36.6 percent of days). This type of privately sponsored remembrance led to Luther's charge that the clergy "ate" off the dead (Strocchia 1992, 225). Payments for masses provided much of the income for most priests, and one modern scholar even observed that late medieval churches had become "veritable mass factories" (Oakley 1979, 118).

For a set fee, donors could pay for a number of masses to be said soon after a funeral. Among the most popular funeral formulas was the Gregorian mass series, which consisted of one mass daily for thirty days after death. In 1490, this option cost about 1 florin (14.3 man-days). Wealthy donors, however, often requested many more masses: in 1411, the testament by the widow of Andrea Cavalcanti left provisions for 1,000 masses, to be held within the first two months after her death, in a chapel in Santa Maria Novella. Across Florence, churches performed thousands of funerary masses each year.

Donors could also set up anniversary masses; these were usually officiated on the date of the donor's death, and on the feast day of the saint to whom the chapel was dedicated. To guarantee these complex and continuing services, testators placed restrictions on their gifts, often including inspection by heirs, with the threat of substituting alternative charities if wishes were not met.[25] In the 1400s, the average bequest for masses was 15 florins per year. Usually donors gave or shared the ownership of a farm or shop with the church; these properties were rented out to third parties, which provided income to pay for the masses. A new development in the late 1400s was short-term anniversary masses, to be performed five, ten, or twenty-five years after death. These less frequent and cheaper services allowed shopkeepers and small tradesmen to provide for their own spiritual well-being and remembrance. At the other end of the economic scale, some very wealthy donors created "chaplaincies," endowed positions designed to guarantee the singing of mass for the souls of specified persons (Colvin 1991, 152–189). A substantial endowment was required to support these chaplains; in 1433, for example, Luca di Marco left 1,000 florins (35 man-years) for the construction of his chapel in the church of San Lorenzo and the support of an associated chaplaincy.[26] To ensure that masses were carried out, donors often left only a small sum as a base salary ("prebend") for the chaplain, and a much higher amount for the performance of liturgical duties. By offering a range of options, from short-term anniversary masses to chaplaincies, price discrimination was introduced into the sale of remembrances.[27]

## Burials and Funerals

Funerals and burials brought considerable sums to local churches. Wealthy patrons regularly spent far more on funerals than on the altarpieces and frescoes that so captivate modern visitors to churches and museums. In the 1400s, the cost of prominent funerals ranged from 300 to 700 florins (8.1–19.6 years), excluding the price of tombs or commemorative masses, but a few exceptional funerals cost far more—up to 100 man-years.[28]

Most of this money was spent on candle wax, funeral clothes, and processions; payment for them did not go to the local churches. The friars and priests were paid directly to participate in the funerary procession, and they also received the appropriate clothes; this fabric could be reused or sold. At major funerals, the large wax candles were often lit for only a brief period, then donated to the church where the event took place. This

---

25. Donors to modern universities have equivalent concerns about fidelity to their wishes, and sometimes stretch contributions over time to establish precedents and make fidelity more likely.

26. For San Lorenzo, see Gaston (1987, 112–13). For prices for chaplaincies, often combined with those for transept chapels, see Elam (1992, 157–80).

27. In the world of academia, these arrangements might be compared to a conference, an annual lecture, and an endowed professorship.

28. The following examples for ceremonies in Florence and Naples are discussed in Strocchia (1992): 1353 (Acciaiuoli), 5,000 florins; 1377 (Alberti), 3,000 florins or 94.8 man-years; 1429 (Medici), 3,000 florins or 93.1 man-years; 1432 (Tornabuoni), 1056 florins or 36.4 man-years; 1491 (Strozzi), 1,222 florins or 64.7 man-years.

constituted a significant tie-in benefit for the church, given the remarkable amount of expensive wax purchased for funerals. The standard amounts were 10 to 20 pounds for artisans and 50 to 60 pounds for physicians and notaries, but wealthy citizens might purchase ten times this amount. At the small church of San Pier Maggiore, burial revenues from cloth, wax, and clerical fees account for 22 percent of the total income in the plague year of 1374, and a respectable 10 percent in a sampling of years with more normal mortality rates between 1374 and 1413 (Strocchia 1992, 91).

### 5.6.3   Private Chapels and Employment

If the Renaissance churches became mass and funeral "factories," they needed increasing numbers of workers to maintain their production. Many churches brought in outside priests on a contrast basis to perform post mortem commemorations. This practice became so widespread that an official decree in 1517 condemned clergy who neglected duties at their own churches in order to celebrate masses at other institutions for pay (Strocchia 1992, 225). Over time, however, the demand for privately sponsored masses and prayers called for an ever expanding number of priests and friars, allowing the religious orders to dramatically increase their numbers. This in turn led to the need for new or enlarged living quarters, and the construction of these convents and monasteries was often supported by private donations. The dramatic growth in the size of the religious orders, and in the number of priests and religions, created many new opportunities for promotion—new churches needed priors, and religious orders needed to fill their hierarchies.

### 5.7   The Demand Side: Benefits to Donors from the Purchase of Chapels

The incentives for churches to sell private chapels are clear. They needed vast funds for the construction, embellishment, and staffing of ecclesiastical structures, and they reaped a handsome profit and a continuing source of revenue from tie-in sales. But why should donors pay significantly above cost, or even just pay significantly, to purchase chapels that were so rarely used by them and their families? Goodwill and altruism would not be sufficient motivation; rather, the purchase of private chapels offered many benefits not available anywhere else. We analyze the two primary benefits: The hope of a speedy passage through purgatory would help the donors in the afterlife; and the status one reaped from being known as a generous donor to the church provided both immediate benefits and posthumous fame.[29]

---

29. Surviving evidence rarely allows us to determine the relative importance of these two benefits for any given donor, although the type of decoration may indicate the weight given to salvation or status.

### 5.7.1  Afterlife

Funerary masses and burial within private chapels offered the possibility of alleviating the pains of purgatory, a service that could not be purchased outside the Church. Donors rarely discussed this point in the surviving statements about chapels. Filippo Strozzi, for example, wrote about why he contributed funds to the renovation of three churches: "God having conceded temporal goods to me, I want to be grateful to Him for them" (Sale 1976, 18).[30] But the owners of individual chapels, familiar with theory of indulgences, must have considered their purchase and embellishment of these spaces to be good deeds that would count in their favor when they died. More directly, they paid for private masses in the expectation that these would advance the exit from purgatory.

Tombs located in chapels could also help donors in the afterlife. Saint Antoninus spelled out three advantages of burials within churches: The saints honored by the church would intercede on behalf of the deceased; the faithful, coming to church, would see the tomb and pray for the deceased; and the dead would be assured of rest undisturbed by demons (Gaston 1987, 131). Starting in the mid-1200s, a series of papal bulls gave Franciscan and Dominican friars permission to bury the faithful inside their churches, an honor previously reserved for the religious. The powerful desire for intramural burials led patrons to buy burial plots in the pavement of churches, and in the crypts below.[31]

For Renaissance Florentines who did not have a personal or family chapel, a prime motivation for acquiring one was to have burial ground—but the wish to be buried in a church does not sufficiently explain the proliferation of memorial chapels. Most families who had chapels in the transepts of Santa Maria Novella, Santa Croce, and Santo Spirito had at least one other chapel in a different church, and only one of these spaces was used for burial. Moreover, an omnipotent God would know who the donors were; a specific chapel associated with one's name was not needed.

### 5.7.2  Status

Girolamo Savonarola, the prior of San Marco in the 1490s, and (in)famous today for his bonfire of the vanities, understood that status was a major benefit of owning a chapel. The Dominican friar complained that he could not convince wealthy men in Florence to give 10 florins to the poor, but they would give 100 florins just to put their coat of arms on a

---

30. In the same letter of 1477, Filippo wrote, "God having granted us His grace, there is no harm in our recognizing it in some way."

31. According to Cohn's (1992, 143) analysis of Tuscan testaments, only 20 percent of wills made in the period before 1363 indicate a specific burial location, but in the early 1400s, about 66 percent are specific.

chapel. He accused the merchants: You do this "for your honor, not for the honor of God" (Gilbert 1980, 158). Statements by donors themselves support Savonarola's view. When Giovanni Tornabuoni drew up a contract for the fresco decoration of the high chapel in Santa Maria Novella (fig. 5.2), he presented this commission as "exaltation of his house and family," as well as "an act of piety and love of God . . . and [for] the enhancement of the said church and chapel" (Chambers 1970, 173–175). High status within one's local community was often identified by Renaissance authors as a goal in and of itself. It also brought other benefits. One could make advantageous marriage agreements for one's self or children. Status fostered the acquisition or retention of power in a period of constantly shifting political alliances; the Medici, for example, were banished from Florence three times over the period studied. Power in turn brought wealth.

Status was predominantly a function of wealth and social ties that often could not be demonstrated directly, particularly since religious leaders advocated humility and self-effacement. Sumptuary laws and local traditions also significantly limited displays of conspicuous consumption. Thus, substantial expenditures on publicly displayed prestigious works were often the best way to signal one's status and wealth. Many Renaissance texts present the construction of buildings, especially religious ones, as a virtuous activity, exemplifying the donor's "magnificence" (Fraser Jenkins 1970). When one paid for a specific commission like a chapel, one's identity could be prominently displayed. Patrons tried to distinguish themselves through the placement, type, and decoration of their chapels.

Private chapels succeeded in signaling status for two main reasons: They were exclusive and they were highly visible. In major Tuscan churches, the price of a chapel was beyond the means of all but the wealthy. According to Cohn (1992, 214), the average sum left for a chapel between 1276 and 1425 was 208.9 florins, excluding costs of masses and decorations; this is more than the total assets of most testators.[32] The even higher cost of decorating, outfitting, and staffing chapels strengthened the signal. Thus, if the chapel was finely decorated with luxurious materials or with works by respected artists, it further enhanced the donor's status. In effect, viewers could calibrate the donor's status by considering the size and intricacy of works, the cost of the materials, the distinction of the artists, and the location within the church.

Although entry into many chapels was blocked by gates, men in the church could easily gaze above and through the barriers at the decorated

32. This figure covers the period 1276 to 1425, during which the florin changed value dramatically, and so it cannot be converted into a single man-year equivalent. These figures apply to several cities and the surrounding countryside, so the price of a chapel in Florence was certainly far higher.

spaces. Private chapels displayed large and colorful indications of owner-ship: names, coats of arms, emblems, and banners. Savonarola himself fumed that donors had their symbols placed "on the back of vestments, so that when the priest stands at the altar, the arms can be seen well by all the people" (Gilbert 1980, 158). In the early fourteenth century, one donor even obliged the friars at Santa Maria Novella and Santa Croce to pro-claim each year, before the congregation, how generous he had been (Cohn 1992, 104–107). The Renaissance patrons who used their chapels and dec-orations to signal and advance their status would have little to learn from modern-day philanthropists.

## 5.8    Conclusion

Many nonprofit organizations have shown themselves to be remarkably durable. Long life for such organizations requires solid financing. Yet such organizations are in the public benefits business, which raises the free-rider dilemma. Many of the most successful modern nonprofits offer donors private benefits, often status and a form of immortality, in exchange for contributions. This mechanism helped drive Harvard University's recent $2.6 billion capital fund drive. The university received 490 gifts of $1 mil-lion or more each. Natural modesty, security concerns, and a desire to avoid solicitations by other nonprofits might motivate many donors to make their gifts anonymously. Those whose goal was merely to "give back to the university" might provide money to general funds such as the schol-arship pool, as opposed to a named specified purpose such as a professor-ship or building wing, which gives lasting recognition. But 94.5 percent of donors chose to be identified, and 84.2 percent of these gifts were made to named purposes.[33] Presumably Harvard's contemporary donors shared some of the same status and immortality goals as did donors to churches in Renaissance Florence. They were securing a permanent link to a presti-gious and long-lived institution.

Starting in the late medieval period, Florence's churches found an es-sential new instrument to raise money that allowed them to build and thrive: the sale of private chapels. This "commodity" was highly valued, could not be produced by others, and brought in considerable related benefits to the church. Since status was a donor goal, more prestigious churches could charge far higher prices. Beyond status, donors received burial locations, a form of immortality, and, with the purchase of accom-panying masses, the hope for a shorter stay in purgatory. The citizenry had their city beautified, their God glorified, and magnificent churches where they could worship. Thus the major nonprofits of Renaissance Florence, its

33. Personal conversations with Sarah Clark and Thomas Reardon, Harvard University Development Office, 19 March 2002.

churches, supported themselves by effecting a market transaction that exchanged private benefits for public goods.

# References

Acidini Luchinat, Cristina, and Elena Capretti, eds. 1996. *La chiesa e il convento di Santo Spirito a Firenze* (The church and the convent of Santo Spirito in Florence). Florence, Italy: Giunti.

Bizzocchi, Roberto. 1987. *Chiesa e potere nella Toscana del Quattrocento* (Church and power in fifteenth-century Tuscany). Bologna, Italy: Il Mulino.

Blume, Andrew C. 1995. Giovanni de' Bardi and Sandro Botticelli in Santo Spirito. *Jahrbuch der Berliner Museen* 73:169–83.

Borsook, Eve, and Leonetto Tintori. 1965. *Giotto: The Peruzzi chapel.* Turin, Italy: Fratelli Pozzo.

Burke, Jill. 1999. Form and power: Patronage and the visual arts in Florence c. 1478–1512. Ph.D. diss. University of London, Courtauld Institute.

Chambers, David S. 1970. *Patrons and artists in the Italian Renaissance.* London: Macmillan.

Ciappelli, Giovanni, and Patricia Rubin, eds. 2000. *Art, memory, and family in Renaissance Florence.* Cambridge: Cambridge University Press.

Cipolla, Carlo M. 1990. *Il governo della moneta a Firenze e a Milano nei secoli XIV–XVI* (The regulation of coinage in Florence and Milan, 14th–16th centuries). Bologna, Italy: Mulino.

Cohn, Samuel K., Jr. 1988. *Death and property in Siena, 1205–1800: Strategies for the afterlife.* Baltimore, Md.: Johns Hopkins University Press.

———. 1992. *The cult of remembrance and the Black Death: Six Renaissance cities in central Italy.* Baltimore, Md.: Johns Hopkins University Press.

Colvin, Howard. 1991. *Architecture and the after-life.* New Haven, Conn.: Yale University Press.

de Tocqueville, Alexis. 1976. *Democracy in America.* New York: Knopf. (Originally published in 1835.)

Eckstein, Nicholas A. 1995. *The district of the green dragon: Neighborhood life and social change in Renaissance Florence.* Florence, Italy: Olschki.

Elam, Caroline. 1992. Cosimo de' Medici and San Lorenzo. In *Cosimo "il Vecchio" de' Medici: Essays in commemoration of the 600th anniversary of Cosimo de' Medici's birth,* ed. Francis Ames-Lewis, 157–80. Oxford, U.K.: Claredon Press.

Fraser Jenkins, A. D. 1970. Cosimo de' Medici's patronage and the theory of magnificence. *Journal of the Warburg and Courtauld Institutes* 33:162–70.

Gardner, Julian. 1994. Altars, altarpieces, and art history: Legislation and usage. In *Italian altarpieces: Function and design 1250–1550,* ed. Eve Borsook and Fiorella Superbi Giofredi, 5–40. Oxford, U.K.: Clarendon Press.

Gaston, Robert. 1987. Liturgy and patronage in San Lorenzo, Florence, 1350–1650. In *Patronage, art, and society in Renaissance Italy,* ed. F. W. Kent and Patricia Simons, 111–34. Oxford, U.K.: Claredon Press.

Gilbert, Creighton E. 1980. *Italian art 1400–1500: Sources and documents.* Englewood Cliffs, N.J.: Prentice-Hall.

Giurescu, Ena. 1997. Family chapels in Santa Maria Novella and Santa Croce: Architecture, patronage, and competition. Ph.D. diss. New York University, Institute of Fine Arts.

Goldthwaite, Richard A. 1968. *Private wealth in Renaissance Florence.* Princeton, N.J.: Princeton University Press.

————. 1980. *The building of Renaissance Florence: An economic and social history.* Baltimore, Md.: Johns Hopkins University Press.

————. 1993. *Wealth and the demand for art in Italy 1300–1600.* Baltimore, Md.: Johns Hopkins University Press.

Goldthwaite, Richard A., and Giulio Mandich. 1994. *Studi sulla moneta fiorentina (secoli XIII–XVI)* (Studies on Florentine coinage [13th–16th centuries]). Florence, Italy: Olschki.

Haines, Margaret, and Lucio Riccetti, eds. 1996. *Opera: carattere e ruolo delle fabbriche cittadine fino all'inizio dell'età moderna* (*Opera:* The character and role of the civic corporations until the beginning of the modern era). Florence, Italy: Olschki.

Hall, Marcia B. 1979. *Renovation and counter-reformation: Vasari and Duke Cosimo in Sta. Maria Novella and Sta. Croce 1565–1577.* Oxford, U.K.: Claredon Press.

Hansmann, Henry. 1990. The role of nonprofit enterprise. *Yale Law Journal* 539:835–901.

Herlihy, David, and Christiane Klapish-Zuber. 1988. *I toscani e le loro famiglie Uno studio sul catasto fiorentino del 1427* (The Tuscans and their families: A study of the Florentine *catasto* of 1427), trans. M. Bensi. Milan, Italy: Mulino.

Höger, Annegret. 1976. Studien zur Entstehung der Familienkapelle und zu Familienkapellen und Altaren des Trecento in Florentiner Kirchen (Studies on the origin of family chapels and on 14th-century family chapels and altars in Florentine churches). Ph.D. diss. Bonn, Germany, University of Bonn.

Kent, Dale. 2000. *Cosimo de' Medici and the Florentine Renaissance: The patron's oeuvre.* New Haven, Conn.: Yale University Press.

Kent, F. William. 1995. Individuals and families as patrons of culture in Quattrocento Florence. In *Language and images in Renaissance Italy,* ed. Alison Brown, 111–34. Oxford, U.K.: Claredon Press.

Le Goff, Jacques. 1981. *La naissance du purgatoire* (The birth of purgatory). Paris: Gallimard.

Luchs, Alison. 1977. *Cestello: A Cistercian church of the Florentine Renaissance.* New York: Garland.

Molho, Anthony. 1994. *Marriage alliance in late medieval Florence.* Cambridge, Mass.: Harvard University Press.

Nelson, Jonathan Katz. Forthcoming. Memorial chapels in churches: The privatization and transformation of sacred spaces. In *Florence: Re-visioning the Renaissance city, Art, patronage, and the dynamics of space,* ed. Roger J. Crum and John T. Paoletti. Cambridge: Cambridge University Press.

Nova, Alessandro. 1994. Hangings, curtains, and shutters of sixteenth-century Lombard altarpieces. In *Italian altarpieces: Function and design 1250–1550,* ed. Eve Borsook and Fiorella Superbi Giofredi, 177–89. Oxford: Claredon Press.

Oakley, Francis. 1979. *The Western Church in the later Middle Ages.* Ithaca, N.Y.: Cornell University Press.

Olson, Mancur. 1965. *The logic of collective action: Public goods and the theory of groups.* Cambridge, Mass.: Harvard University Press.

Saalman, Howard. 1993. *Brunelleschi: The buildings.* London: Zwemmer.

Salamon, Lester M. 1999. *America's nonprofit sector: A primer.* New York: Foundation Center.

Salc, J. R. 1976. *The Strozzi chapel by Filippino Lippi in Santa Maria Novella.* Ann Arbor: Garland.

Spence, A. Michael. 1974. *Market signaling: Informational transfer in hiring and related screening processes.* Cambridge, Mass.: Harvard University Press.

Strocchia, Sharon T. 1992. *Death and ritual in Renaissance Florence.* Baltimore, Md.: Johns Hopkins University Press.

Swanson, R. N. 1995. *Religion and devotion in Europe, c. 1215–1515.* Cambridge: Cambridge University Press.

Trachtenberg, Marvin. 1996. On Brunelleschi's Old Sacristy as model for early church architecture. In *L'Église dans l'architecture de la Renaissance,* ed. Jean Guillaume, 9–40. Paris: Picard.

Trexler, Richard C. 1989. *Naked before the Father: The renunciation of Francis of Assisi.* New York: Peter Lang.

Vauchez, André, ed. 1998–99. *Dizionario enciclopedico del medioevo* (Encyclopedic dictionary of the Middle Ages), trans. Claudio Leonardi. Rome: Città Nuova.

Weisbrod, Burton. 1978. *The voluntary nonprofit sector: An economic analysis.* Lexington, Mass.: Lexington Books.

Zeckhauser, Richard J., and David V. P. Marks. 1996. Sign posting: The selective revelation of product information. In *Wise choices: Decisions, games, and negotiations,* ed. Richard J. Zeckhauser, Ralph L. Kenney, and James K. Sebenius, 22–41. Boston: Harvard Business School Press.

# 6

# Theories of Firm Behavior in the Nonprofit Sector
## A Synthesis and Empirical Evaluation

Anup Malani, Tomas Philipson, and Guy David

Much economic activity occurs in the not-for-profit (NFP) sector of the U.S. economy. Not-for-profit firms—defined primarily by their exemption from certain forms of taxation and by the requirement that the surplus of revenues over expenses not be distributed to the firm's owner or patron (the so-called nondistribution constraint)—are estimated to produce one-fifth of all American research and development, most of the economy's human capital that is not produced by on-the-job training, many important cultural products and services, and most health care services. Within the NFP sector, production is dominated by health care providers, which account for about one-half of NFP employment. Education and research make up the second largest component of NFP employment, at about 20 percent, followed by social services, such as child care and job training, at about 15 percent.

Given the importance of the NFP sector for economic activity, a large body of theoretical and empirical work has emerged to describe and document how NFP firms behave, focusing in particular on how they behave differently than for-profit (FP) firms. (In light of the large share of NFP production accounted for by health care providers, much of this work was developed with the health care industry in mind.) While this literature is extensive, it is not coordinated. There is no accepted theory of NFP behavior, and little of the empirical work is connected to—let alone compares—

Anup Malani is associate professor of law at the University of Virginia School of Law. Tomas Philipson is a professor in the Irving B. Harris Graduate School of Public Policy Studies and a faculty member in the Department of Economics and the Law School at the University of Chicago, and a research associate of the National Bureau of Economic Research. Guy David is a Ph.D. student in business-economics at the University of Chicago.

We are thankful to conference participants and the editor for comments and suggestions.

existing theories. The purpose of this paper is to begin to fill the gap. This paper attempts to synthesize a few of the dominant theories of NFP firms into a common framework, and to connect existing empirical literature on NFPs to this common theoretical framework. We retain the focus on health care. The goal will be to answer two sets of questions:

1. Do existing theories generate different predictions for NFP behavior with respect to a common set of observable outcomes (e.g., factor demand curves, firm size, response to demand or supply shocks) such that empirical work can determine which theory best describes NFP behavior? In short, what is the empirical content of existing theories of NFP firms?

2. Does empirical work exist that examines the behavior of NFP firms with respect to outcomes on which the different theories of NFP firms generate different predictions? In other words, does the existing empirical literature allow one to discriminate among the different theories of NFP firms?

The paper can be outlined as follows. Section 6.1 synthesizes existing theories of NFP behavior into a common empirical framework. The goal is to generate, for each theory, predictions regarding a common set of observable outcomes. The common framework insures that predictions for a given outcome from two different theories are mainly the product of the theories' assumptions regarding NFP firms, and not differences in modeling technology, demand, or the marketplace. A shortcoming of existing theories of NFP behavior is that the predictions of their authors have focused on NFP behavior almost exclusively at the firm level as opposed to at the industry (i.e., equilibrium) level. Section 6.1 concludes with an analysis of such predictions.

Section 6.2 extends existing theories by generating predictions about industry-level behavior in equilibrium under perfect competition. The approach is similar to that in Lakdawalla and Philipson (1998, 2002). Focusing on industry-level predictions is important because most empirical work that compares NFP and FP firms examines the behavior of these firms in equilibrium with mixed production. Section 6.2 concludes that there are few observable outcomes at the industry level with respect to which the different theories of NFPs generate different predictions.

Section 6.3 examines a large number of the existing empirical studies of NFP firms to determine the extent to which they provide evidence comparing the behavior of NFP and FP firms on outcomes with regard to which existing theories generate different predictions. Generally, we find that very few studies examine such outcomes and thus permit us to distinguish theories based on their empirical performance. Producing evidence regarding measures that permit such distinction appears to be a fertile ground for future research.

Section 6.4 concludes that, if forced to choose among existing theories, we would select theories which argue that the distinctive behavior of NFP firms can be explained by the altruistic motives of these firms' principals as most consistent with available evidence. This conclusion is subject to numerous caveats in addition to the limited value of the existing empirical studies to distinguish among existing theories. The most notable is that, because we were interested primarily in theories seeking to explain firm behavior (as opposed to employee or government behavior), the paper does not cover all possible theories of the NFP sector, including those that may potentially perform better from an empirical perspective. For example, Weisbrod (1975) considers the creation of NFP services as a product of imperfect Lindahl pricing of public goods. Another caveat is that our review of the empirical literature focuses exclusively on the health care sector. Our vision is limited in this way because NFP behavior in the health care sector is better studied than NFP behavior in other sectors, because health care providers dominate the NFP sector and because, unlike (say) the education industry, the health care industry is largely characterized by mixed NFP and FP production, which allows direct comparisons of NFP and FP behavior in equilibrium.

This paper relates to and complements existing reviews of the NFP literature (see, e.g., Pauly 1987, Rose-Ackerman 1996, and Sloan 2000). The main difference between this review and others lies in its objectives of attempting to draw out explicitly the differing, testable predictions of existing formal theories and of attempting to point out where the existing empirical evidence allows us to distinguish between those predictions. Although there are many existing surveys of the NFP sector, none of them to our knowledge appear to focus in an explicit and formal way on this objective.

## 6.1  Firm Behavior in the Nonprofit Sector: A Synthesis

This section presents a baseline model of the firm that can, with certain parameter restrictions, capture the essential features of the more dominant formalized theories of NFP firm behavior. The model starts with the standard neoclassical model of the firm, which has the advantage of being familiar to most readers, and adds three features. The firm is assumed to have an owner who may have preferences over the firm attributes other than profits. There may be restrictions on the income that the owner can draw from the firm (nondistribution constraint) and on the output decisions of the firm (implied, e.g., by fiduciary duties imposed by state law). Finally, government tax policies may cause the cost function and after-tax profits of NFP firms to deviate from those of FP firms. Careful specification of these three features permits the baseline model to mimic the essential features of existing theories of NFP firms. Incorporating each of the theories into a common theoretical framework in this manner has a number of advantages. First, it permits us to generate predictions regarding firm behavior that we can be sure are driven by the key assumptions each theory makes about how NFP firms operate, and not by differences in the way nonessential features of the theory (e.g., technology) are modeled. Second, the neoclassical model permits easy derivation of predictions regarding industry-level behavior in equilibrium, a feature that, surprisingly, is missing from most existing theories. Moreover, the formal modeling of a firm's owner allows us to make the choice of organizational form endogenous, also a feature missing in many existing models. This is important, not only because it introduces a dose of realism, but also because it may affect equilibrium dynamics, such as whether each model can sustain an equilibrium with mixed FP and NFP production as is observed in the health care and child care sectors.

This section proceeds in three parts. First, it sets forth the baseline model. Then it demonstrates how the baseline model can capture the essence of the three major theories of NFP firm behavior. One theory is explicitly based on the altruistic preferences of owners; another posits that the NFP firm is operated like a producer cooperative; and the final one is based on the view that NFP firms exist because they mitigate the incentives of firms to take advantage of consumers in market where important product attributes are noncontractible. The third part of this section presents a series of firm-level predictions implied by each theory. The predictions are generated from the baseline model employing the restrictions required to replicate the results of each theory. In many cases these predictions are new and therefore extensions of existing theories. We focus on predictions for a small set of outcomes that are measurable. The goal is to not just to develop testable predictions, but to focus on a common set of outcomes where the theories generate different predictions so that empirical observation can determine which theory performs better than the rest.

### 6.1.1     General Model

Consider a firm that has access to a production technology $F$ and whose owner or patron derives utility $u$ from consumption $z$, a vector of inputs $x$, output $y$ of the firm, and quality $q$ of the firm's output.[1] The firm's type is indicated by the index $i$, where $i = f$ indicates a FP firm, and $i = n$ indicates an NFP firm. Whether the firm is FP or NFP, the firm's profits are given by

$$(1) \qquad \pi^i(y, q) = p^i(y, q) \cdot y - c^i(y, q) + A^i,$$

where $p^i(y, q)$ is the inverse demand function, $c^i(y, q)$ is the cost function for quantity and quality of output,[2] and $A^i$ is donations from any source. We assume that the owner seeks to maximize her utility $u(z, y, x, q)$ subject

---

1. It is useful to think of the agent making decisions in an FP firm as the owner of the firm and in an NFP firm as the charitable donor or patron of the firm or as the head of the board that governs the firm. We assume there is no division between ownership (or patronage) and control.

2. The cost function $c^i(y, q)$ can equivalently be written as $wx^i(y, q)$, where $w$ is a vector of input prices and $x^i$ is the input demand function a firm of form $i$ faces. This alternative formulation permits easy analysis of cases where firms get independent utility (or disutility) from the use of inputs. We will use $c^i$ and $wx^i$ interchangeably throughout.

to the constraint that her consumption $z$ must be covered by income $I$ from the firm as allowed by the government.

If the firm is FP, that income is simply total profits. Thus the owner's/patron's budget constraint is

$$(2) \qquad z \le I^f = \pi^f = p^f \cdot y - wx + A^f,$$

where $w$ is a vector of input prices. (We shall omit the arguments $[y, q]$ of $p$, $c$, and $\pi$ to simplify our exposition, wherever the omission should cause no confusion.)

If the firm is NFP, cash income is constrained to be zero. This is known as the nondistribution constraint. The owner/patron can, however, draw noncash income in the form of perquisites such as a nice office and a company car. We can formalize this regulation of NFP income in the budget constraint.[3]

$$(3) \qquad z \le I^n = d(\pi^n) = d(p^n \cdot y - wx)$$

We assume $d(m) \le m$, reflecting the fact that the utility from cash is at least as high as the utility from perks because all perks can be purchased with cash.[4] Think of $d(m)$ as the income that would provide the same level of utility as $m$ dollars spent on perks. The function $d(m)$ is decreasing in the owner's/patron's relative distaste for perks versus cash and in the legal constraints the state imposes on the sorts of perks NFP firms can purchase for its patrons. In addition to the nondistribution constraint, NFPs may be subject to regulations requiring that they serve (e.g., a religious, charitable, scientific, or educational purpose; see Internal Revenue Code §501[c][3]) or that they satisfy certain fiduciary duties to the putative beneficiaries of the NFP firm. These constraints can be formalized by requiring $(y, q) \in N$, where $N$ represents the set of outputs satisfying this second type of NFP regulation. The benefit of NFP status is that NFP firms get tax breaks from the government that reduce their costs and that, under certain conditions, may be able to command higher prices in equilibrium based on consumer preferences for products produced by NFP firms. Formally, we can write the cost and price benefits of NFP status as

$$(4a) \quad c^n(y, q) \le c^f(y, q), \qquad c_y^n(y, q) \le c_y^f(y, q), \qquad c_q^n(y, q) \le c_q^f(y, q),$$

$$(4b) \qquad\qquad\qquad p^n(y, q) \ge p^f(y, q).$$

---

3. In both the NFP and FP cases, the owner/patron gets a cash wage for his labor. Because the NFP wage is constrained by law to be competitive and because the owner/patron is likely to be paid a salary rather than an hourly wage, we assume that the cash wage drawn from an NFP firm is the same as that from an FP firm and thus that wage can be omitted from the income statements in equations (2) and (3). Of course, if the owner's/patron's cash wage is proportional to output, then we may not be able to make this assumption because the two types of firms may produce different levels of output.

4. We ignore the discount on perks afforded by the tax code, which permits firms to treat perks as deductible business expenses because NFP firms need not pay corporate income taxes.

The owner of the FP firm has the induced utility function $v(\pi^f(y, q), y, x, q) = u(\pi^f(y, q), y, x, q)$ with income $I^f = \pi^f$, and the owner of the NFP firm has the induced utility function $v(d(\pi^n(y, q)), y, x, q) = u(d(\pi^n(y, q)), y, x, q)$ with income $I^n = d(\pi^n)$ and $(y, q)$ constrained to belong to $N$. Let $y^{i*}$, $q^{i*}$ be the optimal output and quality choices of an owner a firm of form $i$ with preferences $v$.

The nice feature of this baseline model is that it permits us to treat as endogenous the choice of organizational form. Thus, before entering a market, the owner/patron can choose whether to organize the firm as FP or NFP. The choice of organizational form requires a balancing of the costs and benefits of FP and NFP status given the owner's preferences. The costs of NFP status are the nondistribution constraint and the NFP regulations embodied in the constraint that $(y, q) \in N$; the benefits are the tax and price advantages. The owner/patron will choose NFP status for the firm if

$$(5) \quad v[d(\pi^n(y^{n*}, q^{n*})), y^{n*}, x(y^{n*}, q^{n*}), q^{n*}]$$
$$< v[\pi^f(y^{f*}, q^{f*}), y^{f*}, x(y^{f*}, q^{f*}), q^{f*}].$$

### 6.1.2  Altruism Models

The oldest and most common formal models of NFP institutions emphasize the role of altruistic intentions of NFP managers. This altruism is captured by including quantity and quality of output in the objective function of the firm.[5] The first paper to do this is Newhouse (1970).[6] That paper models NFP hospitals as maximizing utility over quantity and qual-

---

5. Including quantity or quality in a firm's utility function does not perfectly capture altruism. If a firm were truly altruistic, it would not care whether it supplied the market or another firm did. The only issue would be whether consumers were satisfied. Indeed, Friedman (1970) has criticized the literature for failing to explain why an altruistic firm would not simply take FP status, use its profits to purchase output from the most efficient firm on the market, and distributing this output to the needy.

One can justify the impure-preference assumptions of altruism models, however, in two ways. First, perhaps firms are not truly altruistic. Rather, they may seek the warm glow they get from actually serving the needy directly. Second, perhaps there are logistical problems with Friedman's solution. In markets characterized by information asymmetry between producers and purchasers, simply purchasing output and redistributing it will not insure that the needy get quality products. Or there may be search costs to finding the needy and those search costs may be lower for producers. Preston (1988) makes a similar point in response to the question why workers donate their time to socially beneficial organizations rather than work longer at their regular jobs and donate their wages, a donation which would be tax deductible.

Frank and Salkever (1991) have a model that includes total industry output in the utility function of firms. However, that model does not contrast NFP and FP firms. Rather, it is designed to explain the response of altruistic hospitals to increases in government production of health care.

6. See also Feldstein (1971) and Hansmann (1981). Long (1964) discusses a similar theory about the motivations of NFP firms, but does not formalize his model. Baumol and Bowen (1965) do the same, again without formalization. Baumol (1959) has a theory of a revenue-maximizing firm, but Baumol does not apply his theory to the NFP sector.

ity—but not profits—subject to a budget constraint.[7] The primary prediction of the Newhouse model is that NFP firms will have a bias toward producing in higher-quality markets. The return to the owner's/patron's producing greater quantity of higher-quality products is greater than the return from producing more and lower-quality products.

Lakdawalla and Philipson (1998, 2002) generalize Newhouse's model by including profits in the firm's objective function. Their paper also examines the behavior of NFP firms in equilibrium. As such the paper yields predictions regarding which owners/patrons choose NFP status for their firms, when we should expect to see mixed production versus just NFP or FP production, and for how markets with mixed production respond to demand and supply shocks. Only owners with output or quality preferences choose NFP status. The benefits of NFP status (access to donations) do not provide any advantages to owners/patrons interested only in income. Owners/patrons interested in quantity and perhaps quality start NFP firms only in product markets where there are donations to finance them. If able to secure donations, these owners'/patrons' preference for quantity produces the same equilibrium behavior from NFP firms as a FP firm interested only in profits but in possession of a technology that lowers the marginal costs of producing quantity. Thus FP firms will be the marginal firms in product markets with NFP production. For-profit firms will produce only where donations—assumed to be scarce—cannot sustain enough NFP firms to satisfy total market demand.

Lakdawalla and Philipson note that the response of markets with mixed production to demand and supply shocks depends on whether owners/patrons of NFP firms have, in addition to a preference for profits, a preference for quantity or a preference for both quantity and quality. If quantity only, an increase in demand will induce entry by FP firms (NFP firms are constrained by a limited supply of donations) and thus raise the FP share of output. If firms have heterogeneous costs, price will rise. Supply shocks, such as a reduction in NFP costs due to expanded tax breaks, will increase the share of NFP output. Conversely, an increase in public production, which has the same effect as reducing market demand for private production, trades off one-for-one with FP output. If NFP firms have a preference for quality as well, the results above hold for any given level of quality.

Capturing the altruism models in our general model is straightforward. The objective functions are virtually identical. Lakdawalla and Philipson's model contemplates the introduction of inputs into the owner's/patron's preferences. Because the authors do not explore this avenue, it can be assumed that (like in the Newhouse model) $v_x$ is zero. The main constraint imposed by a status of NFP in Lakdawalla and Philipson is that $N =$

---

7. The analysis is primarily graphical, but Phelps (1997) provides a mathematical formalization.

$\{(y, q) \mid \pi^n(y, q) = 0\}$. As a legal matter this is an unrealistic restriction: NFP firms can earn rents, they just cannot distribute them to owners. Under perfect competition, however, profits are driven to zero and thus the constraint of $N$ does not bind. There are no perks in the altruism models. Both the Lakdawalla and Philipson and the Newhouse models ignore the tax benefits of NFP status[8] and assume that consumers have no preference for products produced by NFPs.

### 6.1.3    Physician Cooperative Model

Pauly and Redisch (1973) propose an alternative to the altruism theory that models the NFP hospital as a physician cooperative. The theory can be justified in the following manner. Because doctors have superior medical knowledge, they have the potential to control resource allocation in the hospital. In an FP hospital there is an outside investor who, due to her claim on residual earnings, has an incentive to acquire the knowledge required to compete with doctors for control over resource decisions within the hospital.[9] Thus the doctors in an FP hospital do not make input and output decisions. In the NFP hospital, however, there is no residual claimant, so no party competes with the medical staff for control. Thus the doctors on the medical staff in an NFP hospital can perfect their authority over the hospital. These doctors treat the medical staff as a partnership and make input and output decisions to maximize the joint income of the medical staff.[10]

Pauly and Redisch analyze long-run equilibrium when all hospitals are NFP but there are three possible forms of organization for the medical staff.[11] The most interesting is the closed medical staff, which restricts staffing privileges (i.e., staff size) and pays each doctor on the staff

8. The absence of tax breaks for NFPs makes the choice of regulatory form trivial in Lakdawalla and Philipson's theory. Without tax advantages to NFP status, there is no reason an owner interested solely in profits would take NFP, even if perks were allowed. Exploring the baseline model with tax breaks and perks reveals a weakness with the Lakdawalla and Philipson model. The baseline model with purely profit-maximizing owners, tax breaks, and perks can yield the same equilibrium predictions as the Lakdawalla and Philipson model. The only difference is that NFP firms rather than FP firms would be the higher-cost firms. Another weakness in the Lakdawalla and Philipson theory is that it assumes NFP market share is financed by donations. Yet, in the hospital market, which is perhaps the largest sector with mixed production, donations make up a tiny fraction of revenue but NFPs dominate market share. Rose-Ackerman (1996, 705). It is hard to imagine that it is the small amount of donations to NFP hospitals that enables such hospitals to dominate the market.

9. In most FP hospitals, the outside investor is herself a physician (Gray 1993). This makes it easier for the outside investor to wrest control over resources from the medical staff.

10. Pauly and Redisch justify their model solely on the grounds that physicians, by virtue of their superior knowledge, have de facto control over hospital resources. They do not attempt to explain, for example, why physicians in a FP facility do not enjoy the same level of control as physicians in a NFP facility. Thus, the story we tell in this paragraph is an attempt to rationalize, as best we can, Pauly and Redisch's treatment of a NFP hospital, but not a FP hospital, as a physician cooperative.

11. Shalit (1977) constructs a model that is related to Pauly and Redisch's. His goal is to describe the equilibrium behavior of what he calls doctor-hospital cartels. The profit function

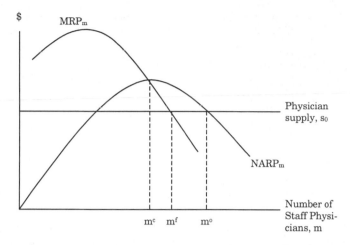

**Fig. 6.1    Long-run equilibrium in the physician cooperative model**

equally.[12] This staff sets the marginal revenue product (MRP) of the physician labor to the net average revenue product (NARP) of the physician. If $p$ is the total price for health care (including the hospital and physician charges), $m$ is physician labor, $k$ is physical capital (with rental price $r$), and $l$ is nonphysician labor (with wage $w$), then the equilibrium condition is

$$(6) \qquad MRP_m = (p + y \cdot p_y) \cdot y_m = \frac{p \cdot y - r \cdot k - w \cdot l}{m} = NARP_m$$

and $m^c$ in figure 6.1 is the closed staff's choice for the size of the physician staff.[13]

---

of these cartels is the same as that of the labor-managed firms of Pauly and Redisch, with doctors as the labor input and hospitals as the capital input. Shalit, however, does not describe or distinguish NFP hospitals as doctor-managed (or cartel) firms and FP hospitals as noncartels. In his model, doctors manage all health care firms, regardless of whether they are associated with NFP for FP hospital inputs.

12. The second type of staff is the open staff. Here the staff is not restricted and any physician who wishes to may join. Each doctor is still paid equally. In this case the staff is a common pool and physicians join until the net average revenue product of physician labor is equal to the marginal or opportunity cost of physician labor. If $s_0$ is the long-run physician supply curve, the result is a staff size of $m^o > m^c$.

The third form of organization for the medical staff is premised on insight that closed medical staffs can increase the rents that they earn if they can add doctors to the medical staff, but treat them as hired or associate physicians and pay them the marginal product of their labor, rather than as partners, who must be paid a pro rata share of residual earnings. (This may fit the division between the medical staff and residents at hospitals.) This sort of medical staff is called the discriminatory sharing staff. This staff will have the same number of partners $m^c$ as a closed staff and retain $m^f - m^c$ physicians as hired staff. The total size of the medical staff will be the same as in the FP hospital, which expands the medical staff until the MRP of the last physician is just equal to the market wage of physicians.

13. Pauly and Redisch also discuss a variant of the closed staff: the closed staff with imperfect cooperation. The doctors control the amount of hospital output (physical capital and

The purpose of Pauly and Redisch's (1973) paper is not so much to produce a model with testable predictions as to provide a model that might explain stylized facts from the hospital market.[14] For example, they claim their closed medical staff model explains why NFP firms tend to use more physical capital inputs and nonphysician labor than FP firms. They also note that with closed staffs one finds hospitals that are too small, as measured by their physician labor inputs. Physicians who are refused entry in existing staffs open new hospitals with their own closed staffs where they can earn more money than if they joined existing open staffs. This, Pauly and Redisch claim, explains both why hospitals are below their cost-minimizing size and why there is duplication of facilities in the hospital industry. Finally, they claim their model explains the positive relationship between hospital insurance coverage and hospital unit prices observed by Feldstein (1971). If cost-based insurance covers part of each patient's hospital bill, the factor prices of hospital inputs (capital and nonphysician labor) that medical staffs face are reduced. This produces an increase in the usage of hospital inputs relative to physician inputs, which in turn raises hospital unit prices.

Pauly and Redisch's closed staff model of NFP hospitals fits neatly into our general model when owners/patrons (physicians) are assumed to care only about income (i.e., $v_y = v_q = 0$); but the NFP form permits owners/patrons to take only a pro rata share of profits home as income (i.e., $I = d[\pi] = \pi/x_0$, where $x_0$ is the total number of owners/patrons [physicians] employed at the firm). This constraint is not imposed by the nondistribution constraint so much as the politics of rent-seeking in a firm without a clear residual claimant. Pauly and Redisch do not discuss the constraints imposed by governmental NFP regulations or the benefits conferred on NFPs by government tax policies. Thus we can assume that $N$ is unconstrained and that there are no cost or price advantages associated with NFP status.[15]

---

non-physician labor). The hospital charges doctors for output such that the hospital just breaks even. So doctors are charged only the average cost of output, which they pass on to patients. Physicians then separately charge patients for their own labor costs plus any rents the hospital foregoes by billing doctors at average cost. Physicians respond by shifting their mix of inputs to favor physical capital and non-physician labor, up to where the marginal revenue product of these inputs equals their average cost.

14. Thus, the Pauly and Redisch model suffers from the limitation that the authors do not derive equilibrium implications from their model in the presence of competition with mixed production.

15. It should be noted that, because the physician's cooperative theory of hospitals is analogous to earlier cooperative firm theories, such as Ward (1958), Vanec (1970), Meade (1972), and Domar (1966), the theory shares some of the troublesome implications of those prior theories, implications for which there seem to be little empirical support. For example, an upward shift in the demand curve for hospital output could result in higher prices, lower output, and smaller medical staffs. An increase in factor prices may lead to an increase in the medical staff, while a lump sum subsidy may decrease output and staff size.

### 6.1.4    Noncontractible Quality Model

The next class of models rests on the view that consumers in many markets cannot contract on product quality. Hansmann (1980, 1996) hypothesizes that NFP firms exist because they can overcome this problem. Easley and O'Hara (1983)[16] and Glaeser and Shleifer (2001) present formal models that use the assumption of noncontractible quality to motivate the existence of NFP firms.[17] The logic of these models is that, when consumers cannot contract on product quality, FP firms have an incentive to shirk on quality because this will lower their costs and increase their unit profits without loss of sales. The nondistribution constraint on NFP firms mitigates this incentive because it limits the ability of NFP firms to distribute profits to the owner/patron. Therefore, consumers of products characterized by noncontractible quality prefer to purchase from NFP firms. In effect, NFP status serves as a signal of noncontractible quality. The signal falls in value if the government does not enforce the nondistribution constraint, allowing FP firms to cloak themselves in NFP status but still operate as FP firms—what Weisbrod (1988) calls "for-profits-in-disguise."

Our analysis of the noncontractible quality theory for explaining NFP production focuses on Glaeser and Shleifer's (2001) model because it is the most streamlined formal version of the theory. Glaeser and Shleifer's model has three periods. In period 1, a consumer agrees to purchase one unit of product at price $p$. In period 2, the firm's owner/patron engages in cost-cutting effort $e$, which reduces costs by $k(e)$, where $k$ is positive and concave. Total costs are $c(q) - k(e)$, where $c$ is the cost of producing a unit of observable quality $q$. Cost cutting reduces unobservable quality according to $-me$, where $m$ is a constant. The firm delivers a unit of the good with observable quality $q$ in period 3. The consumer's willingness to pay, and hence the price, is $q - mE[e]$ and the firm's profits are $\pi = p - c(q) + k(e)$.

In period 0, before any market transactions, the firm's owner/patron decides whether to organize the firm as an NFP or an FP. The owner/patron has preferences over income $I$ and effort $e$ such that $v(I, e) = I - e$. If the owner/patron organizes the firm as an FP, her income is simply profits, $I = \pi$. If she organizes as an NFP, she cannot take profits home as cash. She must consume profits through perks. Hence her utility is the cash value of these perks minus the cost of effort. We can think of this restriction as im-

---

16. Easley and O'Hara (1983) model the NFP firm as the sometimes-optimal solution to the principal-agent problem in which consumers are principals and producers are agents. They find that NFP status dominates FP status as a solution in very rare cases. Therefore, the model is not empirically very relevant.

17. Hirth (1999) extends the analysis by showing the equilibrium relationship between, on the one hand, NFP status as a signal of unobservable quality (measured by the price premium such firms may command) and, on the other hand, the share of the population that cannot observe quality and how well the nondistribution constraint on NFPs is enforced.

posing a discount on the cash value of the entrepreneur's profits: $I = d\pi$. The firm will choose NFP status if

$$d[q - mE(e^n) - c(q) + k(e^n)] - e^n > q - mE(e^f) - c(q) + k(e^f) - e^f,$$

where $e^n$ and $e^f$ indicate choices of effort by NFP and FP firms, respectively. These are chosen to maximize the left- and right-hand sides, respectively, of the previous inequality.

This model yields a number of predictions. First, NFP firms invest less effort in cost-cutting effort because the returns to such investment are lower: $dk(e^n)$ versus $k(e^f)$. Hence NFP firms produce higher levels of unobservable quality: $-me$. Second, NFP firms should dominate markets where consumers value noncontractible quality. This is a direct implication of $e^n < e^f$. Third, NFP status becomes less desirable as the profitability of the industry rises because the utility forgone from consumption of profits through perks is linear in profits: $(1 - d)\pi$. If consumers have heterogeneous tastes for unobservable quality and firms have heterogeneous costs, then we might have mixed production, with NFP firms tending to produce higher levels of noncontractible quality and FP firms tending to have lower costs.[18] If one were to add a taste for (noncontractible) quality to the preferences of entrepreneurs, the model, not surprisingly, yields the conclusion that the greater the entrepreneur's preference for quality, the more likely she is to choose NFP status and the higher is the (noncontractible) quality that NFP firms produce, relative to FPs.

While all these predictions are intuitively pleasing, they are generally difficult to test. (The exception is that low-cost firms choose FP status.) We can, however, mimic the equilibrium behavior of Glaeser and Shleifer's (2001) model with our general theory of NFP firms and use that theory to generate testable predictions. Toward this end, assume that owners/patrons have preferences only over income and cost-cutting effort, $e$, such that $v(I, e) = v(I - e)$. Second, assume owners/patrons of NFP firms can take profits home only as perks, $I = d(\pi)$. Third, assume cost-cutting effort reduces cost, i.e., that $c_e(y, q, e) < 0$, $c_{ee} > 0$, where $q$ is contractible quality, but at the expense of noncontractible quality at a rate of $m$. Since consumers value contractible and noncontractible quality equally, price is proportional to $q - mE(e \mid i)$, where $i$ is the regulatory form of the firm. Consumers cannot contract on effort, but can contract on regulatory form. They offer NFP firms high prices given contractible quality because they know such firms have less incentive to cut costs in ways that reduce noncontractible quality. Finally, assume no regulatory constraints on the out-

---

18. While Glaeser and Shleifer explain situations in which mixed production is possible, they do not derive any predictions regarding the behavior of NFP firms in a competitive equilibrium with mixed production.

Table 6.1                     Parameters Implied by the Three Major Models of NFP Firm Behavior

|  | Altruism | Physician Cooperative | Noncontractible Quality |
|---|---|---|---|
| Induced utility | Preference for $(y, q)$ permitted: $v(I, y, q)$ | No preference for $(y, q)$: $v(I)$ | Preference for effort: $v(I, e)$ |
| Output ($N$) | Zero profits: $N = \{y \mid \pi(y) = 0\}$ | No restriction | No restriction |
| Income | No perks: $I = d(\pi) = 0$ | Pro rata distribution: $I = d(\pi) = \pi / x_0$ | Perks: $I = d(\pi) < \pi$ |
| Price | $p^n = p^f$ | $p^n = p^f$ | $p(y, q - mE[e \mid i])$ Higher price conditional on contractible quality: $p^n(q) > p^f(q)$ |
| Costs | No tax breaks: $E(c^n) = E(c^f)$, etc. | No tax breaks (so equal factor prices): $w^n = w^f$ | $c(y, q, e)$ No tax breaks: $E(c^n) = E(c^f)$, etc. |

put of NFP firms ($N$ unrestricted) and that there are no tax subsidies for NFPs, so $E(c^n) = E(c^f)$.

### 6.1.5   Firm-Level Predictions of Existing Theories

In this section we derive implications of each of the three theories of NFP behavior just described for firm-level behavior. We focus on the differences in behavior between FP and NFP firms along a limited range of observable outcomes. For reference, the constraints on the baseline model implied by the three theories discussed in sections 6.1.2–6.1.4 are summarized in table 6.1. Table 6.2 summarizes our predictions. Implications of the altruism theory are developed assuming owners/patrons have a preference only for income, quantity, and perhaps quality. Our analysis of the physician cooperative theory examines only closed staff hospitals. The exposition is organized by outcome; with respect to each outcome we derive predictions for the altruism, physician cooperative, and noncontractible quality models, in that order. The discussion focuses on the intuition behind each prediction. The results can easily be derived in a more formal manner.[19]

*Shape of Firm Supply Curve*

In the altruism model, the supply curves are upward sloping. The supply curve for an FP firm is standard: the marginal cost (MC) curve in the relevant range (upward-sloping section above intersection with the average

---

19. Readers interested in more formal demonstration should refer to Lakdawalla and Philipson (1998, 2002), which works through the baseline model (albeit only under the assumptions implied by the altruism theory of NFP firms).

**Table 6.2    Predictions of Firm-Level Behavior on NFPs Under the Three Major Models of NFP Firm Behavior**

| | Altruism | Physician Cooperative | Noncontractible Quality |
|---|---|---|---|
| Shape of firm supply curve | NFPs supply more elastic than FPs supply | Supply may be backward-bending for NFP firms | No strongly predicted difference |
| Conditional factor demand | Identical as long as no input preferences | Labor demand smaller for NFPs than FPs | NFPs have higher conditional factor demands |
| Unconditional factor demand | Larger for NFPs than FPs | Labor demand smaller for NFPs than FPs | No predicted difference |
| Firm size | Controlling for quality, total output of NFPs larger than that of FPs | Smaller number of staff physicians, controlling for capital inputs | No prediction possible without information on interaction between production of quantity and quality |
| Quality | NFPs produce higher quality than FPs | NFPs have lower quality as measured by labor-capital ratio; no predicted difference on other measures of quality | NFPs produce higher unobserved quality than FPs |
| Average cost | NFP firms have higher average costs controlling for quality | NFP firms have higher average costs controlling for quantity | NFP firms have higher average costs controlling for quantity and contractible quality |

cost [AC] curve). The supply curve for the NFP firm, however, is given by the AC curve above the intersection between the AC and MC curves. This is because of the nondistribution constraint or of NFP regulations that are assumed to constrain NFP firms to have zero profits ($N = \{(y, q) \mid \pi(y, q) = 0\}$). Because the AC curve lies below and has a smaller slope than the MC curve in the relevant range, the supply curve for individual NFP firms is more elastic than that for FP firms.

In the physician cooperative model, the supply curve for individual firms may be backward bending under common conditions such as diminishing returns to scale (see Meade 1972). The reason is that an increase in the price of output raises both the marginal product of physician labor and the average product of physician labor. However, the marginal product of labor rises less than the average product of labor when there are diminishing returns. This means that average earnings could be further raised if physicians were dismissed from the medical staff.[20] This in turn reduces output.

In the noncontractible quality model, all firms will have identical upward-sloping supply functions. Without more information on the economies between production of quantity and quality, one supposes that the supply curves for quantity are the same. In the case of an increase in the price of quality, however, the reaction of NFP firms is expected to be stronger as such firms are constrained by the nondistribution constraint from distributing rents as cash profits. (NFPs can pay rents only as perks.)

*Factor Demand Behavior*

Although there may be great differences between the output behavior of firms run by owners/patrons with traditional income-maximizing preferences and those run by owners/patrons with nonstandard preferences, the differences in owners'/patrons' preferences over output may not affect input demands. In general, the predictions of cost minimization for the FP firm apply to a firm run by an owner/patron with preferences over the quantity and quality of output as long as we are talking about conditional factor demand, that is, demand for inputs for a given level of output. The unconditional factor demand is simply the conditional factor demand at the optimal level of output. This implies that output predictions translate into factor demand predictions whenever the conditional factor demand behavior, as implied by cost minimization, is identical for both types of firm. In the altruism model the NFP firm produces along the AC curve,

20. In the discriminatory sharing case described in note 12, the total number of physicians in the hospital will increase as output price increase, but the mix of "member" to "hired" physician would change (lower number of members and higher number of hired physicians). This result coincides with the analysis presented by Ben-Ner (1984), who shows that as long as the income per member is higher than the competitive wage, the labor-managed firm would gradually replace its members with perfectly substitutable non-member labor. By so doing, that the labor-managed firm will become a competitive firm (with one member as the owner).

which is always further out than the MC curve; therefore all factor demand curves of NFPs are further out. It is unclear whether there is a difference in shape.

In the physician cooperative model, NFPs are inelastic to changes in physician wages. We can see this in figure 6.1. The closed staff hospital chooses output based on the intersection between the hospital's MRP and NARP. That choice does not depend on the market wage, which is given by the intersection of the MRP curve and the physician supply curve, $s_0$. Contrast this to the FP hospital, which clearly reduces demand for physician labor as $s_0$ slides up. The marginal conditions for capital and nonphysician labor in the closed staff NFP are same as in FP firms (e.g., choose capital such that the marginal product of capital equals the rental price). Hence, conditional on quantity and physician-labor input, factor demands for other inputs are identical to FP firms. Conditional only on quantity, however, demand for capital and nonphysician labor may be higher in NFP firms depending on the economies between physician labor and other inputs. The NFP firm produces less quantity than FP firms, so unconditional demand for physician labor is lower. Unconditional demand for other factors depends on the firm's technology.

In the noncontractible quality model, NFP firms produce higher levels of quality. Because higher quality requires more inputs and because the cost functions of FP firms are at least as low as those of NFP firms after owners/patrons select organizational form, NFP firms have higher conditional factor demands. No prediction can be generated regarding unconditional factor demand without knowing more about the exact nature of the firm's technology for joint production of quantity and quality.

*Firm Size*

In the altruism model, since owners/patrons of NFPs draw direct utility from quantity, NFPs are bigger controlling for quality. If we do not control for quality, we might get larger FP firms as owners/patrons of NFPs with preferences for quality substitute quality for quantity. This is more likely the stronger is the NFP owner's/patron's preference for quality relative to quantity.

In the physician cooperative model, NFP hospitals have smaller labor forces than FP hospitals, controlling for capital inputs. It is evident from figure 6.1 that with a closed staff, size is given by intersection of the MRP and the NARP of physician labor curves. With FP hospitals, size is given by intersection of the MRP curve and the physician supply curve. That suggests that closed staff NFPs should be smaller than FPs, as measured by their physician labor forces.[21]

21. We may observe this result even if the physician cooperative model does not accurately describe reality. NFP hospitals get tax breaks on capital inputs (e.g., property tax breaks).

In the noncontractible quality model the NFP firm is expected to deliver higher quality; in this sense size or production should be measured in levels of quality produced and not in (for example) patients' days. The noncontractible quality model does not supply any insight into the physical level of production. For a given volume of patient, the quality of service per patient is higher in NFP hospitals, yet the volume of patients might be higher or lower depending on the relative attractiveness of NFP versus FP hospitals to patients and the duration of high- versus low-quality treatment (i.e., if patients receiving high-quality treatment have longer hospitalization periods, controlling for the size of the hospital, a high-quality hospital would treat fewer patients).

*Quality*

In the altruism model, NFP market shares at each level of quality depend on the total demand for that level of quality. Not-for-profit firms, due to donations, satisfy initial demand at each level of quality. Because a limited number of owners/patrons prefer quality of output or a limited amount of donations finance the preferences of such owners/patrons, once NFP output rises to the level where the average costs of such hospitals exceeds the minimum average costs of FP hospitals, the latter will begin to enter. Due to the scarcity of altruism, FP firms are the marginal firms at each level of quality.

In the physician cooperative model, there is no difference between NFP and FP firms because quality considerations are omitted from the analysis. Still, one commonly used measure of quality is the number of physicians per bed. This measure is closely related to the physician-to-capital ratio, which the model predicts would be lower in NFP hospitals because physician cooperatives use less physician labor at each level of output.

In the noncontractible quality model, NFPs produce higher levels of noncontractible quality because they have less incentive (rents distributed as perks rather than cash) to exert effort to cut costs by reducing such quality.

*Average Cost*

In the altruism model, NFP firms have higher average costs controlling for quality. They produce where the market price equals average cost due to the inability of owners/patrons to take profits home as income (or due to the restriction that profits must be zero). For-profit firms produce where market price equals marginal cost. Since the AC curve lies below the MC

---

Therefore, these hospitals choose an input mix that favors capital, controlling for the level of output. To test whether the smaller size of NFP physician labor demand is due to the cooperative model or simple profit maximization in the face of tax subsidies for capital inputs, one ought to regress labor force size on an indicator for organizational form, total capital inputs, and the state property tax rate.

curve, this implies lower-quantity output and thus average costs for the FP firms.

In the physician cooperative model, because profit distribution encourages inefficiently high use of capital for every given level of output, average costs are higher for NFP firms, conditional on output. One cannot make a clear unconditional prediction because NFP firms tend to produce less than FP firms. With efficient capital-labor ratios, average costs rise with output in the region to the right of the intersection of the AC and MC curves. Therefore, it is possible that a lower-output but inefficient NFP firm has lower average costs than a higher-output, efficient FP firm.

In the contractible quality model, NFP firms have higher costs controlling for quantity and noncontractible quality because they exert less cost-cutting effort (and thus produce more noncontractible quality). Without controlling for quantity and contractible quality, it is hard to predict relative average costs. Higher noncontractible quality may be associated with higher levels of quantity or lower levels of quantity, and thus higher average costs or perhaps lower average costs even taking into account the additional noncontractible quality produced.

## 6.2   Industry-Level Predictions of Existing Theories

In this section we derive predictions concerning industry-level behavior of NFP firms in markets with mixed production under the assumptions of each of the three primary models described in section 6.1. Table 6.3 summarizes our findings. The first row examines whether each of the theories supports an equilibrium with both NFP and FP production. The remainder of the table examines relative NFP behavior in response to four shocks (to demand, to labor supply, to tax rates, and to public production) and with respect to one outcome variable (quality-adjusted price).

*Is Mixed Production Possible?*

In perfect competition under the altruism model, mixed production is possible if altruism is scarce either because donations are limited or there is a limited number of owners/patrons with preferences for quantity or quality in addition to profits. If total demand cannot be satisfied by firms run by output-preferring owners/patrons (who are aided by donations) at a cost lower than the minimum average cost of FP firms (which are not aided by donations) then FP firms will enter the market.

The physician cooperative model does not rule out mixed production as long as there is a market for "memberships" in closed medical staffs. For mixed production to exist, the income per member, in equilibrium, should be at least equal to the market wage. If it is below the market wage, all physicians would prefer to work for FP hospitals. If it exceeds the market wage, all physicians would want to work for NFP firms. However, if there

**Table 6.3    Derived and Conjectured Predictions of Industry-Level Behavior in Equilibrium under the Three Major Models of NFP Firm Behavior**

| | Altruism | Physician Cooperative | Noncontractible Quality |
|---|---|---|---|
| Is mixed production possible? | Yes, if altruism is scarce and demand is sufficiently large | Yes, if cost of membership in closed staff varies across physician population | Yes, if heterogeneous costs of production or heterogeneous tastes for noncontractible quality |
| Response to a positive demand shock | Higher FP share of production | Assuming NFPs exist, higher FP share | Higher FP share |
| Response to a negative (labor) supply shock | Lower FP share | Lower FP share (but perhaps exit of all NFP firms) | Lower FP share |
| Response to an increase in the tax rate (on FP firms) | Lower FP share | Effect on FP share ambiguous; should reduce size of medical staff in NFPs | Lower FP share |
| Response to a reduction in government production | Higher FP share | Higher FP share | Higher FP share |
| Prices | Equal across FPs and NFPs, controlling for quality | No reason prices would differ | NFP price larger than FP price, controlling for contractible quality |

are costs to membership in a closed staff (e.g., limited mobility in the market for the "member" as opposed to the "hired" worker) and these costs vary across physicians, mixed production is possible. Doctors who face high costs of membership will prefer FP hospitals. Doctors who earn greater profits from membership, even after deducting the costs of membership, will choose to join NFP hospitals.

For the remainder of this section, we will assume that the conditions for mixed production under each of the three theories are satisfied and that firms are in a mixed-production equilibrium.

*Response to a Positive Demand Shock*

In the altruism model a positive demand shock would induce entry by FP firms, which we explained above are the marginal firms. One should see a higher FP share of total market production as a result. In the physician cooperative model, assuming NFP firms exist, the reaction of NFP firms to positive demand shocks is contraction of output. (Recall that the cooperative's supply function is backward bending if there are diminishing returns to scale.) Thus, demand shocks are met by entry or expansion of FP firms. In the noncontractible quality model a positive demand shock will increase profitability. Since higher profitability increases the cost of taking NFP status, the share of FP production will rise.

*Response to a Negative (labor) Supply Shock*

In the altruism model a positive labor supply shock (positive shock to wages) increases production costs. Since FP firms are the marginal firms, such a supply shock would lower FP share of production because FP firms would exit. In the physician cooperative model FP firms reduce their labor forces in response to supply shocks. Not-for-profits do not, however, because they are indifferent to increases in physician wage. Thus NFP share would rise after a supply shock. Note, this prediction holds only if there is mixed production. If the shock is severe enough, the market wage will exceed the optimal income per member, and all firms should convert to FP form.[22] In the noncontractible quality model a positive supply shock will decrease profitability, so the cost of taking NFP status decreases. Due to the selection of owners/patrons into organizational form, a supply shock will result in a lower FP share.

*Response To an Increase in the Tax Rate (on FP firms)*

In the altruism model an increase in the tax rate increases the production costs. Since FP firms are the marginal firms, this would lower FP share of production, as FP firms would exit. In the physician cooperative model,

---

22. In the open staff model (see note 12) you may get the opposite result, depending on the relative elasticities of the NARP and MRP functions. The NARP is flatter than the MRP, so an inward (or upward) shift of the physician supply function causes the size of the open staff at the NFP to fall more than the size of the staff in a FP hospital.

the effect of a hike in the tax rate on NFP share is ambiguous. There are two countervailing effects. Initially FP firms will exit the market as their costs rise. As supply falls, price will rise. This in turn may induce NFP firms to cut their labor forces. This will result in an increase in the scale or entry of FP firms (which negates, at least in part, the initial exit of FP firms). In the noncontractible quality model an increase in the tax rate will decrease profitability, so the relative cost of taking NFP status decreases. This will result in the selection of more owners/patrons into the NFP form, resulting in a lower FP share.

*Response To a Reduction in Government Production*

In the altruism model, since the FP firm is the marginal firm this would increase the share of production in FP firms. Not-for-profit production is unaltered. In the physician cooperative model a reduction in output by public hospitals resembles a decrease in supply. For-profit firms are likely to enter as they face higher residual demand. In the noncontractible quality model, exit of government firms would decrease supply and hence increase the new equilibrium price for any given level of observable quality. The higher profitability would result in a higher cost of taking NFP status. This would result in a higher FP share.

*Prices*

In the altruism model, prices are determined by the marginal firm, which is FP. The NFP firms charge the same prices but use excess revenues to fund the production—actually consumption from the perspective of the owner/patron—of greater quantity and perhaps quality. In the physician cooperative model, there is no reason for the cooperative to charge a higher price than the FP hospital. From the consumer's perspective, both types of firm produce the same level of quality. In the noncontractible quality model, because consumers expect that NFP firms will provide higher level of noncontractible quality, consumers are willing to pay more for NFP output.

*Summary*

The main lesson to draw from the analysis in this section is that there are few equilibrium-level outcomes regarding which the three theories of NFP behavior discussed in this paper generate differing predictions. This limits our ability to use empirical evidence to discriminate among the theories. From a methodological perspective, this reduces the value of the different theories, ceteris paribus. Indeed, the analysis suggests that the noncontractible quality model generates virtually the same predictions as a variant of the altruism model, which supposes that some owners/patrons have a preference for the production of noncontractible quality. The only outcomes along which the noncontractible quality story might generate different predictions than this modified altruism model are the effect of a reduction in donations (which we do not study in this paper), the shape of firms' supply curves, and unconditional factor demand. If donations dried up, the noncontractible quality model would predict that NFP firms might still exist as signals of noncontractible quality. The altruism model would predict that there would be no NFP firms in equilibrium because there would be nothing to finance their owners'/patrons' consumption of quantity or quality. With respect to the shape of firms' supply curves and unconditional factor demand, the noncontractible quality model has no strong predictions, whereas a modified altruism model would predict the same outcomes as the altruism model with output- or quality-preferring owners/patrons.

### 6.3   Empirical Evidence

In this section we address two questions: whether there exist empirical studies that permit us to discriminate among different theories of NFP firm behavior, and what such studies actually suggest about the relative performance of different theories. Superior performance is defined by the ability to generate predictions on a set of common outcomes that are more consistent with the data than the predictions generated by competing theories. The main lesson of this section is that more empirical work is required comparing NFP and FP firms on those outcome measures for which the different theories generate different predictions. Our focus here is on the health care sector in the United States, although we suspect our conclusion about the state of the empirical literature would be the same if we examined other sectors of the economy that have mixed production. This section develops in two parts. The first examines evidence on firm-level behavior of NFPs and FPs. The second examines evidence on industry-level or equilibrium behavior.

#### 6.3.1   Firm-Level Comparisons

Table 6.4 summarizes the empirical evidence on the six firm-level outcome variables. These variables (output supply, conditional and unconditional factor demand, firm size, quality, and average cost) are the same ones for which table 6.2 listed the predictions of the three NFP theories examined in section 6.1. The stub column lists the outcome; the first column then indicates which of the three theories generate differing predictions regarding that outcome; the second summarizes the empirical evidence we have on that outcome; and the third reconciles the empirical evidence and the predictions of each theory.

*Shape of Firm Supply Curve*

Altruism models predict that NFP supply is upward sloping but more elastic than FP supply. The physician cooperative model, however, predicts that the supply curve may be backward bending. Unfortunately, we are not aware of any studies that attempt to compare the output supply curves of NFP and FP firms.

Table 6.4                     **Empirical Evidence on Firm-Level Predictions**

| Outcome | Theories Generate Different Predictions? | Summary of Empirical Evidence | Conclusion |
|---|---|---|---|
| Shape of firm supply curve | Yes | No data | None |
| Conditional factor demand | Yes | NFPs have higher conditional factor demand for nonphysician labor | Data tend to support the non-contractible quality model |
| Unconditional factor demand | Yes | NFPs have larger labor forces | Data supports the altruism model and rejects physician cooperative model |
| Firm size | Yes | NFP hospitals generally larger; NFP nursing homes may be smaller | Data are inconclusive |
| Quality | Yes | Uncertain whether NFPs produce higher or lower quality | Data are inconclusive |
| Average cost | No | Uncertain whether NPFs have higher or lower costs | Data are inconclusive |

## Conditional Factor Demand

While altruism models predict identical conditional factor demands regardless of ownership status, the physician cooperative model predicts that conditional demand for physicians will be smaller in NFP firms and the noncontractible quality model predicts that conditional factor demand for inputs generally will be larger in NFP firms. Available studies suggest that NFP health care providers have higher conditional demand for labor. Philipson and Lakdawalla (2000) examined data from the 1995 National Nursing Home Survey and found that FP homes employed fewer registered nurses, aides, and total employees than FP homes, holding total beds (for example) constant. They also found that NFP homes also used fewer doctors, but that result was not statistically significant. This result is consistent with that of Sloan and Steinwald (1980), who examined much older data (from 1969 to 1975) and found that NFP hospitals employ more registered nurses and non-nurse employees than FP hospitals. These studies, for obvious reasons, cast some doubt on the altruism theories (unless some sort of labor-input preference on the part of owners/patrons is assumed).[23]

23. This inference requires a caveat. Philipson and Lakdawalla (2000) control for price and output. In the altruism models, FP firms produce the same output and price as NFP firms only if they are more efficient than NFP firms. In such circumstances, it is possible that FPs use fewer labor inputs because of technology, not owner preferences. The predictions in Table 2 assume identical technology. Thus the findings of Philipson and Lakdawalla (2000) can be squared with the altruism models if owners have heterogeneous production technology.

Philipson and Lakdawalla (2000) indirectly casts doubt on the physician cooperative theory because it does not find that conditional demand for physicians is significantly smaller in NFP homes.

*Unconditional Factor Demand*

The altruism models predict that unconditional factor demand will be larger in NFP firms, while the physician cooperative model predicts that that unconditional demand for physician labor will be smaller at NFP hospitals. Because the noncontractible quality model makes no prediction about quantity of output, it has no prediction for unconditional factor demands. The available evidence suggests that NFP hospitals have larger unconditional demand for labor.

Existing studies indicate that NFP hospitals and NFP nursing homes have larger labor forces than their FP counterparts. For example, Gentry and Penrod (2000) examined nearly 5,000 short-term hospitals from the Health Care Financing Agency's (HCFA's) 1995 Medicare Cost Reports and observe that the median NFP hospital has more employees than the median FP hospitals (see also Rose-Ackerman 1996). Philipson (2000) studied the National Nursing Home Surveys from 1989 to 1994. He found that the FP homes tend to have 86 to 91 percent as many full-time equivalent employees as NFP homes.

These data support the altruism models and reject the predictions of the physician cooperative model. There is one caveat, however. Predictions regarding conditional and unconditional factor demand are generated holding quality constant, but the existing data on conditional and unconditional factor demand do not control for quality. This fact also reduces the ability of existing empirical studies to discriminate among theories of NFP firms based on their prediction regarding firm size.

*Firm Size*

The predictions of the three theories of NFP behavior regarding firm size, as measured by quantity output, mirror the theories' predictions regarding unconditional factor demand because the latter predictions are based on quantity output. Altruism-based theories predict that NFP will be larger; the physician cooperative model predicts they will be smaller; and the noncontractible quality model has no prediction.

The empirical data on firm size are, however, a bit more complicated than data on unconditional factor demand. Numerous studies demonstrate that NFP hospitals have more beds, admissions, and discharges than FP hospitals (see Frank and Salkever 2000 and Gentry and Penrod 2000). The former examines American Hospital Association (AHA) data on all hospitals from 1970 to 1995. David (2001) examined the same data from 1960 to 1999, however, and found that NFP and FP hospitals are converging in hospital size. For example, the ratio of average NFP to FP beds has gone from around 3.0 in 1960 to around 1.5 in 1999. The same can be said regarding average admissions. David reports that this convergence is due to the growth in the average size of FP hospitals.[24] To complicate matters further, Philipson (2000) reported that, between 1989 and 1994, FP nursing homes tended to be more than 10 percent larger than NFP homes, as measured by average number of beds or patient days.

Thus data from hospitals tend to support the altruism theories (although less and less each year), but data from nursing homes tend to support the physician cooperative theory. It should be noted that the data from each of the studies discussed in the last paragraph were presented in summary statistic form; they were not subject to rigorous analysis.

*Quality*

Ironically, the two firm-level outcomes—quality and average cost—on which there is the least difference in predictions across the three theories of NFP behavior are those on which there has been the most (and the most rigorous) empirical work. With respect to quality, the altruism models predict that NFP firms will produce high quality if owners/patrons who chose the NFP form have a preference for quality, and the noncontractible quality models predict that NFP firms will produce higher noncontractible quality because the nondistribution constraint softens incentives to shirk on such quality. The difference between these predictions—the noncontractible quality model predicts only higher noncontractible quality—may not be amenable to testing because whether any measure of quality observable to an econometrician is truly noncontractible for consumers is questionable. The physician cooperative model also generates a prediction for quality, but it is no different than its prediction for conditional factor demand for labor: NFP firms have lower physician-capital ratios. This is a prediction about quality only if physician-capital ratios are a measure of quality.

The empirical literature comparing the quality output of NFP and FP health care providers can roughly be divided into three classes based on how they measure quality. One class focuses on health outcomes; a second on third-party assessments, such as regulatory violations and accreditation; and the third on intensity of use of certain quality-correlated inputs, such as physician labor. The most widely accepted measure of quality is health outcomes, so we focus more on this class of empirical studies.

Studies of outcomes do not provide a decisive answer to the question of whether NFP's provide higher quality of care. Early studies were limited because they employed cross-sectional data and lacked great controls for

---

24. David hypothesizes that the convergence might have been induced by the creation of the Medicare and Medicaid programs in 1966. These programs may have made previously unprofitable patients profitable to FP hospitals, encouraging their growth.

unobserved severity (see, e.g., Shortell and Hughes 1989 and Hartz et al. 1988). If patients select higher-quality hospitals when they have more severe illnesses and this severity is not observable by the econometrician, then estimates of the quality of high-quality hospitals will be biased downward. Keeler et al. (1992) tried to address this problem by gathering extensive clinical data on patients in their sample. Their study looked at elderly Medicare patients diagnosed with congestive heart failure, acute myocardial infarction (AMI), stroke, or hip fracture at 297 hospitals in 1981–82 and 1985–86. They found no difference in health outcomes between NFP and FP hospitals on average, but noted that FP hospitals appeared to have better outcomes on average than NFP nonteaching hospitals. The problem with Keeler et al.'s approach is that, because gathering detailed data is so expensive, their sample size is quite small.

Gowrisankaran and Town (1999) tried to address the patient selection problem by using a patient's distance to the hospital as an instrumental variable. Looking at data from Southern California between 1989 and 1994, they found that elderly patients admitted for pneumonia at NFP hospitals have 10 percent lower mortality than those admitted to FP hospitals. However, when Geweke, Gowrisankaran, and Town (2001) returned to the sample—actually a subsample of 78,000 Medicare patients admitted to Los Angeles County hospitals for pneumonia between 1989 and 1992—with more sophisticated estimation methods and separated NFP into teaching and nonteaching hospitals, they reached a different conclusion. While they found teaching hospitals were better than nonteaching hospitals, they also found no statistical difference between FP and nonteaching NFP hospitals. This distinction between teaching and nonteaching NFP hospitals is important because it is unclear whether NFP status or teaching status induces hospitals to provide higher quality in the samples.

McClellan and Staiger (2000) tried a different method to control for patient selection. They restricted their sample to patients hospitalized for AMI or ischemic heart disease. Such ailments progress rapidly, requiring patients to go to the nearest hospital. Looking at a sample of 550,000 patients at 4,000 hospitals, they initially find that, on average, FP hospitals have higher ninety-day mortality rates. However, the authors note that, just as estimates of quality differences may be biased by patient selection, they may also be biased by hospital selection (e.g., the choice by hospitals of where to locate). To control for this, they looked in detail at three counties with mixed production. This analysis reveals that, if anything, FP hospitals perform better than NFP hospitals. They also note that the small difference between NFP and FP hospitals masks huge variation within these types of hospitals. Shen (2002) tried to extend McClellan and Staiger by looking not just at a few markets but at the entire United States and by grouping NFP and FP hospitals for comparison, based on (for example) a distance-matching scheme. She found that FP hospitals have at least 3 percent higher AMI mortality or complication rates than NFP hospitals. Her analysis did not, however, draw a distinction between NFP teaching and nonteaching hospitals.

The mixed conclusions of the health outcome studies can also be found in studies that examine patient complaints, violations of government quality-control regulations, and accreditation. Compare, for example, Mark (1996; NFP psychiatric hospitals experience fewer complaints or violations), Weisbrod and Schlesinger (1986; NFP nursing homes experience fewer complaints but the same level of violations), and Herzlinger and Krasker (1987; no difference in hospital accreditation). A further problem with these studies is that they have small sample sizes and violations and complaints are infrequent, suggesting a low signal-to-noise ratio.

Studies that examine input intensity—in particular, physician-labor-to-output ratios—are no more helpful. Although they find that NFP providers have higher conditional demand for physician labor (as discussed above), it is unclear why a high labor-to-capital or labor-to-output ratio indicates higher quality. It seems a superior approach would be to look at outcomes directly, rather than to make implicit assumptions about the production function for quality.

Overall, it does not appear that the literature on quality differences between NFP and FP health care providers offers much support to any of the three theories of NFP behavior.

*Average Cost*

All three theories of NFP firm behavior predict that NFP firms will have higher average costs than FP firms. Therefore, empirical work on the difference in costs of NFP and FP health care providers theoretically cannot be used to discriminate among the three theories, although it can be used to reject all three theories. Work to date, however, cannot do even the latter. The empirical literature on cost, like that on quality, can be sorted into three groups. Earlier work focused on paired comparisons of NFP and FP hospitals. This literature yielded conflicting results and the data may be too old to have relevance in today's changed marketplace. Compare Lewin, Derzon, and Marguiles (1981) and Pattison and Katz (1983) with Sloan and Vraciu (1983) and Herzlinger and Krasker (1987). The former studies found that FP providers are more costly than NFP providers. The latter studies found that FP providers are no different or less costly than NFP providers. Later studies employed regression analysis. They controlled for case mix, for example, but did not yield clear conclusions. For instance, Becker and Sloan (1985) found that FP hospitals have higher costs per patient day, but lower costs adjusted for admission. The third major group of cost studies used linear programming techniques to estimate frontier production functions. The inefficiency of a given hospital is measured by its distance from (outside) the frontier. The frontier analysis studies used more recent data but still produced mixed results. For example, Wilson and Jadlow (1982) found FP hospitals more efficient; Koop, Osiewalski, and Steel (1997) found them less efficient; and Vitaliano and Toren (1996) and Zuckerman, Hadley, and Iezzoni (1994) found no difference between FPs and NFPs. Moreover, few studies of costs, regardless of the methodology, have serious controls for quality (see Newhouse 1994) or account for changes in payment schemes (i.e., the shift from fee-for-service insurance to managed health care) and the effects these changes have on cost-minimizing behavior.

### 6.3.2   Industry-Level Comparisons

Table 6.5 summarizes the existing empirical evidence on the differences in response to an increase in demand, an increase in labor costs, an increase in tax rates, and a decrease in public production; and the evidence on difference in prices. As in table 6.4, the stub column lists the outcome, the first column then indicates which theories generate different predictions regarding that outcome, the second column summarizes the empirical evidence on that outcome; and the third reconciles the empirical evidence and the predictions of each theory.

*Response To a Positive Demand Shock*

All the theories of NFP behavior examined in this paper predict that an FP's share of market production will rise in response to a positive demand shock. This is roughly consistent with the empirical literature that has explored the question. In an early study, Steinwald and Neuhauser (1970) found that, during 1960s, statewide population growth appeared to drive growth in the market share of FP hospitals. Relman (1980) provided evidence that the 1966 enactment of Medicare and Medicaid subsidizing in-

**Table 6.5     Empirical Evidence on Firm-Level Predictions**

| Outcome | Theories Generate Different Predictions? | Summary of Empirical Evidence | Conclusion |
|---|---|---|---|
| Response to a positive demand shock | No | Probably increases FP share | Data do not discriminate between theories |
| Response to a negative (labor) supply shock | No | No data | Data do not discriminate between theories |
| Response to an increase in the tax rate | Yes | Probably reduces NFP share | Data do not discriminate between theories |
| Response to a reduction in government production | No | Increases FP share | Data do not discriminate between theories |
| Prices | Yes | No evident difference in prices | Data tend to support altruism model |

duced significant growth in the market share of FP hospitals. Finally, Gulley and Santerre (1993) found that government regulation aimed at constraining price depressed FP market share.

The evidence on this issue is not, however, unanimous in its support of the predictions of the three theories. For example, Steinwald and Neuhauser (1970) also found that growth in per capita income is negatively correlated with growth in the FP market share. Moreover, Lakdawalla and Philipson (1998) find that the positive effect of Medicaid subsidies on FP share in the nursing home market is not statistically significant.

### Response To a Negative (labor) Supply Shock

There are no studies we are aware of that examine the effect of such a shock. However, even if there were, they would not permit us to discriminate among theories of NFP behavior because all three that we examine predict an increase in FP share of production in response to an increase in physician wage.

### Response To an Increase in the Tax Rate

The altruism model and the noncontractible quality model predict that an increase in the tax rate on FP firms should reduce FP market share. The physician cooperative model suggests that the effect on FP market share of a hike in the tax rate is ambiguous. However, that model does predict that the size of medical staffs in NFP hospitals should fall after a tax hike.

The empirical literature on NFP behavior generally supports the predictions of the altruism and noncontractible quality models. Using a twenty-year panel of U.S. states, Gulley and Santerre (1993) found in a state-fixed-effects regression that corporate and property tax increases raise the market share of NFP hospitals. Moreover, in a national cross section of several NFP industries by city and by state, Hansmann (1987) finds corporate and property taxes to be jointly significant in raising NFP market share (although their separate significance is not robust). Finally, although Chang and Tuckman (1990) found in a cross section of Tennessee counties that increases in property taxes do not significantly increase the market share of NFP hospitals, their study suffers from problems of small-sample size.

The empirical literature does not permit comment on the physician cooperative model. There are no studies that examine the effect of changes in commercial-enterprise tax rates on the size of medical staffs at NFP hospitals.

### Response To a Reduction in Government Production

All three theories of NFP behavior predict that a reduction of government production should increase the FP share of health care production. This prediction finds strong support in the empirical literature. Gulley and

Santerre (1993) found that, from 1967 to 1987, the aggregate market share of FP hospitals (measured by beds) rose by 5.5 percent, while the aggregate market share of public hospitals fell by 5.3 percent. Lefgren and Philipson (1999) documented the continuation of this trend through the early 1990s and, furthermore, found that the aggregate share of FP hospitals has risen almost entirely at the expense of the aggregate share of public hospitals. Finally, Ettner (1999) found that FP psychiatric hospitals have replaced the output lost to the departure of many public psychiatric hospitals over the last few decades.

*Prices*

Neither the altruism nor the physician cooperative model predicts any difference in price across ownership form, controlling for contractible quality. The noncontractible quality model predicts, however, that NFP hospitals can charge higher prices controlling for such quality because they provide greater noncontractible quality. The data provide little support for this prediction. The only study to investigate the existence of a price premium is Philipson (2000).[25] Using firm-level data from the 1985 and 1995 National Nursing Home Surveys, Philipson estimated a hedonic demand function for nursing homes. He regressed private price per day on a dummy for ownership type, output, input, and quality controls (with quality measured by whether a home is certified) by the amount of services provided and by location in a city. His estimates suggest that NFP homes received about a 5 percent premium in 1985 and no premium in 1995, but neither figure is statistically significant. It should be acknowledged that there are problems with Philipson's study. For example, in order for Philipson's regressions to reveal the hedonic demand function for nursing home care, he must assume that the nursing home market is characterized by perfect competition where all firms are in the same market and there is no heterogeneity among consumers (see Vogt 2000). However, certificate-of-need laws impose barriers to entry into the nursing home market. This lack of competition diminishes the substitution between NFP and FP care.[26] These problems suggest further research is warranted.

*Summary*

Our review of the empirical literature suggests some obvious empirical projects worth an investment of resources by scholars interested in NFP

25. There is a large literature that attempts to answer the question, do NFP hospitals exploit market power as FP hospitals do? It is not immediately clear to us how the answer to this question might permit use to distinguish the theories we examine here based on their predictions regarding pricing behavior.
26. Moreover, it is unclear how informative a home's private price is about the price a home would charge in absence of regulations. Finally, Philipson must assume there are no differences between NFP and FP firms that are observable to consumers, but not to the investigator. This is questionable given the limited controls for quality he employs.

behavior. First, there is a need for data on the differences between the supply curves of NFP and FP firms. The three dominant, formalized theories of NFP firm behavior generate different predictions regarding the shapes of these curves, but to our knowledge there is no analysis of data on this outcome. Second, there is a need for better empirical analysis of the quantity and quality of output decisions of NFP versus FP firms. Again, the three theories generate conflicting predictions, but existing empirical studies have not arrived at a consensus on the difference, if any, between NFP and FP firms with respect to these outcomes.

## 6.4  Concluding Remarks

If forced to choose among the three theories of NFP behavior, we would weakly prefer the altruism theory. It enjoys the most empirical successes and fewest empirical defeats, but only barely. The noncontractible quality model is inconsistent with existing data on prices and on unconditional factor demand for labor. The altruism model is inconsistent only with existing data on conditional factor demand for labor, and studies that examine factor demand (conditional and unconditional) do not control for quality. Data on other firm-level outcomes are inconclusive and both theories generate similar predictions on industry-level equilibrium outcomes. Perhaps the better conclusion is that the physician cooperative model is not empirically relevant. It enjoys no empirical successes over its competitors and it is inconsistent with the data on unconditional factor demand.

It should be stressed, however, that a preference for the altruism theory or a rejection of the physician cooperative theory rests on weak data. Indeed, any attempt to elevate one theory of NFP behavior over others based on the analysis in this paper would be subject to a number of caveats, in addition to the obvious problem of decision making with imperfect empirical data. Obviously we focus only on the health care sector and on a small interval in time, typically the last two decades of the twentieth century. It may be, for example, that the physician cooperative model would enjoy more empirical success if imposed upon data from the first half of this century (Starr 1982). More importantly, this paper examines only a limited array of theories of NFP behavior. We focus on those that attempt to explain NFP firm behavior by examining the preferences of and constraints on the owners/patrons of such firms. There are theories that focus instead on the objectives of the government, of employees, or of donors (see, e.g., Francois 2001). They may generate predictions more consistent with the data.

The real purpose of this paper is to make a simple methodological point. In order to determine why NFP firms exist and behave as they do, scholars should focus on generating equilibrium predictions from competing theories with regard to a common set of measurable outcomes and then gather the data on these outcomes in order to discriminate among theories based on their predictions.

# References

Baumol, William J. 1959. *Business behavior, value, and growth.* New York: Macmillan.

Baumol, William J., and W. G. Bowen. 1965. On the performing arts: The anatomy of their economic problems. *American Economic Review* 55(1/2): 495–502.

Becker, E. R., and F. A. Sloan. 1985. Hospital ownership and preference. *Economic Inquiry* 23 (1): 21–36.

Ben-Ner, Avner. 1984. On the stability of the cooperative type of organization. *Journal of Comparative Economics* 8 (3): 247–60.

Chang, Cyril F., and Howard P. Tuckman. 1990. Do higher property tax rates increase the market share of nonprofit hospitals? *National Tax Journal* 43:175–87.

David, Guy. 2001. The convergence between nonprofit and for-profit hospitals in the U.S.: 1960–1999. University of Chicago. Working paper.

Domar, E. 1966. The Soviet collective farm as a producer cooperative. *American Economic Review* 56:734–57.

Easley, David, and Maureen O'Hara. 1983. The economic role of the nonprofit firm. *Bell Journal of Economics* 14 (2): 531–38.

Ettner, Susan L., and Richard C. Hermann. 2001. The role of profit status under imperfect information: Evidence from the treatment patterns of elderly Medicare beneficiaries hospitalized for psychiatric diagnoses. University of California at Los Angeles. Working paper.

Feldstein, Martin S. 1971. Hospital cost inflation: A study of nonprofit price dynamics. *American Economic Review* 61 (5): 853–72.

Francois, Patrick. 2001. Employee care and the role of nonprofit organizations. *Journal of Institutional and Theoretical Economics* 157:443–64.

Frank, Richard G., and David S. Salkever. 1991. The supply of charity services by nonprofit hospitals: Motives and market structure. *RAND Journal of Economics* 22 (3): 430–45.

———. 2000. Market forces, diversification of activity, and the mission of not-for-profit hospitals. In *The changing hospital industry: Comparing not-for-profit and for-profit institutions,* ed. David Cutler, 195–215. Chicago: University of Chicago Press.

Friedman, Milton. 1970. The social responsibility of business is to increase its profits. *New York Times Sunday Magazine.* 13 September, p. 32.

Gentry, William M., and John R. Penrod. 2000. The tax benefits of not-for-profit hospitals. In *The changing hospital industry: Comparing not-for-profit and for-profit institutions,* ed. David M. Cutler, 285–324. Chicago: University of Chicago Press.

Geweke, John, Gautam Gowrisankaran, and Robert J. Town. 2001. Bayesian inference for hospital quality in a selection model. NBER Working Paper no. W8497. Cambridge, Mass.: National Bureau of Economic Research, October.

Glaeser, Edward L., and Andrei Shleifer. 2001. Not-for-profit entrepreneurs. *Journal of Public Economics* 81:99–115.

Gowrisankaran, Gautam, and Robert J. Town. 1999. Estimating the quality of care in hospitals using instrumental variables. *Journal of Health Economics* 18:747–67.

Gray, Bradford H. 1993. *The profit motive and patient care: The changing accountability of doctors and hospitals.* Cambridge, Mass.: Harvard University Press.

Gulley, David O., and Rexford E. Santerre. 1993. The effect of tax exemption on the market share of nonprofit hospitals. *National Tax Journal* 46:477–86.

Hansmann, Henry B. 1980. The role of nonprofit enterprise. *Yale Law Review* 89:835–901.

———. 1981. Nonprofit enterprise in the performing arts. *Bell Journal of Economics* 12:341–61.

———. 1987. The effect of tax exemption and other factors on the market share of nonprofit versus for-profit firms. *National Tax Journal* 40:71–82.

———. 1996. *The ownership of enterprise.* Cambridge, Mass.: Harvard University Press.

Hartz, Arthur J., Henry Krakauer, Evelyn M. Kuhn, Mark Young, Steven J. Jacobsen, Greer Gay, Larry Muenz, Myron Katzkoff, R. Clifton Bailey, and Alfred A. Rimm. 1989. Hospital characteristics and mortality rates. *New England Journal of Medicine* 321 (25): 1720–25.

Herzlinger, R. E., and W. S. Krasker. 1987. Who profits from nonprofits? *Harvard Business Review* 65 (1): 93–106.

Hirth, Richard A. 1999. Consumer information and competition between nonprofit and for-profit nursing homes. *Journal of Health Economics* 18:219–40.

Keeler, Emmett B., Lisa V. Rubinstein, Katherine L. Kahn, David Draper, Ellen R. Harrison, Michael J. McGinty, William H. Rogers, and Robert H. Brook. 1992. Hospital characteristics and quality of care. *Journal of the American Medical Association* 268 (13): 1709–14.

Koop, Gary, Jacek Osiewalski, and Mark F. J. Steel. 1997. Bayesian efficiency analysis through individual effects: Hospital cost frontiers. *Journal of Econometrics* 76:77–105.

Lakdawalla, Darius, and Tomas Philipson. 1998. Nonprofit production and competition. NBER Working Paper no. 6377. Cambridge, Mass.: National Bureau of Economic Research.

———. 2002. The nonprofit sector and industry performance. University of Chicago. Mimeograph.

Lefgren, Lars, and Tomas Philipson. 1999. The three sectors of U.S. health care. University of Chicago. Mimeograph.

Lewin, L. S., R. A. Derzon, and R. Marguiles. 1981. Investor-owned and nonprofits differ in economic performance. *Hospitals* 55 (13): 52–58.

Long, M. F. 1964. Efficient use of hospitals. In *The economics of health and medical care,* ed. S. J. Axelrod, 211–26. Ann Arbor: University of Michigan Press.

Mark, T. L. 1996. Psychiatric hospital ownership and performance. *Journal of Human Resources* 1 (3): 631–49.

McClellan, Mark, and Douglas Staiger. 2000. Comparing hospital quality at for-profit and not-for-profit hospitals. In *The changing hospital industry: Comparing not-for-profit and for-profit institutions,* ed. David M. Cutler, 93–112. Chicago: University of Chicago Press.

Meade, James E. 1972. The theory of labour-managed firms and of profit sharing. *The Economic Journal* 82 (March): 402–28.

Newhouse, Joseph P. 1970. Toward a theory of nonprofit institutions: An economics model of a hospital. *American Economic Review* 60 (1): 64–74.

———. 1994. Frontier estimation: How useful a tool for health economics? *Journal of Health Economics* 13 (3): 317–22.

Pattison, R. V., and H. M. Katz. 1983. Investor-owned and not-for-profit hospitals. *New England Journal of Medicine* 309 (6): 347–53.

Pauly, Mark V. 1987. Nonprofit firms in medical markets. *American Economic Review* 77 (2): 257–62.

Pauly, Mark, and Michael Redisch. 1973. The not-for-profit hospital as a physicians' cooperative. *American Economic Review* 63 (1): 87–99.

Phelps, Charles E. 1997. *Health economics.* Reading, Mass.: Addison-Wesley.

Philipson, Tomas. 2000. Asymmetric information and the not-for-profit sector: Does its output sell at a premium? In *The changing hospital industry: Comparing not-for-profit and for-profit institutions,* ed. David M. Cutler, 325–45. Chicago: University of Chicago Press.

Philipson, Tomas, and Darius Lakdawalla. 2000. Medical care output and productivity in the nonprofit sector. In *Medical care output and productivity,* ed. Ernst Berndt and David Cutler, 119–40. Chicago: University of Chicago Press.

Preston, Anne E. 1988. The effects of property rights on labor costs of nonprofit firms: An application to the day care industry. *Journal of Industrial Economics* 36 (3): 337–50.

Relman, A. S. 1980. The new medical-industrial complex. *New England Journal of Medicine* 303:963–69.

Rose-Ackerman, Susan. 1996. Altruism, nonprofits, and economic theory. *Journal of Economic Literature* 34 (2): 701–28.

Shalit, Sol S. 1977. A doctor-hospital cartel theory. *Journal of Business* 50 (1): 1–20.

Shen, Yu-Chu. 2002. The effect of hospital ownership choice on patient outcomes after treatment for acute myocardial infarction. *Journal of Health Economics* 21:901–22.

Shortell, Stephen M., and Edward F. X. Hughes. 1988. The effects of regulation, competition, and ownership on mortality rates among hospital inpatients. *New England Journal of Medicine* 318 (17): 1100–07.

Sloan, Frank A. 2000. Not-for-profit ownership and hospital behavior. In *Handbook of health economics,* ed. J. Newhouse and A. Culyer, 1141–74. New York: Elsevier Science.

Sloan, Frank A., and B. Steinwald. 1980. *Hospital labor markets: Analysis of wages and work force composition.* Lexington, Mass.: D. C. Heath–Lexington Books.

Sloan, Frank A., and R. A. Vraciu. 1983. Investor-owned and not-for-profit: Addressing some issues. *Health Affairs* 2 (1): 25–37.

Starr, Paul. 1982. *The social transformation of American medicine.* New York: Basic Books.

Steinwald, Bruce, and Duncan Neuhauser. 1970. The role of the proprietary hospital. *Law and Contemporary Problems* 35:817–38.

Vanec, J. 1970. *The general theory of labor-managed market economies.* Ithaca, N.Y.: Cornell University Press.

Vitaliano, D., and M. Toren. 1996. Cost and efficiency in nursing homes: A stochastic frontier approach. *Journal of Health Economics* 13:281–300.

Vogt, William B. 2000. Comment on chapter 10. In *The changing hospital industry: Comparing not-for-profit and for-profit institutions,* ed. David M. Cutler, 351–56. Chicago: University of Chicago Press.

Ward, B. 1958. The firm in Illyria: Market syndicalism. *American Economic Review* 48:566–89.

Weisbrod, Burton A. 1975. Toward a theory of the voluntary non-profit sector in a three-sector economy. In *Altruism, morality, and economic theory,* ed. Edmund S. Phelps, 171–95. New York: Russell Sage Foundation.

————. 1988. *The nonprofit economy.* Cambridge, Mass.: Harvard University Press.

Weisbrod, Burton, and Mark Schlesinger. 1986. Public, private, nonprofit ownership, and the response to asymmetric information: The case of nursing homes. In *The economics of nonprofit institutions,* ed. S. Rose-Ackerman, 133–51. New York: Oxford University Press.

Wilson, G. W., and J. M. Jadlow. 1982. Competition, profit incentives, and technical efficiency in the provision of nuclear medicine services. *Bell Journal of Economics* 13 (2): 472–82.

Zuckerman, S., J. Hadley, and L. Iezzoni. 1994. Measuring hospital efficiency with frontier cost functions. *Journal of Health Economics* 13 (3): 255–80.

# 7

# The Role of Nonprofit Endowments

Raymond Fisman and R. Glenn Hubbard

Theories of nonprofit organizations have generally centered on the motivations of not-for-profit entrepreneurs.[1] Regardless of the motivations of the nonprofit's founder, however, a key connecting idea among these theories is the assumption of the nondistribution constraint as the defining characteristic of the nonprofit form (Hansmann 1996). In this paper, we take this definition of nonprofits as a point of departure, and discuss the implications for the financial structure and governance of nonprofit organizations, regardless of their underlying motivations. In a for-profit organization, shareholders act as the residual bearers of risk. Because nonprofits, by definition, have no residual claimants, there must be some other means of absorbing shocks that exist in a world of uncertain donations and uncertain needs for program expenditures. One possibility would be simply to allow for shocks to revenue streams to be passed on to program expenditures, thus effectively making the recipients of an organization's services bear the burden. However, a desire for "production smoothing" naturally leads to a search for an alternative buffer. Thus nonprofit organ-

Raymond Fisman is the Meyer Feldberg Associate Professor of Finance and Economics at the Graduate School of Business, Columbia University, and a faculty research fellow of the National Bureau of Economic Research. R. Glenn Hubbard is the Russell L. Carson Professor of Economics and Finance in the Graduate School of Business and professor of economics at Columbia University, and a research associate of the National Bureau of Economic Research.

1. More precisely, most theories of nonprofits are based on one of two ideas: (a) a desire to provide a product at the low marginal cost of production, perhaps due to externalities created by the good (see, e.g., Weisbrod 1988), or (b) an interest in signaling the production of a high-quality good where quality is difficult to observe or verify (e.g., Hansmann 1996; Glaeser and Shleifer 2000).

izations will hold precautionary savings in the form of endowment fund balances, to protect against adverse revenue shocks.

In this paper, we take a preliminary step in analyzing empirically the role of the endowment in nonprofit organizations. We begin by describing, across industries, the endowment characteristics of nonprofit organizations. We further provide some preliminary regression results on endowment intensity that are suggestive of a precautionary saving motive for endowments. This need to maintain a fund balance to smooth the provision of services potentially leads to problems of governance and managerial discretion. This observation is obviously related to familiar themes in corporate finance, which has often focused on the agency problems created by giving managers access to discretionary funds in for-profit organizations (e.g., Jensen 1986). The problem is that, given the opportunity, for-profit managers will "steal" from the firm, by consuming perquisites in one form or another. A similar question arises for donors to nonprofit organizations. On the one hand, there is a need for a fund balance to smooth consumption. On the other hand, managers may take advantage of these funds to pursue pet projects or even pay themselves higher salaries. Two possible solutions exist: Donors may insist that funds be spent right away, thereby ensuring that their donations are put to good use at the expense of the production-smoothing ability of the organization.[2] Alternatively, donors may rely on monitoring technologies that guarantee that all funds, both present and future, are spent appropriately. We describe some of the modes of oversight and monitoring that might be used to curb malfeasance, and suggest some empirical implications of our framework for future work.

The rest of the paper is structured as follows: In section 7.1, we describe the process of endowment generation and donor behavior that we believe governs nonprofit organizations. Section 7.2 provides a discussion on potential measures of governance in nonprofits. In section 7.3, we provide details on the Internal Revenue Service (IRS) data that we use to examine organizations' endowments. Our results on patterns of endowments and precautionary savings are presented in section 7.4. In section 7.5, we undertake a preliminary investigation in the link between governance and endowment intensity; section 7.6 concludes.

## 7.1  Donations and Endowments in Nonprofit Organizations

Consider first the problem faced by a not-for-profit entrepreneur who derives utility from providing a good for which the equilibrium market price will not cover average cost. This entrepreneur must therefore raise

---

2. Note that this more commonly takes the form of donations of products (e.g., medicine to aid organizations, or books to a library) rather than cash donations that must be spent immediately. From a saving perspective, the effect is the same.

donations from like-minded donors, who similarly obtain utility from the provision of this good. By assumption, consumers and donors of the non-profit's output are not identical.[3] Donors are therefore required to provide funds to the entrepreneur, with the assumption that he or she will use them to further the stated mission of the organization (i.e., by producing the good that the organization was established to provide).

Within this model, we introduce the following complication: Very often, an organization is faced with uncertain circumstances with regard to revenue and cost streams. This may be driven by uncertainty over future demand for the organization's services, future donations, or changes in input prices. For example, consider the circumstances of the Riverside Church Soup Kitchen, whose mission is to feed the homeless of upper Manhattan, following the stock market decline of 2000–2001. This simultaneously increased the demand for its services and reduced the capacity of its donor base to provide funding. Assuming that this is a temporary shock, the organization may be forced to cut back services exactly when the need is greatest. An alternative is for the entrepreneur to hold funds in reserve, as precautionary savings, for situations where the organization faces a shortfall. This is what is commonly referred to as an endowment, or fund balance. This may be used as a buffer in circumstances where there exists a gap between what donors provide and what is required for program services. Endowments are often described in these terms, as a fund to protect the organization from "rainy days."

However, as noted in the introduction, providing managers with this precautionary savings device may allow them to "steal" from the organization, by pursuing interests that diverge from those of the donors, by consuming perquisites, or even potentially by taking inappropriate financial compensation. Having recognized this danger, donors and society more broadly may wish to impose conditions that restrain nonprofit management from taking inappropriate actions. This may include monitoring by the government or by donors; we consider some of the mechanisms in use in the following section, in some greater detail. Furthermore, if donors know that they will be expropriated by providing endowments to entrepreneurs they may choose to limit the discretionary funds available to managers in the first place.

Now, the preceding story is premised on two basic assumptions: (a) that it is easier for managers to pursue personal interests with endowment funds rather than with streams of revenue, and (b) that donors have some incentive to provide managers with endowments, rather than simply providing funding on an annual basis. We now provide some evidence in support of these assumptions.

3. See preceding references, such as Hansmann (1996) and Glaeser and Shleifer (2000), for reasons that this might be the case.

### 7.1.1  Expropriation of the Endowment

Application of our argument to endowment expropriation closely follows agency models, which emphasizes that providing managers with discretionary funds may lead to governance problems. In such a setting Jensen (1986) argues, for example, that an organization should hold a high level of debt, so that all cash inflows must be used to service this debt and stave off the bankruptcy that would cause the manager to lose his or her job. Analogously, in a nonprofit firm, if the organization has very little cushion in the form of an endowment, all cash inflows will be required to meet the organization's basic mission requirements, leaving relatively little scope for expropriation. Furthermore, to the extent that the organization faces binding constraints and that donations are made for particular purposes,[4] expropriation may be difficult.

The popular press is littered with examples that illustrate this distinction between endowment and revenue expropriation. For example, in a particularly high-profile case in 2000, three former officials of Alleghany Health Education were arrested and charged with diverting $52 million in charitable endowments, for "inappropriate and personal uses." The case of the Bishop Estate, a charitable trust created in 1884 by one of the last members of Hawaii's royal family, provides a particularly compelling illustration of these ideas. The Bishop Estate held an endowment, worth $10 billion in 1997, proved to be too much of a temptation for the estate's five trustees. Funds were diverted for purposes that furthered the financial interests of the stewards of the endowment, through such mechanisms as political donations and direct investment in trustee-owned companies.

### 7.1.2  Endowment Expropriation and Donors

Given this potential for expropriation, the question arises of why donors ever allow for endowments in the first place, rather than simply promising to make up for shortfalls in the future. One answer draws once again on an analogy from research in corporate finance. One of the difficulties with Jensen's arguments for constraining managers is that management may have preferential information on the nature of investment opportunities, so it will be useful to provide them with some discretionary resources. Similarly, nonprofit managers may have a better sense of the needs of their organizations, so it may be beneficial for them to have some discretionary funds available when needs arise. It may be costly for management to have to petition donors for additional funds whenever there are unexpected

---

4. For example, in a case related to one of the authors, a donor told of donating storm windows to his daughter's private school because he was sure that this would not be a fungible donation.

needs. More generally, the transactions costs associated with the "meeting the shortfall" could be substantial.

Another possibility comes from a closer consideration of what exactly the nonprofit is "selling" to its donors. Casual observation suggests that much donation revenue is motivated by a desire for fame in perpetuity. This factor could lead to endowments for two reasons: Nonprofit managers may thus be better positioned to extract endowment funds from donors, through techniques such as "naming rights"; and the willingness of others to give to a nonprofit may increase with the endowment of the nonprofit, which guarantees its permanence. Hence, any individual donor can get other donors to commit more if the first donor commits his or her own money, not only for current expenses but for future expenses as well. In either case, a discretionary fund results for the manager, which may allow for the aforementioned expropriation to occur. We then must consider what steps may be taken to limit the extent of this expropriation.

## 7.2   Modes of Governance

There are a number of potential watchdogs that could mitigate the endowment-expropriation potential described in the preceding section. We consider here three possibilities: government oversight, media oversight, and donor oversight.

### 7.2.1   Government Oversight

Society, broadly defined, may choose to monitor nonprofits to prevent expropriation. Just as the Securities and Exchange Commission was established to prevent the expropriation of investors in for-profit firms, several governmental organizations exist to mitigate expropriation in nonprofits. Both federal and state-level bodies exist to oversee nonprofits. These bodies essentially enforce laws that are meant to ensure that the organization's resources are used to pursue the organization's stated mission, and to prevent the expropriation of value by insiders.[5] For example, the IRS regulations passed in 1998 provide specific guidance to charitable organizations on what constitutes appropriate financial compensation of executives, and further provides for penalties if these regulations are not followed.

Primary responsibility for the legal oversight of nonprofits, however, devolves to the level of the state.[6] While IRS oversight may be uniform across

---

5. More details on regulations from Minnesota may be downloaded from the website of the Minnesota Attorney General: http://www.ag.state.mn.us/charities/Default.htm. The website also contains links to the sites of other attorneys general. Internal Revenue Service regulations may be downloaded from http://www.irs.gov/exempt/display/0,,i1%3D3%26genericId%3D15048,00.html.

6. Most legal actions are initiated by state attorney general offices (private communication, Marion Fremont-Smith, Harvard University).

the country, there exist vast differences across the states in the extent of local oversight. The Office of the Ohio Attorney General carefully documented these differences in a report in 1974. As the authors of the report emphasize, there remain dramatic differences in the resources allocated to oversight of nonprofits, as well as the scope for actions against nonprofits by the state attorneys general.[7] The report emphasized eight possible powers, spelled out in appendix A of this paper; each state's score is listed in appendix B. These figures are based on the regulation of nonprofits in 1974, which is the most recent information available. There have been almost no changes since then in state-level nonprofit statutes (personal communication, Marion Fremont-Smith, Harvard University).

There is considerable variation in the extent of state-level oversight, and this variation does not seem to be easily explained by income, or by simple geographic proximity. We consider below how some measures of governance vary across states with different levels of oversight.

### 7.2.2  Media Oversight

While the state attorney general are the primary enforcing bodies for nonprofits, very often cases come to light because of the activities of the media. This may be in the form of traditional investigative reporting; for example, the Bishop Estate case described above was originally brought to light through the work of a journalist. Furthermore, the media may play a disciplinary role in managerial discretion that is inappropriate, although not strictly illegal.

This element to oversight has increased in visibility recently, as several watchdog organizations have taken advantage of the Internet to disseminate information about the quality of nonprofit governance. The most prominent among these include the Better Business Bureau and Guidestar. Generally, these organizations provide basic accounting information on charitable organizations, and also attempt to evaluate their governance structures. This includes information on program spending (relative to fund-raising) ratios, executive compensation, and the structure of the board, which may also be relevant for the extent of expropriation.

We have not yet compiled data that might be used to examine the media as a source of oversight. Numerous possibilities exist, however, including

---

7. One may be concerned that nonprofit regulation is of limited relevance, unless states devote significant resources to enforcing these regulations. In the same report cited above, the Office of the Ohio Attorney General also collected data on the human resources devoted to the enforcement of nonprofit regulation. The number of full-time employees devoted to enforcement, deflated by state population, is highly correlated with the extent of regulation, as measured in our study. Moreover, when we use this as a measure of governance, it yields similar (although slightly weaker) results to our law-based definition. Alternatively, examining actual convictions for misconduct is unlikely to be revealing, because effective enforcement will increase the proportion of illegal acts that are uncovered but will reduce the number of such acts that are committed.

media penetration, by city or state; coverage by media watchdogs; and ratings from these watchdog organizations.

### 7.2.3    Board and Donor Oversight

Underlying much of the discussion on donor oversight is the role of the board of directors, who are owners of the organization in the sense that they are given ultimate decision-making rights over the organization's assets. Thus, just as the board of a for-profit organization acts on behalf of shareholders, nonprofit boards may act on behalf of donors. Furthermore, just as large shareholders may demand representation on for-profit boards, large donors may demand representation on nonprofit boards.

The analogy between for-profit and nonprofit boards further allows us to develop some hypotheses as to the characteristics that may promote good governance. These include representation of large donors on the board ("shareholder representation"); the presence of large donors that may be expected to monitor on behalf of the broader donor community, thereby overcoming the free-rider problem in monitoring ("ownership concentration"); outside representation on the board; noncompensation of board members; and so on. Many of the latter examples are spelled out in the governance guidelines for boards given by the Better Business Bureau. We therefore expect to be able to collect information on these dimensions of governance in the future. At this point, we can only loosely say that there appears to be considerable variation among organizations in the choice of governance structures.

Examining the various dimensions of oversight and governance described above is an important avenue for research. For example, do varying degrees of state oversight lead to different levels of monitoring by other bodies—that is, are boards more active in the absence of strong government pressure? Alternatively, one could easily imagine that different oversight mechanisms act as complements (e.g., the media is effective in bringing about change only if accompanied by strong legal enforcement).

### 7.3    Data

For this paper, we concentrate on charitable nonprofit organizations (so-called 501[c][3] organizations, named for the section of the U.S. federal income tax code that gives them tax-exempt status), making use of the IRS Statistics of Income files. This is a data set compiled by the National Center for Charitable Statistics (NCCS) at the Urban Institute and derived from data taken from the Form 990 that tax-exempt organizations must file with the IRS. These data contain all 501(c)(3) organizations with more than $10 million in assets, plus a random sample of approximately 4,000 smaller organizations. Most financial variables on the Form 990 are included, and the data are considered to be more reliable than the data in the IRS's unedited files because of the substantial error-checking by the NCCS.[8]

Our measure of the endowment, or net assets, is from the Form 990; this is simply total assets less total liabilities (ENDOWMENT).[9] Research on nonprofit organizations generally uses the term "endowment" to refer to a restricted fund for which, at least in theory, the principal cannot be spent. They are therefore careful to make a distinction between restricted (endowment) and unrestricted (fund balance) funds. We do not believe that such a distinction is necessary here: Restricted (endowment) funds are held primarily by large educational institutions and hospitals. These organizations are generally able to borrow against the value of their endowments, and may furthermore use the interest generated by the endowments to make interest payments on their loans. Particularly given that these organizations are generally able to issue tax-exempt bonds, it would appear that the restriction on endowment payout is not binding.

We require some means of scaling endowment size; we deflate by annual total expenses (EXPENSES), which lends itself to a natural interpretation: ENDOWMENT/EXPENSES reflects the number of years that the organization may continue to operate at its current scale, finance solely by the endowment.

In examining the determinants of endowment size, we require variables that are related to an organization's ability to cope with financial shocks, other than using the endowment as a buffer. We focus on labor intensity and access to alternative financing. We measure labor intensity by the ratio of total wages to total expenses (LABIN).[10] To proxy for access to financing, we use a dummy variable that takes on a value of 1 if the organization obtained a loan during the decade 1987–1996 (DEBT). Obviously, there is an offsetting effect here: Organizations with large endowments may borrow against their endowments, thereby generating a positive relationship between DEBT and endowment intensity. Hence, in this case, there is a bias against finding a negative relation.

The Statistics of Income files contain annual observations on 10,000 to 12,000 organizations per year, varying by year, for 1987–1996, with approximately 18,000 organizations filing in at least one year. Prior to 1987, the data were collected on a much smaller sample of organizations. We

8. For more details, see the NCCS Web site at http://nccs.urban.org/index.htm.
9. An alternative, and perhaps more direct, measure of the endowment is the organization's holdings that could potentially be used to finance program expenditure. More precisely, we may use the following equation: ENDOWMENT = CASH + BANK DEPOSITS + SECURITIES + REAL ESTATE INVESTMENT. This measure is very highly correlated with reported fund balance ($\rho = 0.96$), and using it as an alternative yields virtually identical results (available from the authors).
10. An alternative measure of labor intensity would be to deflate by physical capital. However, because physical capital is a significant part of the endowment, it would be almost tautological to have such a variable on the right-hand side of the regression.

**Table 7.1**          **Summary Statistics**

|  | Mean | Standard Deviation | Minimum | Maximum |
|---|---|---|---|---|
| ENDOWMENT ($1,000) | 39,736.24 | 159,664.90 | 0 | 5,207,517 |
| Endowment/Expenses | 3.17 | 6.75 | 0 | 98.62 |
| Log(Endowment/Expenses) | 1.00 | 0.77 | 0 | 4.60 |
| Expenses ($1,000) | 33,436.97 | 101,734.80 | 9.671 | 4,039,460 |
| Revenues ($1,000) | 36,431.88 | 108,203.10 | 6.608 | 4,108,413 |
| Private donations/Revenues | 0.14 | 0.21 | 0 | 1 |
| (Labor costs)/(Total expenses) | 0.41 | 0.20 | 0 | 0.89 |
| Loan dummy | 0.67 | 0.47 | 0 | 1 |
| Private donations ($1,000) | 2,642.20 | 14,095.07 | 0 | 667,663 |
| Observations | 4,546 | | | |

*Source:* Authors' calculations.

limit our analyses to the approximately 5,300 organizations that filed with the IRS every year during this period. After removing mutual organizations (dominated by TIAA-CREF), grant-making foundations and trusts, and organizations whose industry is "unknown," the sample is reduced to 5,007 organizations. We also limit the sample to organizations that consistently report sensible values for the variables that are central to our analyses. We remove organizations with negative reported revenues or expenses, a 1987 endowment rate of greater than 100, and a negative ratio of private donations to revenues. These omissions result in a further reduction of 461 firms, leaving a total of 4,546 organizations.

Table 7.1 presents summary statistics for the entire sample, while table 7.2 presents the distribution of median values by industry for a subset of variables. As table 7.2 makes clear, the sample is dominated by health care organizations, which are primarily hospitals. Because hospitals tend to be larger than other nonprofits, health care is even more dominant in the revenue-weighted distribution of organizations (see column [1]). However, the representation of hospitals does not increase, relative to the simple headcount measure, when organizations are weighted by their endowments (see column [2]); rather, the endowment weighting shifts the focus to educational institutions. This is a reflection of educational institutions' large organizational size as well as their relative endowment intensiveness.

## 7.4   Endowment Intensity and Precautionary Savings

In the estimates presented in table 7.3 and 7.4, we move from examining the distribution of organizations across industries to looking at organizational characteristics, by industry. We begin by looking at the variable of primary interest: endowment intensity (Endowment/Expenses). Not surprisingly, given the results from table 7.2, endowment intensity is by far the

Table 7.2                Distribution of Organizations, Weighted by Size (%)

| | Total Revenue | Total Value of Endowment | Total Organizations |
|---|---|---|---|
| Arts | 2.25 | 4.17 | 6.03 |
| Education | 26.67 | 49.32 | 29.45 |
| Environment | 0.11 | 0.26 | 0.86 |
| Animal-related | 0.21 | 0.38 | 0.81 |
| Health | 61.89 | 34.53 | 37.62 |
| Mental health | 0.31 | 0.23 | 1.36 |
| Diseases | 0.76 | 0.51 | 1.08 |
| Medical research | 0.53 | 3.43 | 0.97 |
| Crime, legal-related | 0.12 | 0.08 | 0.37 |
| Employment, job-related | 0.07 | 0.07 | 0.66 |
| Food, agriculture, and nutrition | 0.01 | 0.01 | 0.09 |
| Housing, shelter | 0.06 | 0.06 | 1.21 |
| Public safety | 0.04 | 0.02 | 0.24 |
| Recreation/sports | 0.18 | 0.23 | 0.79 |
| Youth development | 0.16 | 0.25 | 1.19 |
| Human services | 2.76 | 3.66 | 11.92 |
| International/foreign affairs | 1.11 | 0.65 | 0.99 |
| Civil rights/social action | 0.04 | 0.03 | 0.15 |
| Community improvement | 0.18 | 0.28 | 1.12 |
| Science research | 1.86 | 1.06 | 1.32 |
| Social science research | 0.15 | 0.18 | 0.33 |
| Society benefit | 0.27 | 0.29 | 0.48 |
| Religious | 0.26 | 0.28 | 0.92 |

lowest among hospitals. Of the other categories, we observe a particularly high rate of endowment intensity among arts organizations. The second column in Table 7.3 suggests one element to this pattern: A much larger proportion of revenues comes from donations (rather than generated income) in arts organizations, relative to hospitals. However, health care appears to be systematically different from other nonprofit activities; in particular, the median donation rate is significantly below that of other sectors. In general, as numerous scholars have noted (see, e.g., Weisbrod 1998), hospitals behave increasingly like for-profit organizations; accordingly, we also report empirical results for nonprofit organization samples including and excluding hospitals, where appropriate.

The data in table 7.2 and 7.3 are suggestive of relatively high endowment-to-expense ratios in many industries; moreover, there is considerable variation across industries. We may tentatively examine whether there may be systematic industry differences that could possibly lead to differences in endowment intensity, by comparing industries' (a) potential to take on debt, (b) ability to maintain a labor-intensive production process, and (c) level of cash flow volatility (proxied by standard deviation of revenues). Table 7.4 reports these patterns. Again, we focus on the three largest in-

Table 7.3    Median Endowment Intensity and Donation Intensity, by Industry

|  | Endowment Expenses | Donations Revenues |
| --- | --- | --- |
| Arts | 3.56 | 0.345 |
| Education | 2.41 | 0.196 |
| Environment | 3.54 | 0.404 |
| Animal-related | 4.06 | 0.323 |
| Health | 0.63 | 0.033 |
| Mental health | 0.68 | 0.079 |
| Diseases | 0.83 | 0.188 |
| Medical research | 2.43 | 0.297 |
| Crime, legal-related | 0.66 | 0.284 |
| Employment, job-related | 0.82 | 0.037 |
| Food, agriculture, and nutrition | 2.24 | 0.421 |
| Housing, shelter | 0.92 | 0.108 |
| Public safety | 2.83 | 0.159 |
| Recreation/sports | 1.86 | 0.235 |
| Youth development | 2.01 | 0.264 |
| Human services | 1.38 | 0.149 |
| International/foreign affairs | 0.83 | 0.380 |
| Civil rights/social action | 0.94 | 0.664 |
| Community improvement | 1.82 | 0.128 |
| Science research | 1.08 | 0.102 |
| Social science research | 2.32 | 0.277 |
| Society benefit | 0.99 | 0.216 |
| Religious | 2.50 | 0.440 |

dustries: arts, education, and health care. Systematically, arts and education organizations appear to have a greater need for endowments, relative to health care organizations: They have less labor-intensive expense ratios, are less likely to have taken a loan, and have more volatile revenue streams.

Table 7.5 presents results describing industry median endowment intensity and the effects of the three aspects of precautionary savings described above. Each measure of endowment need enters with the expected sign; however, when all measures are included simultaneously, the loan dummy variable is no longer significant.

## 7.5   Endowment Intensity and Governance: Preliminary Results

The extent to which an organization has precautionary savings requirements will depend upon its specific circumstances. However, as a rough guide for examining the summary statistics, we take the National Center for Nonprofit Boards guidelines that "not more than two years' expenses" should be held as an endowment. By this measure, the median organization in many industries in our sample already exceeds the suggested level of endowment intensity. Furthermore, the distributions within each industry suggest that there are relatively fat tails in the range of endowment in-

**Table 7.4**      **Organizational Characteristics that Affect Endowment Intensity: Medians**

|  | Received Loan | Labor Intensity | Volatility |
|---|---|---|---|
| Arts | 0.38 | 0.40 | 0.24 |
| Education | 0.67 | 0.45 | 0.14 |
| Environment | 0.41 | 0.41 | 0.30 |
| Animal-related | 0.24 | 0.44 | 0.19 |
| Health | 0.81 | 0.48 | 0.15 |
| Mental health | 0.65 | 0.55 | 0.18 |
| Diseases | 0.39 | 0.31 | 0.12 |
| Medical research | 0.27 | 0.43 | 0.21 |
| Crime, legal-related | 0.18 | 0.39 | 0.17 |
| Employment, job-related | 0.53 | 0.59 | 0.19 |
| Food, agriculture, and nutrition | 0.00 | 0.38 | 0.28 |
| Housing, shelter | 0.87 | 0.17 | 0.19 |
| Public safety | 0.73 | 0.10 | 0.14 |
| Recreation/sports | 0.22 | 0.20 | 0.20 |
| Youth development | 0.37 | 0.48 | 0.21 |
| Human services | 0.64 | 0.51 | 0.15 |
| International/foreign affairs | 0.36 | 0.25 | 0.23 |
| Civil rights/social action | 0.43 | 0.47 | 0.20 |
| Community improvement | 0.35 | 0.22 | 0.25 |
| Science research | 0.42 | 0.30 | 0.18 |
| Social science research | 0.27 | 0.36 | 0.19 |
| Society benefit | 0.41 | 0.35 | 0.19 |
| Religious | 0.50 | 0.24 | 0.23 |

**Table 7.5**      **Determinants of Endowment Intensity**

|  | (1) | (2) | (3) | (4) |
|---|---|---|---|---|
| Volatility | 28.81 |  |  | 23.41 |
|  | (5.54) |  |  | (7.45) |
| Loan dummy |  | −3.14 |  | −0.77 |
|  |  | (1.19) |  | (1.48) |
| Labor intensity |  |  | −7.73 | −5.10 |
|  |  |  | (2.69) | (2.68) |
| CONSTANT | −1.64 | 5.09 | 6.46 | 1.51 |
|  | (1.00) | (0.75) | (1.06) | (1.99) |
| $R^2$ | 0.36 | 0.14 | 0.15 | 0.43 |
| N | 23 | 23 | 23 | 23 |

*Notes:* Standard errors in parentheses. All regressions use robust standard errors. Volatility is the standard deviation of revenues for each organization during 1987–1996. Loan dummy reflects whether an organization received a loan during 1987–1996. Labor intensity is the ratio of labor expenses to total expenses in 1987. In all cases, the dependent variable is the 1987 ratio of endowment to total expenses.

Table 7.6                Endowment Intensity, 10th and 90th Percentiles

|  | 10th percentile | 90th percentile |
|---|---|---|
| Arts | 0.66 | 12.70 |
| Education | 0.91 | 7.46 |
| Environment | 0.35 | 12.19 |
| Animal-related | 1.15 | 16.61 |
| Health | 0.29 | 2.88 |
| Mental health | 0.11 | 2.56 |
| Diseases | 0.15 | 4.42 |
| Medical research | 0.55 | 13.78 |
| Crime, legal-related | 0.09 | 6.87 |
| Employment, job-related | 0.19 | 5.04 |
| Food, agriculture, and nutrition | 0.26 | 15.75 |
| Housing, shelter | 0.19 | 5.97 |
| Public safety | 0.14 | 18.42 |
| Recreation/sports | 0.38 | 10.88 |
| Youth development | 0.75 | 7.80 |
| Human services | 0.20 | 6.23 |
| International/foreign affairs | 0.09 | 10.13 |
| Civil rights/social action | 0.58 | 4.38 |
| Community improvement | 0.32 | 26.56 |
| Science research | 0.23 | 8.05 |
| Social science research | 1.05 | 6.11 |
| Society benefit | 0.27 | 10.39 |
| Religious | 0.41 | 14.24 |

tensities. This point is illustrated in table 7.6, which lists the 10th and 90th percentiles of endowment intensity, by industry. In particular, among both arts and educational organizations, the top 10 percent of organizations by endowment ratio have more than ten years' expenses in endowment.

Our measure of the extent of oversight comes from variation in oversight across states, as described in section 7.3 above.[11] Table 7.7 presents results relating endowment intensities by level of oversight, where "oversight" is measured by the number of powers accorded to the state attorney general in monitoring and punishing nonprofits.

Somewhat surprisingly, there are no systematic differences across states in terms of a relationship between oversight and endowment intensity. This finding likely reflects a differential composition of industries across states; the role of substitute modes of governance in low-oversight states; donors' reaction to poor governance by "starving" nonprofits so that they are unable to grow to have sizeable expenses (the denominator of the dependent

11. Unfortunately, collecting appropriate information on board oversight is not feasible at this time. We obtained measures of media presence, by state, such as newspaper circulation per capita, and number of newspapers, by city. We do not believe that these are reliable indicators of the *quality* of media presence, and leave each of these areas as possible avenues for further research.

Table 7.7          Median Endowment and Donation Intensities, According to Oversight by
                   State Attorney General

| Level of Oversight | Endowment Intensity | Donation Intensity | Observations |
|---|---|---|---|
| 0 | 1.05 | 0.01 | 125 |
| 1 | 1.17 | 0.03 | 349 |
| 2 | 1.03 | 0.02 | 1,029 |
| 3 | 1.41 | 0.08 | 635 |
| 4 | 1.67 | 0.06 | 193 |
| 5 | 1.00 | 0.01 | 150 |
| 6 | 1.23 | 0.05 | 1,478 |
| 7 | 1.00 | 0.05 | 493 |
| 8 | 1.05 | 0.01 | 125 |

*Notes:* Oversight is defined by the number of powers accorded to the state attorney general in overseeing nonprofits; see appendix A for further details. Endowment Intensity is the 1987 ratio of endowment to total expenses. Donation Intensity is the 1987 ratio of donation revenue to total revenue.

variable); and the result of the endogenous development of state oversight (i.e., enforcement is strongest where self-dealing by nonprofits is most likely). The first of these factors does not seem to explain this nonresult; oversight is still insignificant in a regression that controls for industry affects. Better data on other modes of governance are necessary to differentiate among the various other competing explanations.

In table 7.7, we also examine a related margin—donation intensity, defined as the ratio of an organization's donations to total revenues. The summary statistics again do not show a clear pattern. However, in table 7.8, in which we control for industry effects, a systematic relationship emerges. While the simple binary regression does not suggest a significant relationship between state-level oversight and donation intensity, after we add basic controls, the estimated coefficient on Oversight is statistically significantly different from zero at the 5 percent level, allowing for state-level clustering of standard errors. Thus, in states with higher oversight, we observe more donation-intensive organizations. This is at least suggestive that better oversight by the state encourages donors to provide resources to nonprofits.

Unfortunately, data availability constrains our ability to estimate the relationship between governance and the endowment. We are now collecting the data described in section 7.2, but we intend to examine the endowment-governance link more closely in future research.

## 7.6   Conclusion

Nonprofit organizations constitute an extremely important part of the U.S. economy. It is therefore surprising how little attention economists have paid to the behavior of such organizations. In this paper, we examine some fundamental issues of governance in nonprofits that stem directly

Table 7.8            **Determinants of Donation Intensity**

|                        | (1)       | (2)       | (3)       | (4)       |
|------------------------|-----------|-----------|-----------|-----------|
| Oversight              | 0.0037    | 0.0047    | 0.0053    | 0.0036    |
|                        | (0.0025)  | (0.0023)  | (0.0023)  | (0.0016)  |
| Log(per capita income) |           |           | −0.027    | −0.084    |
|                        |           |           | (0.039)   | (0.024)   |
| Log(revenues)          |           | −0.040    | −0.040    | −0.024    |
|                        |           | (0.0020)  | (0.0020)  | (0.0026)  |
| CONSTANT               | 0.12      | 0.77      | 1.03      |           |
|                        | (0.015)   | (0.041)   | (0.39)    |           |
| Industry fixed effects? | No       | No        | No        | Yes       |
| $R^2$                  | 0.002     | 0.11      | 0.011     | 0.30      |
| $N$                    | 4,456     |           |           |           |

*Notes:* Standard errors in parentheses. All regressions use robust standard errors, allowing for state-level clustering. Oversight is defined by the number of powers accorded to the state attorney general in overseeing nonprofits, and takes on values from 0 to 8. See appendix A for further details. Log(per capita income) in state per capita income in 1987. Log(revenues) is the log of total revenues in 1987. The dependent variable in all cases is Donation Intensity, the 1987 ratio of donation revenue to total revenue.

from the nondistribution constraint that defines the nonprofit form. A precautionary-savings model of the endowment is supported by the data. We further examine the possibility that endowments may be the source of potential governance problems in nonprofit organizations. In particular, we draw parallels between the functioning of for-profit and nonprofit organizations, and on this basis, lay out a framework for examining governance concerns raised by nonprofit endowments. We discuss steps that governments and donors may take to mitigate these concerns, and discuss potential data sources for work in this area.

# Appendix A
## *Powers of the State Attorneys General in Nonprofit Oversight*

Thanks to the United States' common-law heritage, most regulation of nonprofits devolved to the states, which exhibit a very large amount of variation in their extent of oversight. Almost uniformly, the power to monitor and prosecute nonprofits has been allocated to the state attorneys general. The Office of the Ohio Attorney General has documented the basic legislative enactments that allow the state attorneys general to oversee nonprofit organizations, and how these basic enactments vary across states. The eight statutes covered by the report are listed below; for further details, see Office of Ohio Attorney General (1977).

1. Is the attorney general the enforcing authority?
2. It is the attorney general a necessary party for enforcement?
3. Does the attorney general have the power to institute suits to enforce the charitable trust?
4. Is registration with the attorney general required?
5. Are periodic reports to the attorney general required?
6. Does the enforcing authority have subpoena power?
7. Does the enforcing agency have rulemaking authority?
8. Are probate judges required to notify the enforcing authority whenever a will containing a charitable bequest is admitted?

## Appendix B
### State-Level Oversight by Attorneys General

| | | | |
|---|---|---|---|
| Alabama | 0 | Montana | 0 |
| Alaska | 0 | Nebraska | 1 |
| Arizona | 0 | Nevada | 8 |
| Arkansas | 1 | New Hampshire | 2 |
| California | 8 | New Jersey | 2 |
| Colorado | 2 | New Mexico | 2 |
| Connecticut | 3 | New York | 7 |
| Delaware | 1 | North Carolina | 3 |
| Florida | 1 | North Dakota | 2 |
| Georgia | 7 | Ohio | 7 |
| Hawaii | 2 | Oklahoma | 1 |
| Idaho | 3 | Oregon | 7 |
| Illinois | 7 | Pennsylvania | 2 |
| Indiana | 2 | Rhode Island | 8 |
| Iowa | 4 | South Carolina | 5 |
| Kansas | 1 | South Dakota | 3 |
| Kentucky | 3 | Tennessee | 2 |
| Louisiana | 0 | Texas | 3 |
| Maine | 3 | Utah | 1 |
| Maryland | 2 | Vermont | 2 |
| Massachusetts | 7 | Virginia | 4 |
| Michigan | 7 | Washington | 8 |
| Minnesota | 3 | West Virginia | 1 |
| Mississippi | 1 | Wisconsin | 5 |
| Missouri | 2 | Wyoming | 1 |

*Source:* Office of Ohio Attorney General (1977).

# References

Glaeser, Edward, and Andrei Shleifer. 2001. Not-for-profit entrepreneurs. *Journal of Public Economics* 81 (1): 99–115.

Hansmann, Henry. 1996. *The ownership of enterprise.* Cambridge: Harvard University Press.

Jensen, Michael. 1986. Agency costs of free cash flow, corporate finance, and takeovers. *American Economic Review* 76 (2): 323–29.

Office of the Ohio Attorney General. 1977. The status of state regulation of charitable trusts, foundations, and solicitations. In *Research papers sponsored by the commission on private philanthropy and public needs.* Washington, D.C.: Department of the Treasury.

Weisbrod, Burton. 1988. *The nonprofit economy.* Cambridge: Harvard University Press.

———. 1998. *To profit or not to profit.* Cambridge: Cambridge University Press.

# Contributors

Jason R. Barro
Harvard Business School
Baker Library 184
Boston, MA 02163

Michael Chu
30 Newport Parkway, #1504
Jersey City, NJ 07310

Guy David
Graduate School of Business,
    Ph.D. Office
University of Chicago
1101 East 58th Street
Chicago, IL 60637

Burcay Erus
Department of Economics
Room 345
Northwestern University
2003 Sheridan Road
Evanston, IL 60208-2600

Raymond Fisman
Uris 823
Graduate School of Business
Columbia University
3022 Broadway
New York, NY 10027

Edward L. Glaeser
Department of Economics
315A Littauer Center
Harvard University
Cambridge, MA 02138

William N. Goetzmann
Yale School of
    Management
135 Prospect Street
P.O. Box 208200
New Haven, CT 06520

Henry Hansmann
Yale Law School
P.O. Box 208215
New Haven, CT 06520

R. Glenn Hubbard
Graduate School of Business
Columbia University, 609
    Uris Hall
3022 Broadway
New York, NY 10027

Daniel Kessler
Graduate School of Business
Stanford University
Stanford, CA 94305-5015

Anup Malani
University of Virginia School of Law
Office WB351
580 Massie Road
Charlottesville, VA 22903-1789

Mark McClellan
Department of Economics
Stanford University
Economics Building, 224
Stanford, CA 94305-6072

Jonathan Katz Nelson
Department of Fine Arts
Syracuse University in Florence
Piazza Savonarola, 15
Florence 50132
Italy

Sharon Oster
Yale School of Management
135 Prospect Street
P.O. Box 208200
New Haven, CT 06520

Tomas Philipson
Department of Economics
University of Chicago
1155 East 60th Street
Chicago, IL 60637

Burton A. Weisbrod
Department of Economics
Northwestern University
2003 Sheridan Road
Evanston, IL 60208

Richard J. Zeckhauser
John F. Kennedy School of
    Government
Harvard University
79 John F. Kennedy Street
Cambridge, MA 02138

# Author Index

# Subject Index